The Phenomenology and the Philosophy of Running

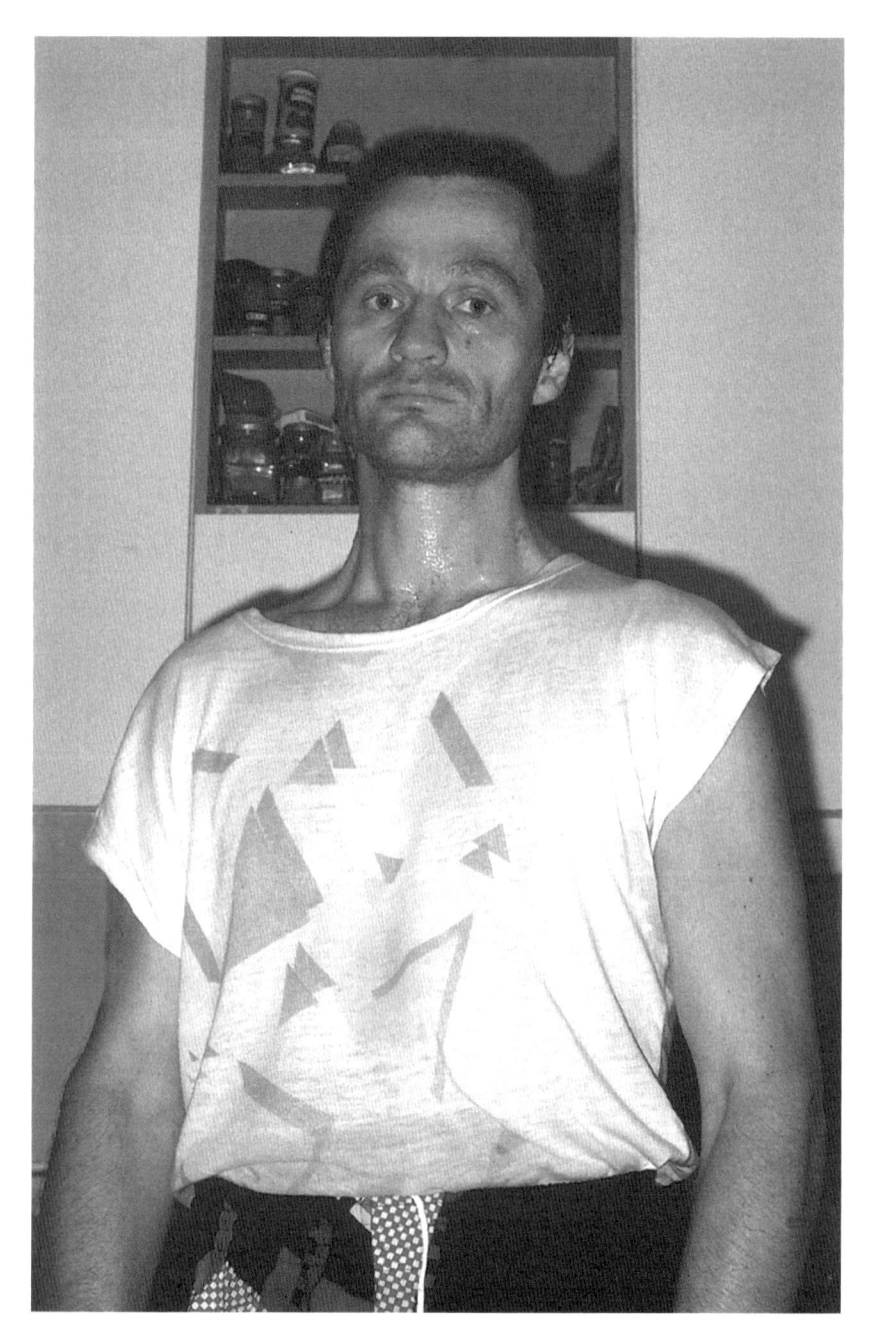

This is what the author Tapio Koski looked like right after his first marathon in May 1999. He ran alone, left for the run at 8:00 PM, and arrived home shortly after midnight at 0:19 AM. Koski's intended 24 km run turned into a full marathon, underprepared for the energy consumption with only 1 l of water and a couple of sweets. The book contains a detailed description of the experience

Tapio Koski

The Phenomenology and the Philosophy of Running

The Multiple Dimensions of Long-Distance Running

Springer

Tapio Koski
University of Tampere
Kaukovainio, Oulu, Finland

ISBN 978-3-319-15596-8   ISBN 978-3-319-15597-5 (eBook)
DOI 10.1007/978-3-319-15597-5

Library of Congress Control Number: 2015935330

Springer Cham Heidelberg New York Dordrecht London
Translation from the Finnish language edition: *Juoksemisen filosofia* by Tapio Koski, © Tampere University Press, Tampere, 2005. All rights reserved
© Springer International Publishing Switzerland 2015
This work is subject to copyright. All rights are reserved by the Publisher, whether the whole or part of the material is concerned, specifically the rights of translation, reprinting, reuse of illustrations, recitation, broadcasting, reproduction on microfilms or in any other physical way, and transmission or information storage and retrieval, electronic adaptation, computer software, or by similar or dissimilar methodology now known or hereafter developed.
The use of general descriptive names, registered names, trademarks, service marks, etc. in this publication does not imply, even in the absence of a specific statement, that such names are exempt from the relevant protective laws and regulations and therefore free for general use.
The publisher, the authors and the editors are safe to assume that the advice and information in this book are believed to be true and accurate at the date of publication. Neither the publisher nor the authors or the editors give a warranty, express or implied, with respect to the material contained herein or for any errors or omissions that may have been made.

Printed on acid-free paper

Springer International Publishing AG Switzerland is part of Springer Science+Business Media (www.springer.com)

For the first 38 years of my life I did not do any kind of physical exercise.
My hobbies had more to do with drinking beer and smoking. Now I'm almost 43.
Five years ago, at the darkest winter period I found it difficult to fall asleep in the evenings and, consequently, very difficult to get up from the bed in the morning.
I had a constant flu and my back was aching.
The doctor could not name any illness to explain my condition.
He only made a discrete suggestion that someone doing light office work should do at least some kind of physical exercise in order to stay in good health.
Since I felt obliged to change my lifestyle somehow, the idea was to discover a physical exercise that would make sense to me.
There was no sport from the youth that I could have restarted, and none of the ball games appealed to me. The idea of going to a gym sounded repulsive.
The only thing that I could think of was jogging.
Or, that's how I called it then. I don't use that word any longer.

Today, I call myself a runner.

The first running attempts 5 years ago were quite a challenge. Jogging turned into walking only after a couple of 100 m. The experience made me angry;
I could not bare such wretchedness in myself. So, I set myself a target.
I chose one silver birch not far from home and decided to run there from home without stopping. It was only the third attempt that finally proved successful. I had, however, reached the first target and gotten my reward.

I had beaten the inner loser in myself, which plead for mercy and asked me to stop running. The next target was to reach a rock a little further away. That is how it got started. Eventually the distances grew. The pain I used to feel had been replaced by joy and warmth.

My legs, my lungs, and the rest of my body were getting accustomed to physical exercise and sent the message about good feeling instead of pain and fatigue that used to be the case.

I was totally hooked. The mental pleasure about my capability and strength introduced by muscular exercise were like a drug to me.

Written by my friend Jorma Peussa, thank You, Jorma!

Foreword

Nine years ago I was sitting contentedly on my porch reading a book which Tapio Koski, a brand-new friend, had brought to me the day before. Dr. Koski had come to interview me for a popular Finnish Quarterly because of my forthcoming seventieth birthday and we had had a nice conversation about the possibilities of phenomenological philosophy in these modern days in this modern world.

At first sight the new book Tapio had brought to me had appeared somewhat elusive and tantalizing. For me its topic was very different from the usual and normal. It was his first book on the philosophy of running.

I am not very familiar with running but soon I found the subject utterly fascinating. It was obvious that philosophers had once again neglected a highly attractive phenomenon. Of course, running had tended to be approached occasionally in a fragmentary manner as part of some larger enterprise. Seldom had the topic of running been handled in a comprehensive manner as a subject of intrinsic interests. This certainly is the case because running itself is making it difficult to achieve a synoptic view on the subject and the role it takes in our *Lebenswelt*.

In the light of Tapio Koski's book it was obvious that a philosophical investigation of running could be worked up from the simplest examples to its most sophisticated manifestations. Koski's personal habit of discussing the topic also appealed to me. We have never lost contact.

Today I am happy to have the possibility to say these few words about Tapio Koski's new book, now about its English Edition and the new form it has taken in these 9 years, very much advanced in understanding of the human body and mind, presenting his exceptional research, which fascinates me not only because of the topic itself, which still is out of the ordinary. Tapio Koski has been fortunate to discover a topic which offers immensely great opportunities to be explored, at the same time presenting basic human philosophical themes in a new, fascinating conceptual environment.

Koski exploits the structural description of the human mode of being introduced by Martin Heidegger initially in his *Sein und Zeit*, known as existential analysis. Another source of inspiration comes from Maurice Merleau-Ponty.

He and Heidegger form together a new type of exciting and prominent basement of a conceptual building which I constantly find so illuminating and promising. Koski works here in an exceptionally skillful and original way.

From the viewpoint of Koski's work, it is not important whether his reading of Heidegger and Merleau-Ponty is thoroughly right and generally acceptable as an interpretation of their ideas. Rather, it is more important to see what he manages to make out of those ideas.

In my opinion Koski is one of those very few who have managed to present interesting and insightful views on a topic which has not been formerly covered in philosophy. Having familiarized myself with the work I can only wonder the lack of former understanding how fascinating connections the philosophy of running may have with the more traditional motifs of philosophical thinking. Koski introduces these connections in an elaborate yet unassertive way. The work is of high standard methodologically as well. In the philosophy of running attentiveness to one's own inner life is vital. It is a phenomenon of the human mind that needs to be analyzed. Based on what I have seen so far, I dare to expect Koski's work to fulfil the highest standards in this respect as well.

Emeritus Professor of Art Education and Philosophy,   Lauri Olavi Routila
University of Jyväskylä, Chairman of the Finnish
Society for Philosophy and Phenomenological Research,
SFFS, Jyväskylä, Finland
25 November 2014

Preface

Years ago, when I was young and had started my studies in sociology and philosophy at Tampere University, Finland, I was also regularly exercising running and karate-do. I came to notice that I was reflecting my perceptions of my own experiences and of the human being as an exercising being. I came to realize that the human body contains particular wisdom from which one can learn. One would only need to start looking for this wisdom. I was struck by the feeling that when I reshape my ideas in the form of research, it may be of some value for philosophical and physical education. My desire to clarify the nature of my own exercising coupled with the above triggered the idea to further investigate this area, leading me to the path of doing research. In this way the starting point for my research became settled on its own. My doctoral dissertation[1] was published in the year 2000, followed by *The Philosophy of Running* in Finnish in 2005. The extended edition of the latter is what you are reading at the moment. The translation process was long and demanding, and getting a publishing contract took several years.

The philosophy of physical exercise is a new research area in occidental academic philosophy. There are not many philosophers and researchers who at the same time are themselves part of the subject of their study. This is probably why after 2005 I have not been able to locate but one book in which the connection between running and philosophy has been investigated from a participatory point of view. In book *Running and Philosophy: A Marathon for the Mind* (2007) contains 18 articles the authors of which are all runners. There isn't a single monograph that I know of. Thus, I have been forced to explore unknown waters of philosophy.

---

[1] *Physical Exercise as a Way of Life and a Method for Spiritual Growth* – with Yoga and Zen-budo as Examples. Only in Finnish. Abstract: http://tampub.uta.fi/handle/10024/67035?show=full.

The publishers expressed the wish to shorten the subtitle to its current form. The purpose of the original subtitle (The multiple dimensions of long-distance running – how to challenge oneself through the flesh) was to bring up both the role and significance of the body in running and taking one's life into possession, the will and the spirit.

Kaukovainio, Oulu, Finland   Tapio Koski
28 November 2014

Acknowledgements

I dedicate this book to my son Roope and wish to express my gratitude to Timo Klemola Ph.D. for explicating the research topic, Annamaija Leinonen who appeared as a new star in my life towards the end of the translation project, translator, Janne Rissanen MA, with whom we formed a dynamic ensemble, and Tere Vadén Ph.D. for his valuable expertise in commenting on the translation.

The work was supported financially by Polar Electro Ltd, Esju Ltd, Timo Tarvainen Ph.D., Matti Parkkali MA, and Finnish Ministry of Education and Culture, which is gratefully acknowledged.

I wish to express my deepest gratitude to professor emeritus Lauri Routila who at the finalizing phase of the translation reviewed the manuscript and wrote the foreword.

Contents

1 Introduction 1
2 Running as Phenomenological and Bodily Inquiry of the Self 17
3 The Philosophical Foundation of Running 25
   3.1 The Groundwork of Maurice Merleau-Ponty's Philosophy 26
   3.2 Merleau-Ponty's Philosophy of the Body 28
   3.3 Martin Heidegger's Fundamental Ontological Philosophy 35
4 Long-Distance Running as the Subject of the Study 45
5 Running as a Way of Life 53
6 Viewpoints to a Long-Distance Runner 61
   6.1 The "They", Authentic Being and Inauthentic Being 61
   6.2 Authenticity and Inauthenticity of Running 68
   6.3 Running as "Care" 69
   6.4 Prerequisites of Physical Exercise 75
   6.5 Uncovering and Covering of the World for a Runner 80
   6.6 The Distant Is Far and Near 83
   6.7 Repetition 87
   6.8 Running, False Devotion, Fanaticism and Dependence 89
   6.9 Ready-to-Hand and Present-at-Hand as the Dimensions
       of Human Relationship with the World 91
   6.10 The World as Present 103
7 The World Is Running 107
   7.1 Running Experiences 107
   7.2 The Buddhist Marathon Monks of Mount Hiei 112
8 Experiential Cores 119
   8.1 Disappearance of the Contradiction Between
       the Subject and Object 120
   8.2 Calming Down One's Mind, Quietness 121

	8.3	Attunement	123
	8.4	Presence	125
	8.5	Power	126
	8.6	Joy	129
	8.7	Devotion, Gratitude	129
	8.8	True Self, Enlightenment, Absolute	131
9	**Going Beyond the Reason and the Wisdom of the Body**		**135**
	9.1	Running as Meditative Thinking	135
	9.2	The Call of Conscience	140
	9.3	Active-Passive Process	150
10	**Conclusion**		**159**
Literature			**169**

Chapter 1
Introduction

When I started to run, the sun was high up in the sky.
I ran for one hour, two hours.
At four o'clock there was a traffic jam, and a moment later it was gone.
The sun has already moved a long way in three hours and I just keep on running.
The light is turning reddish and the sun is not as warm as it was at the beginning.
Running exists.
The landscape is a scene in which I as a runner remain unchanged.
The landscape is temporal, and the time seems to have stopped.[1]

Physical exercise has in highly industrialized countries with a high standard of living a very different relationship to an individual and one's awareness than before. As an activity running is not dependent on technology. One's own body and a terrain suitable for running suffice. This may initiate the experience of the autonomy and "freedom" of ones actions. Unless you deliberately want to use your body and muscular strength, you choose an instrument that suits the purpose. Today, taking a physical exercise or a sports activity is a conscious choice. The conscious choice to take an exercise means challenging your bodily self. The goals of the challenge naturally depend on your motivation. For example, climbing the stairs to the fifth floor calls for a deliberate choice to walk up instead of taking the lift. It calls for entertaining the possibility to see yourself as someone climbing the stairs instead. The degree of difficulty in realizing the challenge determines its nature. It means challenging oneself in relation to an achievable goal. The starting point is the idea that you can challenge your bodily and mental self through the "flesh". Challenging yourself through the flesh is a conscious choice to be a sportive (mobile?) person. The conscious choice to take an exercise means challenging your bodily self.

This book deals with running and philosophy. Someone may ask the question what does running have to do with philosophy, what is philosophy needed for? Running involves running, a concrete physical and sweaty activity, rhythmic breath-

---

[1] An extract from my running diary.

© Springer International Publishing Switzerland 2015
T. Koski, *The Phenomenology and Philosophy of Running*,
DOI 10.1007/978-3-319-15597-5_1

ing, gasping – whereas philosophy is about philosophy and thinking, a somewhat secondary activity compared to running. One does not learn to run by reading books. Rather, one learns by running only. However, we must bear in mind that a human being is (also) a thinking creature who by thinking is capable of adjusting one's body to certain conditions and situations. A human being makes a conscious decision when and how long to run, what factors need to be taken into account in order to make the activity to best benefit and suit oneself. Each and every running experience increases our understanding about the former exercises. The increased understanding also affects the way we understand the subsequent exercise. A runner will notice the changes in her health and well-being inflicted by running. In short, running affects both one's body and one's mind.

When running or performing some exercise, a human is in a different relationship to the world compared to one's everyday activities. While in motion, the runner will face herself one on one in a sense. When running becomes important to you, you may raise the question about its nature and significance to your physical and mental health, hence your life as a whole. A runner may end up experiencing running as a positive activity and become curious to know, for example, what happened during the latest exercise when the feeling was light and euphoric and everything happened as if by itself, at ease and so naturally. Where did the experience of delight come from, without any obvious reason? And when such an experience continues after the exercise, you may easily come to ask the question what this experience means to your life and your running. At that point we are already quite far in the philosophical pondering.[2] Again, do your fellow runners share similar experiences with you?[3] This is philosophy regardless whether one thinks of it as such or not. One exercises philosophy even when denying it as useless for humans!

Running is a bodily-mental event in the corporeal world in which a runner goes through and takes a grip on an experience individually, yet partially in a way that is specific to humans, and thus common to all people. It is this common part that I wish to explore. What are these experiences that are common to all, and what is it that is so important and significant in them?

I will discuss the nature of the experiences evoked by long-distance running, how they occur and how to conceptualize and express them. Many of the experiences can be expressed with everyday language, even though they or their nature often remain unconscious. Philosophers have not investigated those hidden experiential levels (except for a few), neither have they been studied in relation to the analysis of human existence. One of those is the aforementioned experience of delight, which is apparently familiar to those who have been running long distances. Those who do not run themselves may think that this is a result from the runner's personality, from the fact that "she is a joyful person". Such experiences are probably shared amongst runners. Those who do not run are not, however, involved

---

[2] And like Amby Burfoot (2007) says in the foreword (p. ix) in *The Running and Philosophy*, "running provides a great time and space for thinking", too.

[3] See Kabasenche (2007, 103–113), where he writes about internal and external goods.

in those discussions, leaving this aspect or dimension unknown to them, which means that their understanding about running remains quite thin. What I mean to say is that you may gain your own experiences about running only by running, or else your relationship to running is formed by conceptual means only. J.P. Roos,[4] a Finnish scholar and runner, writes about the thin understanding in his Internet book *Marathon man's life* as follows:

> In his travel book America the French novelist Jean Baudrillard handles running as one of the central features of being American. For him running is an entirely inconceivable new form of masochism, suicidal behaviour, pursuit of death, volunteer slavery, and even infidelity. Mouth dribbling, eyes empty and focused on one's own internal countdown, runners represent to Baudrillard the degradation of human species, an apocalyptic atmosphere. Slightly similar tones can be identified in Antti Eskola's short notions on running as he expresses his aversion to joggers. I have met them both and I can rest assured that they would truly kill themselves if they started to run (as far as I know, Eskola is into some peaceful jogging these days!) The views presented by Baudrillard and Eskola are, however, interesting in the sense that they demonstrate how wrong the idea about the symbolic significances of running can be amongst outsiders. Especially the theme of suffering is entirely faulty: to the contrary, running is one of the forms of physical and mental self development and enjoyment in a modern society, not to mention easy social collaboration! Until this day I have not come across a runner with a dribbling mouth (although in winter your nose may dribble). Running is fun and enjoyable once you learn it.

A little bit later in the same chapter Roos states the following:

> Running in the morning or at night both have great attractions of their own. It is an unforgettable experience to run at sunrise in a quiet town, or running on empty streets under the streetlights which make the asphalt shine. – I must admit that the attraction of running does not open up in an instant. Most joggers I know complain how dull it is to run and how they actually do it against their will only because they believe they could sleep better that way, lose some weight, or the like. However, I can assure you that at some point runners will find in running the enjoyment, ease and momentum, combined with nice scenery and attractive tracks. – Only someone who does not run may imagine that it's monotonous, constantly the same. – After all running is an extremely versatile activity that you learn first after practicing it for a long period of time.

What does it tell about running and the various aspects involved with it when learned men like Jean Baudrillard and the Finnish professor Antti Eskola, respected professionals of thinking, look at running as described above? Does it really mean that those who do not run themselves cannot understand by means of mere observation and thinking the versatile experiences generated by running? I'm tempted to understand it this way.

The American journalist and experienced long-distance runner George Sheehan, who has written a lot about the philosophical aspects of running, says "moments of sudden illumination that come effortlessly and without trouble, this will become the most valuable hour of your day –".[5]

---

[4]Roos (1995), Chapter 1, first paragraph; only in Finnish.
[5]Sheehan (1978, 95).

And, in addition to everything that is directly experienced in running, the regular exercise may change one's attitude towards life: Sheehan puts it this way: "If you think that life has passed you by; or, even worse, that you are living someone else's life, you can still prove the experts wrong".[6]

Running causes a great variety of feelings and experiences. Some of the experiences are strange, lack concepts or are difficult to conceptualize and to clarify in an inter-subjective sense (unless the physical pre-understanding speaks for the same).[7] They may also give the impression that the person doing the running is peculiar, someone known for his strange experiences is easily considered strange himself. Generally speaking, things happen and do not happen. The relationship between an experience and its reflection is not a natural causal relationship, since it happens always in a personal, qualitative world.

As a physical exercise long-distance running is quite simple. The movements are not complicated, nor hard to learn. From that point of view, again, long-distance running appears to be a somewhat boring activity. What is interesting, however, is the fact that it generates such a variety of experiences. The challenge of the philosophy of running is in conceptualizing the running experiences and in learning to understand their nature in the best possible way. This is related to (1) what is the nature, true character and the essence of those experiences and (2) what do they mean to us?

There are several reasons for running. A former Finnish national level athlete Ari Paunonen[8] has analysed the purposes of running, and he has identified the following six reasons related to four stages of life:

	Childhood	Youth	Adulthood as an active runner	Adulthood after the running career
Play	xxx	x		
Competitivity	x	xxx	xx	
Targetfulness/being goal-oriented		xxx	xxx	
Way of life		xxx	xxx	xx
Well-being		x	xx	xxx
Fitness and health			x	xxx

As we can see, in childhood playing is the driver, and in youth it is competition, being goal-oriented and having a way of life, targetfulness and way of life, whatever it may mean here (probably in view of the forthcoming important career as a runner),

---

[6]Sheehan (1978, 51).

[7]See Murphy and White (1995, 103–106). The book describes hundreds of non-everyday experiences related to different sports and physical exercise in the light of various Asian philosophies, for example.

[8]Paunonen (1999, 32–33).

are the leading motives. As an adult the same factors are central, yet with well-being gaining more emphasis. After the active, competitive running career the stress is clearly on the way of life, well-being, fitness and health.

Ari Paunonen's competitiveness awoke alongside with participation to competitions. By targetfulness he means the desire to achieve something, which I understand to be good performance in competitions. Way of life refers to the importance of running, adding to the content and order in one's life, which he also considers part of spirituality. Well-being, fitness and health are close to one another. They have to do with good constitution and the lighter, stronger and more relaxed feeling caused by running. As he puts it, "after the exercise life always looks better".[9]

When you ask people about the reasons for running, they may say that they cannot tell why – it only is fun or feels good.[10] Or, they may reply that you are allowed to think of your own things in peace and be alone with your own thoughts. Surely this is true. In addition, one potential answer is that one's mind is emptied of thoughts, and there are no thoughts left in your "head". There is just quietness and emptiness. Marko Vapa describes "runner's ecstasy", a concept of sports psychology, as an indescribable

> sense of lightness during the physical exercise. The term "runner's ecstasy" is explained by the fact that runners come across this experience significantly more often than other athletes, although the sensation is quite similar. In such an ecstasy one does not usually feel pain nor have any rational thoughts rather an internal calmness and sense of balance are prevalent. The mechanism causing this state is considered to be the rhythmical and monotonous movement altering one's consciousness even long after the running exercise is over.[11] – Runner's ecstasy develops through a peaceful state of mind and typically deepens towards the end of an exercise.[12]

Sheehan writes that the benefits of running are physical grace, psychological ease and personal integrity. Among the best experiences are the peak experiences which allow you to experience unity.[13]

These factors are one reason to run. Such ways of expressing the ideas presuppose a philosophical way of thinking and looking at the experience very closely. The sensation of quietness and emptiness, being here and now, internal calmness and a sense of balance in which the sense of existence is strongly present and one's own being is filled with the sensation of existence, means both mental and spiritual rest, the capacity of which to generate strength and energy is great. Putting this in more philosophical terms, one significance of running is that with it, through a physical activity, through your body and mind, you can reach for personal integrity and being a whole human being. These are big words – and later on I will introduce them in more detail.

---

[9] Paunonen (1999, 33).

[10] An interesting and a playful way of running is the hash run. See DeWitt (2007, 71–80).

[11] Vapa (2001, p. 6/10), ref. Douillard (1994). See Murphy and White (1995, 19).

[12] Vapa (2001, p. 6/10), ref. Vettenniemi (1994), Hänninen (2001).

[13] Sheehan (1978, 72).

Philosophically it is possible to analyze the various levels related to running and in this way cast some light to the versatility of a human being. With the help of philosophical analysis, various elements related to experience can be considered and in this way made more transparent, and the understanding that so improves can be used, for example, to direct the forthcoming exercise into a meaningful direction.

In this philosophical study about long-distance running my target is:

1. to establish some ground for the debate (e.g. by opening up a discussion between runners and researchers);
2. to pursue clarity of thinking and concepts in order to allow discussing the issue on all experiential levels;
3. to analyze, conceptualize and understand the levels of human existence related to the experiences caused by running.[14]

It is important to make an attempt to clarify these targets as well as possible, since they are related to the essential problems of representation, i.e. to the way a human being conceptually takes possession of the world. What can we talk about and how? And when we talk, what are we actually talking about? What is the ontological status of speech[15] (especially when we talk about something that according to the philosopher Ludwig Wittgenstein cannot be talked about)?

This study discusses the following fields:

1. Philosophical view to human being, here pertaining to the phenomenological way of examining the human being with which an attempt is made to conceptualize and understand the sensations and experiences produced by running. Understanding is important especially to researchers of physical education – understanding the human being as multidimensional is an important starting point and viewpoint for everyone involved in humane work. Philosophical research can be utilized when pondering about the guidelines for physical education. In addition, new ways of thinking about physical exercise and experiencing them are often transferred from the parents to the children and the youth. This, again, has an impact on what kind of physical exercise and sports the future adults adopt and feel attracted to. From the point of view of the future of physical culture and physical education the important issues is research that sheds light on the different levels of human being. In this way we can learn to understand the factors that serve as initiators for a lifelong physical exercise;

---

[14] Kari Ilmarinen, former editor-in-chief of the Finnish runner's journal "Juoksija", writes in issue 6/1981, p. 16, the following: "Sports journalism has often been blamed for superficiality, yet not too much attention to its essence has been paid by means of research either. – Nobody can deny the great significance of sports, but very few can tell us why it is so important."

[15] The ultimate way of existence and significance of the issues, phenomena and entities under discussion in the hierarchy or our existence.

1 Introduction 7

2. Participative method in the philosophy of physical exercise which means that the researcher himself practices the sport being the subject of the study, making him a research subject as well[16];
3. In order to study running on a relevant basis, we must outline the (human) way of being in the world (Martin Heidegger), the existential basis of one's bodily nature and its significance (ontology) – here in reference to Maurice Merleau-Ponty's philosophy of the body.[17]

I will not discuss topics like doping, problems of competitive sports, commercialism, nor differences between the sexes. Neither will I concentrate on any technical analysis of running, but rather on the experiences produced by it and their significance – making an attempt to look at running very closely. These include an increased understanding of one's own body as a result of exercise, increased vitality and the existential and ethical experiences related to one's existence. These topics bear an important relation to spiritual relaxation and increasing tranquillity – which could also be called increased peace of mind and spiritual growth. The Finnish philosopher Lauri Rauhala,[18] defines spiritual growth as clarification of the sense of values, responsibility for oneself, fellow humans and nature, ability to feel love and empathy, increased sense of beauty, reduced selfishness and reduced amount of negative ways of thinking and acting. When defined in this way, spiritual growth is inseparably related to increased self-knowledge and self-understanding, as well to peace of mind, and experience of oneness and holiness. This theme is visible already in my doctoral dissertation in which I claimed that with the help of physical exercise it is possible to explore oneself.

In research related to sports we often talk about the "mental growth" of an athlete and how sport helps grow. What this means in practice is mostly better perseverance, improved ability to concentrate to avoid giving up, which is the psychic impact of exercising the biological-physical part of the human being. The fact that one can act with better perseverance and concentration a.s.o. may serve one in managing everyday life, but this has nothing to do with the ethical level of the person. Seeing the impact of exercise and sports in the truncated way described above only refers to the human ego, and not any "deeper" down to what lays the foundation for the ego, too. This foundation is, as I see it, the birthplace of ethicalness.

As a starting point we may point out that a physical exercise in relation to knowing oneself and one's own body better could be both conscious and subconscious – by a subconscious exercise I mean that an individual's conscious attitude towards the goal sought (such as good physical condition or loss of weight) may bring along something that is not consciously targeted at. In other words, a

---

[16]This viewpoint of research has been thematized largely through the fact that I run long distances such as marathon myself. Tai-Chi (or Taiji), yoga and karate-do have been part of my way of life for many many years.

[17]When Heidegger and Merleau-Ponty talk about ontology, they refer to the ways in which a human being exists in the world.

[18]Rauhala (1990, 207).

runner does not very often reach for better self-knowledge rather for better physical condition and health. Running produces experiences that add to the understanding of one's body and mind, and in case they are strong enough and gain attention, the person may come to see the significance of running in a new light. Generally speaking, with the help of exercise you become more aware of your existence in the world, since the act of running takes place only by starting to do it, by setting your body to do it. The basis for this setting is that the human body is the centre of one's existence. The touch of the body and the world, the ontic[19] touch, the concrete exercise, serves as a basis for the experiences.

On the other hand there is the exercise in which the conscious target is to increase the understanding of one's own body and oneself. By regarding a physical exercise as a workout you can seek towards experiences which dissolve and reduce alienation and separation between man and the world. In many of the physical-spiritual traditions targeting at spiritual growth the idea is to consciously seek for a whole and solid experience in which existence is felt to be peaceful and tranquil. Such experiences are valuable existential experiences, adding to the quality of life. With the help of exercise and living in relation to it you can understand more about yourself, human relationships and the world, which is also reflected in your everyday life.[20]

As a way of investigating oneself, long-distance running can be seen as active work in order to increase self-knowledge, serving at the same time as improved consciousness and understanding of the reality. By doing this the purpose of a physical exercise is not only to acquire a good physical condition, physical competitiveness and skill. It is important to become aware of one's own potentials. **Mere knowledge is not sufficient as such, since it is important for us to experimentally understand the creative basis of the liberated activity on the basis of which also the potentials are realized**! By "experimental understanding" I mean the conception that develops through one's own concrete action, whereas by "mere knowledge" I refer to the conceptual structure evolved solely from rational thinking.

I hope that the results of this study could help runners identify their own structures of meaning in their reasons why to run. This is to say that if running is based merely on external target setting (winning, success, social esteem, rewards, etc.), the runner may, after the end of her career, fall into an existential vacuum in which the meaningfulness of life is lost when everything that the life was based on ceases to exist. This may have some negative impact on a runner's (athlete's) life. In case the runner has been able to explore her inner self and such structures of meaning that allow the analysis of her existential being in the world, life is not over at the end of the career. Rather a new phase in life opens up.

In Finland there was a project in which the target was to help athletes at the end of their sports career and to prevent them from falling into the trap of a vacuum in

---

[19] See Chap. 2.
[20] Koski (2000, 179).

their lives. The most apt to alienation are those athletes whose entire childhood and youth has been bound solely to sports, says Ritva Söyring who was in charge of the project. According to her we have a national duty to make sure that athletes have a chance to continue a decent life after their careers.[21]

It is important for a runner's life that experience and the self-understanding about one's own realized potentials improved by experience, widens and thematizes the operational horizon into the future as well. That being the case, the runner's existence and understanding of the experience are not limited to the present, but rather let her be open to the world and feel confident about the future.[22]

When running is considered to contain this dimension, the target is no longer merely to gain and maintain a good physical condition and health rather improved self-knowledge as well. If and when a human being finds a state of true creativity and freedom through one's inner experience, the reality will open up as a sphere of individual activity. This can be seen as a means of personal, unalienated and authentic being in the world. It is an active and individual process in which a human being makes an attempt to realize everything that originates from the self to gain a life that looks like the self.

It is in the interest of this study to encourage and make people run. Long-distance running may be a philosophical way of self-exploration (as love of wisdom and as "fronesis", i.e. an activity driven by common sense to seek for wisdom and a good life). This means that long-distance running is approached as a subject through one's own experience, after which it is put into proportion with the intersubjective reality.

The idea of challenging yourself through flesh, mentioned at the beginning, is a provocative expression in which I exploit the dualistically evolved understanding about the relationship between the body and the mind (based on the dualism of the body and the soul). Challenging the flesh should be understood as challenging both the body and the soul, as challenging human existence, monistically, and not dualistically. In other words, as the body and the soul are one, challenging your flesh also means challenging your mind. From a philosophical point of view the starting point is an incarnated[23] human being, a material and extensive mental being with a consciousness.

When answering this provocative question one must ask why is it something to reach for and what is the significance of this type of challenging. Answering the question presupposes

(a) mapping the conditions of bodily human existence in the world, mainly through Merleau-Ponty's philosophy. Challenging the self through the flesh takes place
(b) in certain forms of existence that are analysed by Heidegger's fundamental ontology. To support my analysis, I use

---

[21] Aviisi (2004, 8).

[22] Koski (2000, 178).

[23] A bodily human being, not the kind of being whose bodilyness is considered secondary and a burden from the viewpoint of the spiritual essence which is seen as primary and real.

(c) the phenomenological method and my own experiences as a runner, which means that the study proceeds also
(d) supported by the participatory method of philosophy of physical exercise.
(e) The concrete sports discussed in this study is long-distance running, the description and analysis of which is interpreted from the viewpoint of challenging oneself through the flesh.

Challenging the flesh can be both active and passive. Active challenging is conscious. Passive challenging means staying alive, to put it simply. Using the terms of Spinoza, it is the motivating action of "conatus" (power that maintains the existence of a being).

Conscious challenging means conscious setting of the self in its situation. Situation means here the situatedness of life. "The basis for this term is the situation, the moment in life, which pertains to everything that the human body and consciousness are related to. Thus, the term situation comprises climatic and geographical conditions, culture, nationality, social and economical conditions, fellow humans, values, norms, God, hell, etc. Situatedness of life means man's entanglement to the structural elements of his life situation".[24] Conscious challenging is about self-exploration in the chosen situation as well as conscious submission of the body into a certain relationship with the world. Conscious challenging of the flesh is a concrete physical exercise. Thus, I want to emphasize the difference compared to just thinking about the issue. It is essential, important and significant to concretely, bodily and functionally perform the exercise, **to run and not only think about doing it**.

By choosing to consciously challenge the flesh it is possible to influence the way one's life is built. This is the positive impact of a physical exercise. A relationship with the world that is not actively sportively thematized constitutes an individual in a passive way from the sportive point of view (negative impact). Passive challenging of the flesh means being without a conscious sportive thematization of the self.

Challenging, whether conscious or not, has a constitutive meaning for an individual. A conscious exercise constitutes an individual to the consciously chosen direction which is adopted via pre-understanding.

Active challenging may take place when you are motivated, happy, eager, etc. The significance of challenging lies in the fact that it shows the meaning of physical exercise to our lives. In other words, you can choose to challenge yourself through running as one means of existence. In this case the targeted self is principally ahead of you. It is something important and worth reaching for.

In short, I choose myself in my life to challenge myself and to reach for something greater than my existence at that moment.

It is somewhat problematic to write about the experiences of physical exercise, and it is hard to make a philosophical analysis merely by adhering to one's own experiences. In order to extract something more structured, they must be seen as

---

[24]Rauhala (1991, 40).

part of another, larger entity, which in this case is philosophical study of man. Such research is intersubjective, which means that the research tradition has evolved over a long period of time through several generations – each philosopher who has added his own flavour to the tradition is in a way standing on the shoulders of his predecessors. This entails the burden of theoretical concepts that over the years has developed into jargon. If written without the support of those traditions, the text often remains flat and thin and fails to carry those meanings which in the long tradition of philosophical thinking have been considered important and significant and which best describe the nature of human existence and have been tested and thought through by in-depth and drawn-out pondering of several philosophers.

With all this I refer to the fact that in this study I utilize the thinking of Maurice Merleau-Ponty and Martin Heidegger, of which especially Heidegger's philosophy is quite difficult to "tackle". One must bear in mind, however, that all ideas about the human being and one's being in the world embedded in theoretical thinking are in a broad sense based on human experience, which allows us to think that it cannot be very different even from the viewpoint of a present-day human being. Thus, everyone's experiences are based on the body as the centre of being in the world. By being in the world the body forms the basis for pre-understanding, which principally is the same for all of us.

Another fact that adds to the difficulty of writing about this subject is the fact that no philosophical phenomenological analysis (a monograph) of running has formerly been made, thus there is no-one whose shoulders to lean on.

He takes life as it comes and says yes[25]

This study emphasizes the importance of the body and the mind and their mutual relationship. It is important, through physical exercise, to gain an increased ability to experience reality, understand the nature of one's existence and increase understanding of the self.

The factors related to personal experiential meaningfulness neglected e.g. by the traditional supercompensation theory have been considered in modern sports coaching. Marko Vapa,[26] Finland, writes: "Contemporary learning theories have notified the importance of enjoyment, having fun and personal experience." Experiencing frequently the runner's flow in endurance training and the joy related to an athlete's entire life could be the solution for continuous, day-to-day high performance. The healthier the athlete, the better are the chances to reach the top. At least there would be fewer problems on the way.[27]

Occidental tradition does not contain any philosophical types of physical exercise, yet Plato in his philosophy presents the paideia theory according to which it is also essential for versatile human growth to undergo physical exercise. The

---

[25] Sheehan (1978, 207).

[26] Vapa (2001, p. 8/10).

[27] Vapa (2001, p. 8/10).

former professor Raili Kauppi[28] from Tampere University, Finland, writes about the significance of philosophy to people: "Throughout the history of philosophy, from the very beginning, there has existed the conception that philosophy is not only about theoretical thinking, pure general science, rather it has a profound practical significance to human communities and above all to the individual."

First after the Asian traditions of physical exercise had spread to the West, the connection between physical exercise and philosophy became apparent. Yoga, for example, spread to the West in the early 20th century. The latest of them are the Japanese martial arts (budo) developed for fighting and self-defence. In the West we have also become familiar with the so-called holy dances. In these philosophic-religious traditions physical exercise and spiritual growth are connected to one another. In the light of philosophical analysis we can say that in these traditions the target is to overcome the limited individual and to realize in oneself what a human being potentially is. This is the target of all "perennial" traditions of physical exercise: to become more like oneself, to become a whole.

In the philosophical tradition perennial philosophy targets at identifying all that is in common to all philosophical schools despite their mutual contradictions. This view was presumably first presented by Augustinus Steuchus in his work *De perenni philosophia* in 1540.[29] Generally speaking, perennial philosophy investigates philosophical, scientific, religious and any systems and mental structures with the help of which people have throughout times been reaching for constituting themselves and the world. This includes, for example, people's endeavours to pursue peace of mind, becoming a whole, and wisdom.

The significance of exercise lies in the fact that it could lead to changing the way you experience the world and your existence.[30] In this sense the perennial techniques serve as a kind of psychotherapy, an idea supported by Lauri Rauhala, for example. For runners who have discovered the spiritual aspect of the exercise, running "is not a test but a therapy, not a trial but a reward, not the question but an answer", as Sheehan[31] felicitously puts it. Murphy & White[32] claim that sports reveal to a human being the nature of one's existence just as it is presented in the perennial philosophy.

My understanding is that the experiences which (also ethically) constitute an individual must be investigated ontologically (in the sense presented by Heidegger and Merleau-Ponty), since we are talking about "preobjective" experiences. These experiences precede information and a conceptual representation of the world and serve as a basis for knowledge. When looking at the experiences constituting an individual, it is essential to understand that the question is not about conceptual

---

[28] Kauppi (1990, 1).

[29] Nasr (1976, vii); see Kauppi (1978, 1–2, 6).

[30] Koski (2000, 22–23).

[31] Sheehan (1978, 75).

[32] Murphy and White (1995, 127).

relationships, which are the operational area of the ego, rather about the relationship between the body and the world, about the touch between the body and the world. As physical exercise has more than just physiological effects, it is important to study the levels of human existence in which a person is realized and becomes a social being.

Sports and physical exercise have their ethical aspect as well. The ethics of sports has been under a debate over and over again. This study will focus on the primary and fundamental experiences which the whole debate on the ethical is (or should be) based on. By this I mean the preobjective experiences that emerge from the touch between an individual and the world, all of which do not have a conceptually clear expression in everyday language. These experiences form the basic substance which an individual can become aware of. One of the special instances is the existential or "peak" experiences which I consider ethical by nature.

The long-distance runner George Sheehan has written about running and its significance, intending to answer the question "why". Sheehan's family writes that he thought that runners didn't run just to stay fit. They weren't out there to lower their cholesterol or blood pressure. Although that might have been the reason they started, most continued because they had discovered a greater fulfilment – the physical morality that one develops through exercise and sport. This, he believed, would lead to a greater morality in one's life in general.[33] This morality, which can be discovered by running, is based on the same experience that I'm writing about in this context (preobjective and bodily physical experiences). Sheehan[34] writes: "Sport will not build character; it will do something better. It will make a free man. It has this tremendous potential for self-revelation. What we want to know is who we are, and sport can tell us quickly, painlessly –."

In other words, bodily experiences can be seen as a basis for ethical ones, of which the peak experiences may be of great importance to an athlete. Their significance lies in the fact that they act as inner indicators guiding an individual, something that external memorized ethical norms fail to do. Long-distance running can be characterized with the same elements that call for articulation.

The Finnish ultra-distance runner Pekka Lehto ran through the U.S. in 50 days, the daily mileage varying from 50 to 75. When he was asked for a reason to his running, he replied that he wanted to become alike with his soul. Intuitively this is quite understandable, yet in a philosophical sense it is difficult to define accurately. I call such a goal and process an existential-ontological metamorphosis of a living body, one of the unuttered targets of which could be living a good life. By this I mean peace of mind and "wisdom", also known as transcendental wisdom and wisdom of the heart (gnosis). Sheehan,[35] on the other hand, claims that his training regime was not a training regime rather a campaign, a coup, taking a new direction. He tells about his decision to find himself; "how do you want to live the rest of your life"?

---

[33]Sheehan (1978, 7).
[34]Sheehan (1978, 10).
[35]Sheehan (1978, 62, 64).

In that process he discovered his body and the soul that comes along with it. In this way he started a new life by discovering his body in a new way. Little philosophical research of such experiences in connection with sports and physical exercise exist.

I consider an individual's (living) body the starting point for this study. The experiences from physical exercise are analyzed and interpreted by means of a phenomenological method, giving emphasis on individual experience. It is essential to study what these experiences mean to the individual himself and what they have been considered to mean in different cultures throughout the history. This kind of study combines the traditions of physical exercise with the meaningfulness of an individual's life.

The Finnish philosopher Timo Klemola also puts emphasis on the bodily experience in his study.[36] One of the aspects of his study is the criticism of the dualistic way of thinking. The core of his critique is found in bodily experience through which "these divisions can be broken by experience. This process is largely conducted by exercising the body, especially breathing. The point is about a kind of deep dive into the bodily experience and return from there equipped with a new kind of understanding."

For my research I have chosen from the selected philosophers such concepts that best convey the desired meanings. I have used personal matters to interpret source literature and hence what is personal.[37] I have made an attempt to select the concepts so that their intersubjective significance would be as much in line as possible. Thus, I'm not looking at the philosophers or philosophical traditions from the viewpoint of their internal consistency, neither do I investigate the relationship between individual concepts and theories. Historical connections are likewise not under the scope of my research. Instead, I use the concepts of the philosophers and traditions to introduce my own ideas. In a way, I have selected the maximally matching conceptual tools from a philosophical toolkit. The above can in poetic phenomenological terms be crystallised as follows: based on my understanding and perception I have made an attempt to pave the way for the reader to ease one's own understanding.[38]

In addition my work involves the philosophical problem how to present something beyond conceptual in conceptual terms. This problem is related to the primary nature of personal exercise in an individual's constitution in comparison to the understanding achieved with the help of concepts. Since this is a written work, I'm making an attempt to do something that is impossible to reach. In other words, how to conceptualise the experiences generated by exercises, which due to their nature are sometimes out of the reach of the conceptual? If an experience is rare,

---

[36]Klemola (2004, 10). (*Taidon filosofia – filosofin taito* [The Philosophy of Art – A Philosopher's Art]. The book is available only in Finnish.)

[37]Compare this to the two aspects of intentional relation, subject-in-relation-to-the-object and object-in-relation-to-the-subject, which cannot be understood without the relationship to one another (Schmitt 1967, 67).

[38]See Koski (2000, 34).

it is personal for a small minority only. The reader lacking this kind of experience will only read the term without understanding its substance – the intersubjective connection is missing. Confusion may also arise from the many different traditions dealing with experiences remaining outside the conceptual which, however, use different concepts and terms about them due to their fundamental ontological commitments. The purpose of this work in this respect is to give hints and show direction. This idea also arises from the Zen tradition – even though spoken words and (minimally constricted) literature is used to support the teaching, ultimately the texts are, as understood by the tradition, waste paper which can only be used for wiping out the intellectual garbage.[39]

---

[39] See Koski (2000, 35).

Chapter 2
Running as Phenomenological and Bodily Inquiry of the Self

Running a marathon is a process in which the body and the psyche go through a certain experiential curve: the experience of long-distance running. It involves the desire to win, fatigue, sensations of dehydration, i.e. both things that you may experience without running a marathon, and also the kind of experiences which you may come across only by running a marathon, experiences that are unique to that kind of physical exercise.[1]

A basic assumption for the study is that running produces a variety of experiences. *My most central point of view is that it is possible to conceptually uncover various levels of human experience and experiential cores.* The intensity of the levels varies. The strongest of them always have to do with existential questions. The problem with them is that the foundation of experiences is always preobjective by nature, which means that they do not automatically become articulated in a runner's mind as intersubjective, adequate concepts (in other words, an experience is not automatically transformed in people's minds into common and shared concepts that everyone would understand the same way). Therefore experiences are often hard to express by language. They are understood through cultural connotations and are conceptualized, for example, as pleasure, relaxation, pain, distress, tranquility, peace of mind, joy, thankfulness, devotion, etc.

I analyse the experiences produced by running also by means of Martin Heidegger's fundamental-ontological philosophy. He uses the term Dasein to describe a human being as a process. Rauhala[2] states that Dasein is an auxiliary concept of philosophical analysis,

> which is a mere moment of potential for humans. It has no real qualifiers yet. When Dasein faces its existential condition in its experiential situation, the existence, i.e. the true human being is realized. – In the view of existential phenomenological analysis a human being is continuously in the process of becoming something. Therefore it [Dasein] serves as an

---

[1] Kitti (1997).
[2] Rauhala (1990, 131–132).

© Springer International Publishing Switzerland 2015
T. Koski, *The Phenomenology and the Philosophy of Running*,
DOI 10.1007/978-3-319-15597-5_2

objection toward such schools of research in which human existence is frozen to be static, an entity that also in its occurrence would always and everywhere follow the same pattern.

Running is a versatile physical exercise which, however, does not immediately reveal all of the dimensions it has. Those dimensions are not exposed to outside spectators who do not run themselves[3] and are not always exposed conceptually to the runner. Rather, they appear mostly as sensations, feelings and experiences. Running can serve as a peaceful passage and self-exploration, as quality time that brings you joy. It can be more and something else than just keeping fit or competitive sports. These levels hidden from the direct look can be investigated in order to uncover the meanings embedded in experiences. By means of a hermeneutic approach I make an attempt to uncover some of those hidden meanings related to human experience. *The purpose is to conceptualize experiential levels that remain beyond everyday language.*

The goal of this study is to investigate the experiences produced by running by using phenomenological and hermeneutical means. The research problem is how to describe, conceptualize, analyse and interpret these experiential phenomena. This means that the experiential structures of long-distance running are opened up and analysed. The research involves the following: (a) what kind of experiences long-distance running produces, (b) what dimension and "levels" (experiential cores) they contain and (c) what is their status in the hierarchy of experiences (significance to an individual). The analysis is an attempt to find out how those experiences represent the different aspects of human experience. In terms of content, it involves, e.g., the following questions:

1. The ontic relation between the body and the world in a factual exercise: the significance of the senses, temporality and ecstasity of the body (the touch to the ground, the sun on the skin, sweat, wind, rain, frost, movement, etc.).

    The ontic touch is an ontological (in the traditional ontological sense) structure related to man's being in the world, where the human being together with other entities is realized. There is a structure that is in common to all humans. This real touch to the world contains and produces all the means of experience which the entities involved in it can come to experience. When seen from the human point of view, I mean primarily the touches that affect an individual through bodilyness. In this way the ontic touch is considered in the research of the philosophy of physical exercise from the human point of view, and so can be used to describe man's preobjective structure in which experiencing takes place. The experiential that forms the foundation emerges solely from this ontic touch. When you exercise regularly and methodically, your senses become more sensitive, allowing you to perceive the elements transmitted through them

---

[3]Kari Ilmarinen (1981, 17) writes about his amazement when the claim "sport with its victories and defeats thus describes something essential about human existence" in his seminar presentation at Tampere University made the listeners react in a way which was a total surprise to him: some of them did not buy the idea at all. Having spent more than half of his life with various sports this reaction was incomprehensible."

in a richer and more delicate and versatile way. At the same time man's internal experiential horizon is broadened and opened up – "the world enters into a human being" more completely, i.e. the world is seen as more complete.

The term ontic refers to the kind of being that man is in touch with (Merleau-Ponty calls it the preobjective world), which forms the factual foundation of human existence.[4] This is what I believe Heidegger refers to when he writes: "The kind of Being which belongs to Dasein is rather such that, in understanding its own Being, it has a tendency to do so in terms of that entity towards which it comports itself proximally and in a way which is essentially constant – in terms of the 'world'." Meyers kleines Lexikon Philosophie[5] defines ontic as follows "the difference to ontological is the true being in its individuality or in its spatial-temporal factuality; it is indeed already readily understood (as a phenomenon) by the spirit, although not yet a (rationally) unfolded being". I myself see ontic as such an entity which we can be in touch with and from which we can derive a sensation. In this way ontic also refers to such entities that are dimensional and concrete.[6] For example, an ontic piece is a (principally tangible) dimensional entity (as a distinction from a rounded cube to name one). Heidegger[7] writes about man's ontic way of being as follows: "ontically, of course, Dasein is not only close to us – even that which is closest: we *are* it, each of us, we ourselves." This refers to the primarily experiential nature of man's bodily being-in-the-world.

2. Experience and analysis of the running exercise and "lived body" using the idea of the "ontic touch". In this way an individual can set a thematization horizon which helps her to pay attention to the versatile elements produced by running.
3. Feelings, states of mind, experiences: the lightness vs. strain of the exercise, pain, joy, ease, tranquillity, peace, thankfulness, unity, change in the experiential horizon, etc.
4. How a long-lasting physical strain and the spiritual concentration it requires impact a runner's experiential horizon?
5. How is one's consciousness related to the idea of the exercise?
6. How does the meaning of an exercise get set?
7. What factors constitute the essence of an exercise?
8. How to interpret changes in the states of consciousness?

I will analyse and uncover also those experiences which make a competing athlete or an enthusiast exercise, the factors that give the motivation to go on. By analyzing the different levels of experience we can distinguish between the meaningful and meaningless experiences. With the help of this analysis an individual can become more aware of the nature of her experiences and their significance. This also

---

[4] See Heidegger (1978, 32–36).
[5] Meyers kleines Lexikon Philosophie (1987, 299).
[6] Cf. Kaelin (1988, 29).
[7] Heidegger (1978, 36–37).

helps one in focusing an exercise in a more meaningful, adequate and personally suitable way. In this way exercise can turn into a hermeneutic circle in which pre-understanding, increased self-understanding and exercise are in a dialogical relationship with one another.

One important aspect is how long-distance running can bring an individual experientially closer to the world in such a way that it allows the emergence of ethical experiences. In what circumstances do such experiences emerge? Where do those experiences originate from? How can you influence their emergence?

I also investigate what long-distance running means as a way of life and as a perennial exercise. Perennial philosophy proposes possible ways of uncovering experiences and values that add to the quality of life. The foundation of perennial philosophy lies on all those thinkers, manners, beliefs and traditions with which phenomena considered perennial have been approached in the history of mankind. The themes of perennial wisdom have also been part of the European philosophical tradition for thousands of years starting from philosophers prior to Socrates and ancient Greece. Empedocles, Plotinos, christian mysticists (e.g. Augustine, Eckhart, Juan de la Cruz, Silesius, Böhme) have all been reaching for wisdom, the connection to the foundation. Reaching for wisdom has also given rise to several schools (such as Pythagoreanism, Gnosticism, Neo-Platonism). Later European seekers have been, for example: Spinoza (who has written in his work Ethics about wisdom and free man), Schopenhauer, Weil, Heidegger, Levinas, and Scheler. In the original sense or, one of them, philosophy can be said to be wondering about the surrounding world and man's search for one's own position, which has nothing to do with dogmatism.[8]

"At all stages of the problem setting of 'philosophia perennis' the ethical question of leading a good life is present. In the classical tradition the good is usually seen as something that can be known, at least in some sense of the word 'to know'."[9] The research of the formerly mentioned questions falls under the scope of the philosophy of exercise in terms of the philosophy of value in the sense that through the perennial perspective physical exercise as a human practice reaches some existential depth. By perennial exercise I refer to all types of exercise in which the goal is not only to maintain and improve physical condition but to provide a means to explore oneself and the world around us and in this way to strive for wisdom and peace of mind. An exercise is not perennial if the understanding it provides remains merely on the level of non-experiential conceptual relationships.

Perennial philosophy deals with basic questions like what is a good life, what is the meaning of being ethical, what does it mean to strive for perfection and how is this related to wisdom. Perennial philosophy provides a physical exercise enthusiast a conceptual framework for interpreting one's experiences. *The significance of the experiences gained through physical exercise is essentially the way they affect people's means of experiencing and seeing the world. Consequently, the experience*

---

[8]See Kauppi (1978).

[9]Kauppi (1978, 7).

produced by exercise and all that is of importance in a human sense finds it realization in everyday life.[10]

There are physical exercise traditions in which the aim is to systematically reach for growth as a human being and for the ideal of an ethical human being. As an example of such traditions I discuss the Japanese "marathon monks" later in this study. In other words, running can be seen as a perennial exercise or as a part of it. During an exercise and/or after it, an individual may experience peace and tranquillity which she may wish to deepen further (either by continuing to do the same exercise or by seeking for more efficient ones in this respect, such as the traditional meditation techniques). In this situation essential are the kinds of experience that are existentially constitutive by nature to humans, such as flow and peak experiences.

The aim in meditative traditions is to strive for the good, variously called by terms such as "finding the true self", "enlightenment" – Spinoza's "intuitive knowledge", "free man" and Heidegger's "authentic self" refer to a similar spiritual experience.

We have all the reason to claim that flow as a meditative experiential state opens out a human being and makes her more and more open to the experiential nature of the world and provides the world some space and a route to "enter into a human being". This event is part of an individual becoming a whole and her realization – not from the ego out but rather from the relationship between the individual and the world. Another way to express the issue (not from the point of view of how the phenomenon is constituted, but from the viewpoint of the individual) is to say that it is about the realization of some latent aspects of the essence of your being or about the opening of the horizon set by them, when an individual has a real opportunity to realize her potentials and in this way set herself as something ever more complete.

In perennial physical exercise traditions, exercise and bodily training are a way of life. It is helpful to an individual that she has a tradition to lean on when training. This tradition – as a theoretical crystallization of thousands of years old experience – guides us amidst the new kinds of experience created by the exercise. From the point of view of running, in order to consciously direct the training to a certain direction, support from a tradition is needed to conceptually tell what kind of experience a runner could face, what she may have experienced already and what is the nature and status of the experiences.

Running can be seen as a way of life. An exercise tradition becomes a way of life when it is no longer performed in order to gain some immediate benefit but to develop the psychophysical totality of a human being. The question is what kind of attitude you take towards training. Through an attitude of holistic development, an exercise is no longer merely an exercise, but a natural part of one's way of life.

You can improve your self-understanding by training. One of the central tasks, then, is to deconstruct anything that prevents this (the process also involves

---

[10]The Japanese philosopher Shinobu Abe (1985, 4) writes that experience as such is sufficient to a human being herself, yet there is the danger that she interprets experience in a wrong way and gets distracted (see Merleau-Ponty 1987, 250).

reconstruction). Here the most important factor is the ego of an individual. I call this process of deconstruction and reconstruction the *deconstruction of the ego*, which can be exercised by long-distance running – I see the deconstruction of the ego as an important step in developing as a human being which to me represents authentication of the individual. Studying the nature of this process using the problem setting of Heidegger's fundamental ontology shows that a running exercise is of significant existential importance.

The question is about the deconstruction and construction of the ego – here ego means the conscious self of an individual. The deconstruction of the ego is fundamentally an ontic experience, which is a preontological experience that takes place in the touch between man and the world (the ontic touch thus refers to an experience that occurs before conceptualization). In this experience the dualism of the subject and the object is "exceeded". The deconstruction means that the ego is not and does not get destroyed, rather its organisation and being in the world is modified. The deconstruction of the ego has an impact on one's way to experience reality, which changes the way of being in the world entirely. In the end of this study I will analyse the deconstruction of the ego with the help of the concept of active-passive process.[11]

To sum up: how can a runner investigate by means of exercise her own existential potentials and how is it possible through this to realize the potentials and make oneself more whole, which, for example, Heidegger analyses in his problem of the *authentic self*. The idea of authenticity, which is related, for example, to the call of conscience, is an important theme throughout this study. Here we can do with the following simple idea: a common target in people's lives is that they could live as themselves with their potentials fully realized and having control over themselves, their lives and the world.

In 29 Nov 2003, when I was running, the question why Heidegger writes about "authenticity" and the "call of conscience", what these concepts actually mean, suddenly occurred to my mind. As I see it, Heidegger makes an attempt to describe an important and significant process that takes place deep in an individual, yet his way of writing about the "call of conscience" is difficult to follow and very far from everyday language.

The most central theme in this study is the question how the life of an individual is organized and realized through running? What parts of life does it involve, what ways of existence is it related to? In all, how does a human being exist (for oneself) as a running being? Naturally, the question comprises not only the act of running but also those moments when one is not running. Tentatively I see that the question covers at least those conscious thoughts that in one way or another have to do with running and the issues related to it. What if running made you change for a more healthy diet? When healthy eating habits become a way of life, you do not consciously think about running or that, for example, "now I eat healthily because it promotes my vitality, improves running, etc."

---

[11] See Koski (2000, 132–142, 153–157, 177, 205–212).

Before moving on to discuss Maurice Merleau-Ponty and Martin Heidegger, a few words about Wilhelm Dilthey (1833–1911) and his philosophy.

Dilthey made an attempt to create a *Geisteswissenschaft* which could take the special nature of the human into account. He claimed that the theory of knowledge of his time explained experience and knowledge purely from an ideal and abstract point of view. "No real blood flows in the veins of the knowing subject constructed by Locke, Hume, and Kant, but rather the diluted extract of reason as a mere activity of thought".[12] Dilthey made an effort to raise the issue of individual and concrete experiences into philosophical discussion.

Dilthey makes a separation between (a) experience as it is before it becomes conscious in reflective thinking (Erlebnis) and (b) experience as reflected (Erfahrung). Erfahrung as part of reflective consciousness is a kind of second-level experience. According to Dilthey it is an experience which has been submitted to evaluation or some concept and therefore belongs to the area of representative knowledge. Erlebnis, to the contrary, belongs to the preconscious area.[13] Erlebnis could also be characterized as an asubjective experience, which means that the difference between the self and the world is not conceptually realized in the subject. Speaking in traditional terms, there is no subject-object distinction.

Erlebnis finds its roots in Fichte's philosophy. To Fichte an experience means the subjects state of being unreflectively taken by a given state.[14] This corresponds to the above-mentioned experiential state before consciousness takes it reflectively into possession. Consequently, we may also call Erlebnis or lived experience as the immediate, original experience.

The conceptual pair Erfahrung–Erlebnis makes a distinction in relation to consciousness as well. Dilthey separates them as refle**ct**ive and refle**x**ive consciousness. Erlebnis belongs to the state of preconsciousness in which the subject is not separated from the object through reflection. "Erlebnis is the level of consciousness where the experiencing subject and the content of the experience are one", writes Oesch.[15] In reflexive consciousness the subject is not yet separated from what is to be perceived. This state is called immediate consciousness. Reflexive consciousness is the primary fact of being-for-oneself (Für-sich-sein) which, like life itself, does not yet make a distinction between the subject and the object but serves as a basis for that purpose.[16]

Oesch explicates Dilthey by stating that "at the level of a lived experience one's mind has not yet reached self-awareness and started reflectively to ponder what lived experiences mean. Thus, the mind has not become an object to itself".[17] Lived

---

[12]Dilthey (1982, 288).
[13]Dilthey (1982, 160).
[14]Dilthey (1982, 159).
[15]Oesch (2002, 296).
[16]Dilthey (1982, 161).
[17]Oesch (2002, 296).

experience is present in its own immediacy as something directly experienced – every one of us experiences our own body as lived, since an individual is the living weft created by the existing in which experiences are realized. A lived experience forms the substance to the reflective consciousness, which in this way can afterwards take possession of the experienced world. Dilthey writes that a lived experience forms the versatility in which reality is present to us. A lived experience is present to me through the fact that I am internally aware of directly possessing something that belongs to me. Only by thinking can it become an object to me.[18]

I take this to mean that lived experiences in a way "get stuck" in the body or the "bodymind", from which they are presented to the experiencer herself (as an epistemic agent). The presentation can be direct and spontaneous or something consciously and thematically set by the experiencer. Spontaneous experiences are presented when they get separated from the ordinary flow of experiences, i.e. are intensive, strong and different by nature, for example. Thematically, the subject can consciously focus one's attention on potential experiences.

In connection with long-distance running the significance of the body together with Erfahrung and Erlebnis becomes clearly visible. The starting point for the significance of running is the ontic touch between the body and the world, which in the lived body becomes internally and directly experienced by the runner (and so is reflexive as a state of consciousness). Roos[19] writes "how enjoyable running can be at its best: a playfully light and relaxed passage in which the mileage is covered without one noticing it and in which running does not disturb enjoying the beautiful scenery or good company in any way – or on the other hand you may concentrate on yourself and feel the perfection of your body." A lived experience is the basic substance of meaning, which in the research after reflection is set as a research object, as the subject of the analysis, the aim being to penetrate under the surface to the original to which the word refers to.

---

[18]Dilthey (1982, 162).
[19]Roos (1995), Chapter 4.

Chapter 3
The Philosophical Foundation of Running

This study is a phenomenological one. Since phenomenology is a very broad area and difficult to define unambiguously, in the following I present the point of view on phenomenology used in this study. In a sense, phenomenology is considered an approach rather than an entity that takes its form by using certain exact methods. My view on the nature of phenomenology relies on the ideas of the French philosopher Maurice Merleau-Ponty and the German Martin Heidegger.

First I will discuss man's bodily being and the basis for being in the world with the help of Merleau-Ponty's philosophy. I will point out the importance of the body and its experiences. How does the preobjective world[1] that derives its meaning through bodilyness constitute an individual and conscious (predicative) understanding of the world, and when it comes to physical exercise and sports, what kind of experiential basic substance the preobjective world gives? This is the most essential and central thematics that provides the basis for everything else in this study.

It is also interesting to see whether the experiences from long-lasting exercises are clearly distinct from the experiences from short exercises, such as bench press, for example. I think they are. My view is based on the idea that long-lasting exercises strain humans in a whole in a different way. We could characterize them using the word meditative, which includes at least the following properties: (a) aerobic, (b) rhythmic (both bodily movements and breathing) and (c) monotonous. These themes I will discuss primarily with reference to Heidegger's philosophy ("letting-be", "meditative thinking", "call of conscience" and so on).

Meditation is self-exploration and taking a closer look at oneself. In a broad sense meditation can be seen as self-performed control of one's mind, to which

---

[1] The preobjective world is the world that forms the foundation of human being, the foundation that precedes all conceptualizations. In other words, the preobjective world provides the starting point of the explanations concerning the world (Merleau-Ponty 1986, 433).

the aspect of spiritual self-education is related.² There are a countless number of meditative schools and methods, wherefore it is impossible to come up with an accurate and common definition for meditation. Conceptually, meditation is a psychophysical training method.³ We can distinguish – as Rauhala does – between religious and profane meditation. "In religious meditation one presupposes – in one way or another a divine reality independent of man to which one seeks for contact by meditation –. In profane meditation experiences are seen as deeply spiritual yet by no means divine."⁴ In religious meditation the divine reality, which we can call an absolute, is considered a personal being. The absolute can also be viewed in a philosophical sense. Rauhala claims that "the absolute which all existence originates from and which every individual is already originally contributing and related to, is not a person."⁵ He writes about meditation as something that "broadens our subjective idea of the world, improves our sensitivity to experience divinity, devotion, enchantment by beauty, love, and passion".

3.1 The Groundwork of Maurice Merleau-Ponty's Philosophy

The motto "To the Things Themselves" used among phenomenologists means studying the world starting from itself and not, for example, from a conceptually formed metaphysical theory.

This would be the case if you either intuitively or "authorized" by a feeling adopted a metaphysical theory as a starting point for understanding, explaining and interpreting the world or the universe on the basis of which individual entities and events took their meaning and positions in the wholeness of the existing. It is to be noted here that in a sense people always rest on some kind of theoretical view to support their understanding and thinking. What is essential, however, is to become aware of the theoretical as well as historical nature of our thinking and existence in order to make the world as transparent to us as possible.

Merleau-Ponty writes that

> to return to things themselves is to return to the world which precedes knowledge, of which knowledge always *speaks*, and in relation to which every scientific schematization is an abstract and derivative sign-language, as is geography in relation to the countryside in which we have learnt beforehand what a forest, a prairie or a river is.⁶

---

[2]Rauhala (1990, 66).
[3]Koski (2000, 105, see 118–128).
[4]Rauhala (1990, 68).
[5]Rauhala (1990, 72).
[6]Merleau-Ponty (1986, ix).

3.1 The Groundwork of Maurice Merleau-Ponty's Philosophy

The aim of phenomenology is

> re-achieving a direct and primitive contact with the world, and endowing that contact with a philosophical status. It is the search for a philosophy which shall be a 'rigorous science', but it also offers an account of space, time and the world as we 'live' them. It tries to give a direct description of our experience as it is, without taking account of its psychological origin and the causal explanations which the scientist, the historian or the sociologist may be able to provide.[7]

Phenomenologists talk about the destruction of traditional ontology, one target of which is to become detached from the old tradition in order to track down the original experiences through which understanding about existence has taken shape.[8] In this sense phenomenological philosophy strives for something fundamental, which we could characterize as a kind of ambitious desire to take possession of the world "from a clean slate" – this should, of course, be understood as a normative project (as a target to be aimed at but which is not necessarily reached).

Merleu-Ponty writes that

> true philosophy consists in re-learning to look at the world –. Phenomenology, as a disclosure of the world, rest on itself, or rather provides its own foundation. Philosophy (is, TK) a dialogue or infinite meditation, and, in so far as it remains faithful to its intention, never knowing where it is going. The unfinished nature of phenomenology and the inchoative atmosphere which has surrounded it are not to be taken as a sign of failure, they were inevitable because phenomenology's task was to reveal the mystery of the world and of reason. If phenomenology was a movement before becoming a doctrine or a philosophical system, this was attributable neither or accident, not to fraudulent intent.[9]

In my opinion the challenge and burden of philosophy lies in being able to understand how we have ended up having, e.g., such views as presented in Merleau-Ponty's main work *Phenomenology of Perception* (i.e. one is forced to read and study almost all of the philosophy written so far).

When Merleau-Ponty writes that "true philosophy consists in relearning to look at the world",[10] I understand him to mean that since the world existed even before we were born to experience it, we take it as self-evident. With the emergence of this self-evident way of looking at the world we lose our capability to see and experience the world as a unique place. This spiritual limitedness must be dismantled in order that we could stand before the world with amazement.[11] The emergence of that limitedness is an inevitable consequence of becoming human and existing in the world, since to start with, our birth takes us so close to the world that we see its versatility as natural. A central aim is to make transparent how to get engaged with the world, how our existence is realized based on engagement and what is our own contribution (based on this engagement) to how the meanings take

---

[7] Merleau-Ponty (1986, vii).

[8] Levinas (1996, 11).

[9] Merleau-Ponty (1986, xx–xxi).

[10] Merleau-Ponty (1986, xx).

[11] See Merleau-Ponty (1986, xiii).

shape.[12] Transparency is increased by interpreting an experience intersubjectively. The intensity of the experience may also have such an impact that it makes itself undeniably and apodictically transparent. Although due to its nature philosophy does not provide exact knowledge, it helps us in becoming more aware of the meanings related to our lives. This kind of understanding is important, because humans make their decisions on the basis of those meanings which they face in the course of their lives.

In short, Merleau-Ponty's phenomenological research has two sides. First, it is about researching the beings/entities[13] and phenomena by identifying their essence. Second, the question is about studying the existing as it is (facticité) and about realizing one's being.[14]

3.2 Merleau-Ponty's Philosophy of the Body

In this chapter I concentrate on man as a bodily and integrated being. The fundamental task is to understand man as a moving being, which gives bodily realization in the world as the starting point.

The foundation and starting point of my study is the world and human realization in it. Understanding human being in an abstract sense and in isolation from the world and other humans is narrow-minded and so we must start from the relationships in which people live their lives. We take shape and are realized as articulated by those relationships. As we as a whole beings are not what we think about ourselves, neither is our existence defined by the way we *think* (by the concepts formed about reality using reason) about being defined.

Bodily existence is revealed to an individual as self-evident, as the foundation for understanding oneself. Ludwig Wittgenstein makes a remark on this self-evidence of bodily existence as follows:

> We teach a child "that is your hand", not "that is perhaps (or "probably") your hand". That is how a child learns innumerable language-games that are concerned with his hand. An investigation or question, 'whether this is really a hand' never occurs to him. Nor, on the other hand, does he learn that he *knows* that this is a hand.[15]

The foundation for this idea is that our immediate relationship with the world is constantly formed through the perceptions produced by the touch between the

---

[12]Heinämaa (2000a, 74). Heinämaa (2002, 275) comments on Husserl's conception on phenomenology as follows: A phenomenologist studies "the ways in which we see the world and the various entities in it. Therefore the analysis takes two sides: the noetic which concerns the acts of consciousness, and the noematic which concerns the objects of those acts."

[13]An entity is anything that can be taken as a research subject. It can be real, imaginative, or abstract. (Everything that exists as it is, is called being.)

[14]Merleau-Ponty (1986, vii).

[15]Wittgenstein (1979, 374).

3.2 Merleau-Ponty's Philosophy of the Body

body and the world. In other words, this touch is constantly giving us experiential implications about the means how our own bodies are situated in the world, how the world is being construed and how it functions in relation to the body. The Finnish scholar Kimmo Jokinen comments on this, clarifying the idea presented by Wittgenstein: "The existence of the body precedes approval of any kind, and if we were to argue the truth-value of this pre-knowledge, we would say goodbye to language."[16]

The experience derived through personal history proves that certain ways of thinking make sense and are such that acting on the basis of them will provide us the security of the continuation of our existence. Wittgenstein thinks that "why do I not satisfy myself that I have two feet when I want to get up from a chair? There is no why. I simply don't. This is how I act."[17] This wording reveals that our experience about the existence of our bodies is coherent (with some exceptions such as the existence of false limbs), since preconsciousness and consciousness covers the entire body.

In the case of a false limb one may have the sensation of itching fingers, for example, even if the whole arm was amputated. Thus, the body is inclined to preserve its original coherence, even if factually this isn't the case. Even if the arm is amputated, the sensation of itching fingers is an indication of their former existence. If, for example, an armless baby was born: could she feel the same? If so, could this be an indication of arms and fingers being included in the human genotype?

Wittgenstein thinks that "if someone said to me that he doubted whether he had a body I should take him to be a half-wit".[18]

Merleau-Ponty sees man as a transcendence, which means the capacity of humans to exceed themselves (in their being in the world).[19] In other words, the starting point is the phenomenological observation that man is an ecstatic being.[20] We are both in our consciousness and bodilyness capable of exceeding the prevailing way of being. From this ecstasy we derive the significance of our temporal existence. The foundation of ecstasity lies in the idea that a human being as a body is actively and functionally orientated to the world.[21] Ecstasity as an ontological structural factor of human being gives us the existential framework in which we are the potential of our own existence. Our possibilities of living have to do with the potentials of being in the world. We can be in the world in many different ways. This is due to our ontological structure.[22]

---

[16] Jokinen (1994, 214).

[17] Wittgenstein (1979, 148).

[18] Wittgenstein (1979, 257).

[19] Merleau-Ponty (1986, xiv).

[20] Ecstasy is about transcending to the world – the Greek word ekstasis means "out" and "a stand", "stepping out".

[21] A newborn is bodily active right at birth – and in fact already in the womb.

[22] Klemola (1998, 100).

As a starting point when we make an attempt to conceptualize the experiences and dimensions related to long-distance running we have the human body which is capable of *moving*. The foundation for conceptualizing it is a bodily experience. Humans already have (except for a very young child) some experience about the world, its structure, relations and ways of being; they have concepts for a variety of entities. This forms the pre-understanding which we use to conceptualize our lived experiences and to give names to the conceptualized.

Every human is in touch with the world through one's own body, which is why the body is considered a reasonable, primary and fundamental starting point for philosophical anthropology. Due to this common foundation (the touch between the body and the world and the body as a presubject) human experiences (preobjective experiences) are principally similar in everyone. Merleau-Ponty[23] writes that "there is – another subject beneath me, for whom a world exists before I am here, and who marks out my place in it. This captive or natural spirit is my body –." Veli-Matti Värri[24] calls this kind of body the "presubject".

According to Merleau-Ponty human experience about one's existence and realization in the world is based on the senses and the experiences transmitted by them. To put it simply, man touches the world through his senses. A sensing body opens up the world to a human being, who through this projection gets connected to it. Senses are the channel through which one orientates to the world, and on the other hand, the world orientates to humans. The touch is active and the body acts as the mediator.[25] Here we must bear in mind that the body is a part of the world. We must not see the situation in such a way that on one hand there is the world and then the human on the other. It is only by the help of conceptualization that we can isolate ourselves from the world.

Anyone who has run in a forest will recognize, say the legendary, gently sweet smell of the forest heated by the afternoon sun. Through this smell our experience connects us to the world, the existence of which has become familiar to us. When we breathe the sweet smell of the forest, the sensation gets us connected to our former ways of being, all the way to our early childhood. Even if we are not aware of this, our senses act as open channels and receive the corresponding experiences from the world. Our minds also react to the messages transmitted by the senses, where upon consciousness can awaken to some of them. If the observed phenomenon is familiar or significant to us, our consciousness can "take hold" of it. In this way consciousness may, owing to ecstasity, get a runner connected to pleasant and significant experiences, for example.

A newborn baby does not start to move consciously. Merleau-Ponty sees the body to have an inborn tendency to take action and move – which he terms operative intentionality. It is the first medium for taking possession of the world in which

---

[23] Merleau-Ponty (1986, 254).

[24] Veli-Matti Värri (1997, 47).

[25] Merleau-Ponty (1986, 52–53).

3.2 Merleau-Ponty's Philosophy of the Body

mobility belongs to as a primary property.[26] Immobility as a constant state is unnatural to a human, unnatural in the sense that it eventually causes deformation, i.e. decomposition and deterioration of the bodily appearance. And, if the vitality of the body is lost, what happens to mental activity?

The bodily way of being in the world is functional. Through motion the body is experientially in touch with the world. What is essential is the change that takes place in the relationship between the body and the world (ontic touch).

To Merleau-Ponty consciousness is primarily an experience of the operational capacity of the body rather than some thinking activity. Consciousness contains the bodily experiences of the world, since they have contributed to its constitution. This is exactly why consciousness in relation to human being in the world is not of the form "I think" but rather "I can". "I can" exists before "I think", and in such a way that operational "capacity" did exist before the idea of "I can".[27] "I can" can be formed only by action and personal effort – a baby is capable of sucking the breast before understanding of being capable of doing it.[28]

Thinking is one of the human activities and it does not make sense to regard it merely as a product of the brain but rather as action at the moment it happens. Thinking is a bodily action that arises from the touch between the human and the world which can be taken reflexively into possession but not understood at the very moment when thinking takes place (Erlebnis). If I make an active attempt to be conscious of my thinking, to take hold of it when it takes place, all that I achieve is a reflective hold of my aim to consciously take thinking into possession. In other words, it is only afterwards when I can get hold of my thinking, which is a different thing than possession at the time when thinking takes place.

On the other hand I can be in a state of mind in which my mind rests empty upon itself without thoughts and in which a thought appears from an empty state of consciousness. Klemola[29] writes:

> We can become conscious of that point in consciousness where a thought is emerging. When our minds are empty at times, a number we utter in our minds (he uses a number as an example of a conscious concept, TK) will have a certain starting and ending point. The word appears in and disappears from our consciousness and we can take a closer look at that very point.

This calls for a lot of exercise, however.

---

[26] Merleau-Ponty (1986, xviii).

[27] Merleau-Ponty (1986, 89–90).

[28] Gallagher and Melzoff (1996/9, 231–236) make a distinction between "body schema" and "body image". Klemola (2004, 82) comments on this as follows: "*A body schema* is a system of motoric capabilities functioning without conscious control. It consists of a variety of physiological systems that enable movement and keeping a position. It functions despite the fact that the intentional target of a perception is something else than the body. – A *body image* is the system of those perceptions, attitudes and beliefs which I attach to my own body. It means not only my own perception and experience about my own body, but my conceptions about it as well."

[29] Klemola (2004, 34).

There is a gap between the pre-predicative (lived experience) and the predicative (conceptualized). Experiences and feelings that occur when running are not manifested directly in consciousness as concepts.

> Humans do not possess any kind of built-in apparatus which could 'translate' or interpret an experience as a constant factor specific to humans as a concept in such a way that all people would understand the nature of the experience on the basis of the term in the exact same way. An experience is always reflected in language as an approximation and from the foundation of common lifeworld experiences.[30]

Similarly, running does not become understood by looking at the brain impulses supposedly causing it or at the distance covered on foot as a consequence. Rather, running is a human action the result of which is the distance covered by running. The brain impulses and the distance covered do not suffice to understand running.

In relation to a running exercise, the basic idea is to understand man as a moving being. The purpose is to uncover the bodily ontological structure of man's being in the world, through which we can justifiably study the relationship between the subject and running. Theoretically, the experiences emerging from this touch are meaningfully interpreted especially from the viewpoint of man's bodily being in the world, and not from the objectifying point of view, for example, in which man is seen merely as an immaterial and rational conscious reified as a subject in isolation from its real lifeworld. Merleau-Ponty[31] makes an explicitly normative statement by claiming that man is not the objective physical body studied in occidental natural science.

The Finnish philosopher Matti Sintonen[32] writes about differences between human and natural sciences: "Science which approaches its subject from an exterior point of view – can never reach the idea what the other entity feels like." Merleau-Ponty[33] writes that the external approach which objectifies man is not the correct means for human research. For him the mistake made in the objectifying approach is the way in which it " reduces all phenomena which bear witness to the union of subject and world, putting in their place the clear idea of the object as *in itself* and of the subject as pure consciousness".

When the research subject touches the world with her own body, it is as an event at a different level than what happens when the consciousness of the researcher "touches" those conceptual relations in which the athlete acting as the research subject becomes realized in her own world and conceptual and semantic relations.

> Since every individual is the centre piece of her own experiential world, this basic relation between humans and the world cannot be disentangled by losing something essential about the reality itself. – The question is not about a purely conscious relationship to entities folded around themselves (things-in-themselves) (das Ding an sich) rather about the relationship between the bodily and subjective human being to the surrounding world

---

[30]Koski (2000, 28).
[31]Merleau-Ponty (1986, 86–89, 108–110).
[32]Matti Sintonen (2003, 22).
[33]Merleau-Ponty (1986, 320).

3.2 Merleau-Ponty's Philosophy of the Body

and the entities in it that you can feel and touch, take a look around, etc. The world begins and is experienced in the body.[34]

The objectifying approach typical of natural sciences towards man minimizes the experiential and living human and fails to uncover the bodily-mental situation of an individual. Although it admits the consciousness that "resides" in the body, it fails to see that body is consciousness.

Like Heidegger, we can state that bodily existence and, for example, the ability to take possession of the world are human means of being-in-the-world which have constituted man from the very beginning. As our existence and understanding are always-already-in-us, all of our actions take place in these forms of realization as well – and the being and action in those forms can never be looked at objectively like the transcendental ego. The point of view cannot rest outside ourselves. A transcendental ego has no ontic touch to the world. Enabled by ecstatic consciousness we can thematize, imagine a viewpoint outside ourselves, but at the same time we lose something. We should always be aware of the constitutive factors of our understanding and carry them with us in our processes of thinking and analysis.

I will make an attempt to bring in the subjective significance of bodily existence. I see the human incarnated existence as a true jackpot of life, since this is how an individual has a personal relationship and perspective to the world.[35] When dimensional entities reveal themselves and become experienced, they are revealed to a subject. They would not be dimensional and "something to get hold of" if they were transparent (thus would not be revealed with perspective) and fully revealed. Running or any other human activity would not exist if the world was absolutely open – that is ontologically fully open and revealed without a chance to be covered.

For the transcendental ego the world is a transparency without perspective. It includes no ontic touch or running as the running of a subject. Here entities would not become exposed by covering and uncovering. I could not run across the hilltop and only then see what is over there, since, everything being-already-exposed, I would always-already be situated everywhere around the hilltop. The perspective movement, act and action would be missing. They could not exist because with the lack of perspective you could not do anything in relation to anything. Thus, there would not be a situation related to the human, no incarnated subject to set a meaningful horizon for being and action.

To crystallize the idea, in phenomenological anthropology the question is not about the relationship of a bodiless human to the entities themselves but rather about the relationship of a bodily and subjective, historical human being to her concrete

---

[34]Koski (2000, 41).

[35]The idea here is that if "gods" (immaterial, conscious) existed, they would be envious of people for their bodies.

situation of realization. The world is shown and experienced and lived in each and every bodily human being.[36]

Edmund Husserl's original division to objective and lived body (Körper, Leib) is analysed by Calvin Schrag. According to him it is important to a make a distinction between the concretely lived, personal body and the objective body as a subject of special sciences. In the latter we are at the level of such abstractions which have no contacting surface with the experiential level of existence which every human, every "ego" concretely experiences in their personal lives. It is abstract and in this sense only thinly associated with personal experientiality, although it in many situations suits to serve as a starting point when studying man in general. "The lived body is self-referential" and contains the experience of the self, writes Schrag.[37] The reference is targeted to the unique and experiential body of each and every individual.[38] In other words, Schrag probably wishes to express that a sentence is understood correctly when everyone who reads the sentence "the lived body is self-referential" understands it to refer to the person himself as a unique entity reading the sentence.[39] This experience refers especially to you yourself, who is now reading these words and to the body you currently experience. Every individual experiences one's body as lived in her own way.

Both of the earlier-mentioned terms, Erlebnis and Erfahrung, are dimensions of the lived body. Erlebnis is prior in time and thus primary by status. When you look inside humans, Erlebnis and Erfahrung are as if they were experiential levels found in them. The lived and objective body are distinct on the basis of one's own experience and the exterior approach toward the body.

Schrag writes, "my body is lived in an existential immediacy and is apprehended as uniquely my own".[40] According to him "the self-referential quality of the lived body is most directly disclosed in my experience of my body as that which individualizes me".[41] When I proportion this idea to myself as someone doing this research on the philosophy of physical exercise, as a participating subject with my personal way of being, I can claim that it is not the body in general in question here but my own personal and unique body.[42]

Sheehan writes about how running affects his experience on his body and mind: "Before I run, I am a Cartesian. The body is simply a machine. I must take it for a run and tune it up. I must improve my body so that I can fulfill my – purpose, which

---

[36]Merleau-Ponty (1986, 320).

[37]Schrag (1988, 110).

[38]Schrag (1988, 112).

[39]Koski (2000, 97).

[40]Schrag (1988, 112).

[41]Schrag (1988, 111).

[42]Koski (2000, 98).

is to think.[43] It isn't until I get on the roads that I know again, as I have known for 15 years, that I am my body and I am my soul, and I exist as a totality."[44]

This clearly reminds me of my own personal experiences of the connection and unity of body and mind. Man's consciousness is ecstatic, which allows for transition of consciousness into a sphere of its own ("before I run, I am a Cartesian"). This, again, gives us the impression that mind is independent of the body, supporting the dualistic view ("the body is simply a machine"). Yet, certain experiences return consciousness to man's totality which consciousness is dependent on (thus realizing that our whole thinking is dependent on the totality). In my doctoral thesis I put it this way[45]:

> The significance of a healthy, vital and well-functioning body reveals itself often spontaneously to consciousness when we fall ill. – An ailment of the body or an ill part of it is like the "Archimedes's point" around which our being is concentrated. An ailment constantly reminds us about its presence, and consciousness becomes entangled around the ideas of an ailment. In an experiential sense man is a whole in this situation.[46]

The significance of the lived body becomes clearly apparent in the idea where we imagine having documents of all possible kinds on sport and physical exercise. This would not, however, tell us anything unless we could not through our bodies understand what we are reading.[47] Without a bodily understanding about physical exercise we could not merely by means of rational thinking and our senses come up with a truthful idea about the different sports and physical exercises in the world.

3.3 Martin Heidegger's Fundamental Ontological Philosophy

> (P)hilosophy is supposed not only, and not in the first place, to be a theoretical science, but to give practical guidance to our view of things and their interconnection and our attitudes toward them, and to regulate and direct our interpretation of existence and its meaning. Philosophy is wisdom of the world and of life, or, to use an expression current nowadays, philosophy is supposed to provide a *Weltanschauung*, a world-view.[48]

---

[43] Here Sheehan refers to his work. He finds his work as a journalist an important task and especially cares about conveying the message of his experiences on running to the readers.

[44] Sheehan (1978, 252).

[45] Koski (2000, 80–81).

[46] Owing to the ecstasy of consciousness we can imagine ourselves as a soul and a body which are separate from one another (dualism). In this sense a headache is an excellent and efficient reminder about the existential entity we are all about.

[47] Heinämaa (2000a, 123).

[48] Heidegger (1982). *The Basic Problems of Phenomenology*. http://www.marxists.org/reference/subject/philosophy/works/ge/heidegge.htm, taken 6 Aug 2014.

Heidegger determines that the task of phenomenology is "to let that which shows itself be seen from itself in the very way in which it shows itself from itself. – The signification of 'phenomenon', as conceived both formally and in the ordinary manner, is such that any exhibiting of an entity as it shows itself in itself, may be called 'phenomenology' with formal justification."[49]

Heidegger's fundamental ontology makes an attempt to explain how a human is realized in her life and through which ways of being, and what is the nature of one's realization in the world. Just as Merleau-Ponty, also Heidegger sees the most fundamental structure of Dasein to be being-in-the-world.[50] When man is in the world, how is he doing it? He is mortal, thinking, socially realized, bodily, aware of his consciousness, dynamic, someone who ponders about his self and existence, and so on. Heidegger makes an effort to understand this enormous entity in his fundamental ontology.

Thus, we ought to reveal running to ourselves from the viewpoint of running itself just as it does to runners through running. Running is always shown as some kind of phenomenon. A runner always experiences running as a variety of experiences. It is only through these experiences that one can become connected to running.

Fundamental ontology is a good means to approach the human ways of being arising from the grounds of the touch between man and world, and in the way it is realized in the incarnated human being. Fundamental ontology is also a good means to approach the touch between man and world and, for example, to the (perennial) experiences in which the touch between an individual and reality takes place in a gentle and subtle way. What is important to the authentic constitution of Dasein are the existential experiences, these ethical-ontic experiences that take place at the level of primordial togetherness which change the way in which the world is experienced.

One possible viewpoint is that the foundation of ethical experiences is a bodily preobjective experience. Klemola[51] also supports this idea. He writes:

> This is most essential from the viewpoint of ethics, since this experience (Klemola refers to bodily experience which has not arisen from conscious articulation, TK) is the bodily basis for empathy and sympathy. Thus, all this takes place in bodily consciousness, in consciousness which is part of the body, in a body which is part of consciousness.

Or – philosophically we may also ask – is the selection of an ethical viewpoint a purely cognitive event in which some human way of existence is seen as good and something to strive for according to which an individual then tries to do one's best?

As I see it, both ways are reality, in other words are the means according to which people "choose" their views. Maybe the latter is generally a more recognized than the view of the bodily nature as the origin of the ethical that I wish to promote.

---

[49] Heidegger (1978, 58–59).

[50] Heidegger (1978, 65). Heidegger writes being-in-the-world with hyphens whereas Merleau-Ponty does not. In this text the practice is loyal to the usage of the two thinkers.

[51] Klemola (2004, 62).

3.3 Martin Heidegger's Fundamental Ontological Philosophy

In ethical-ontic experiences the structure of das Man[52] is temporarily lost. Heidegger writes about

(a) truth as uncovering (aletheia[53]), from which I have separated as a special case the notion of "existential-ontological disclosure of being",[54] and about
(b) a method of waiting, i.e. the releasement (Gelassenheit zu den Dingen) of beings, with which one can strive for experiential confrontation with the world and self.[55]

Heidegger's fundamental ontology is about the different kinds of shapes and structures in which human existence is realized.

Here I come to debate whether Heidegger is actually presenting the structures in which experiencing takes place. Does ontological analysis mean that we analyse the being of a human, since in this way we may uncover the structures populated by experience? It is in being where experiencing takes place.

Heidegger does not, however, mention anything about the experiences that a human will face. My idea is that these existentialia can be "filled up" with human experiences which means to bring the structures into touch with a concrete human being in order to gain a true and real connection and a positive content.

When we start to explain existentialia using concrete examples, we have to use ontologic-ontical examples. Such an experience is e.g. when I feel my existence come close to myself. Here we can distinguish (1) bodily experience, of which Klemola[56] writes: "As the ego-awareness decreases, increases the bodily awareness in which we are faced with life in ourselves very closely. We feel its presence in our bodies, in the beat of our cells, but also in our breath or as a pulse on the neck." Another level in this example is (2) the existential experience of existence becoming crystallized, as if turning into something tangible.

For this study this means that I will make an attempt to fill up the existentialia with experiences that are meaningful to a runner.

"(T)he substance of man is existence", writes Heidegger,[57] and since the characteristics of Dasein's existence are determined by existentiality, Dasein's own

---

[52]Heidegger's term for the way in which an individual looks at himself from the viewpoint of the "they". Das Man is a kind of average, *normal* man who produces the pressure of normality.

[53]When we talk about truth as unconcealment, we mean the world that opens up and appears to Dasein as a location of happening and being. Truth is not situated in any particular location and it is nothing which could be presented by a statement like "it is raining outside". Verifying that clause in order to find out its truth value is not the kind of truth that Heidegger talks about.

[54]Experiences that with the enormity of a lightning strike into the very foundation of an individual's existence.

[55]In addition to long-distance running with the help of Heidegger's philosophy we can analyse such long-lasting means of exercising that are like methods of releasement by their essence (marathon, ultra-marathon, triathlon, cycling, various "ultimate-type" exercises like long hikes, etc.).

[56]Klemola (2004, 64).

[57]Heidegger (1978, 362).

existence, Heidegger[58] calls them existentialia. Steiner[59] interprets existentialia as categories for understanding reality. Are existentialia those "channels" (to Being?) through or in which Dasein is in touch with being? Or, is it so that Dasein is composed of those elements which the existentialia refer to? Has Heidegger articulated all the existentialia?

Factually Dasein's various means of existing may manifest themselves in very different ways. Taking a glass as an example, the existentialia of it could be space, pattern and a certain hardness. A glass can be filled with many kinds of liquids and substances. It can be placed on many kinds of surfaces and viewed from many different points of view in varying lighting conditions. In other words, the ways of existence of a glass are realized on the basis of the existentialia, but factually a glass is realized in very versatile relationships.

Stimmung (mood) means that Dasein in its life situation is always overwhelmed by some kind of mood. *Stimmung*, again, pertains to a particular kind of mood, an ontic-ontological example of *Befindlichkeit*. In other words, the existentiale Befindlichkeit is a pattern, a human way of being that has a subjective emotional content, Stimmung. In brief, existentialia are ways of being and existential levels are feelings or experiences (*Stimmung*). For example, being-towards-death[60] is an existentiale, which can be experienced in very many different ways in people's lives.

Yet death, which from Dasein's point of view points to "being-toward-death", is not an experiential issue related to our own being. Thus, you cannot obtain an experience of your own death, and thus cannot have any experience of it. Therefore, being-toward-death can only be seen as a Dasein's structure of being. However, Heidegger also writes about the touch between Dasein and the world. He writes that our interpretation "merely carries out the explication of what Dasein itself ontically discloses".[61] This statement comprises the idea of interpreting Dasein – including Heidegger himself – primarily from one's incarnated being. The "fleshy" commitment always and primarily as Dasein, within-the-world, being ready-to-hand and present-at-hand,[62] inevitably means being in connection with the world, which determines the location of the exposure.

The theme and main interest of fundamental ontology lies in Dasein, an ontologico-ontically distinctive being.[63]

> In explaining the tasks of ontology we found it necessary that there should be a fundamental ontology taking as its theme that entity which is ontologico-ontically distinctive, Dasein, in order to confront the cardinal problem – the question of the meaning of Being in general. Our investigation itself will show that the meaning of phenomenological description as

---

[58]Heidegger (1978, 70).
[59]Steiner (1987, 84).
[60]"Death is Dasein's *ownmost* possibility" (Heidegger 1978, 307).
[61]Heidegger (1978, 229–230).
[62]See Sect. 6.3.
[63]Heidegger (1978, 61).

3.3 Martin Heidegger's Fundamental Ontological Philosophy

a method lies in *interpretation*. The logos[64] of the phenomenology of Dasein has the character of a *hermeneuein*,[65] through which the authentic meaning of Being, and also those basic structures of Being which Dasein itself possesses, are *made known* to Dasein's understanding of Being.[66]

I understand this thought to contain a requirement to connect the analysis of Dasein to concrete contents also. Shouldn't the interpretation (also) be targeted at the interpretation of experiential contents of individual cases of Dasein? Otherwise, the analysis and interpretation would not concern anyone.[67]

My view is supported by Lauri Rauhala who writes that the purpose of Heidegger's

> analysis is, ultimately, to show how real categories and concepts derive their meaning from the shape, means and quality of human existence. Such – real concepts as home, father, mother, school, work, family, child, a.s.o. derive the limitations and locations of their meaningfulness in people's idea of the world from the fact that their existence is especially about being in or relation to them. The significance of these concepts is essentially determined by the means in which – i.e. in what way of life, in what kind of relationships, how rich, limited or damaged – the structural factors of existence named using these terms "contribute to" the constitution of one's existence. Thus, from the viewpoint of consciousness our factual relationship with the world signifies that our experientiality derives its content from the facticity into which we are related. – An experience cannot be about nothing but rather has to do with some phenomenon or some state of affairs. For example, the meaning of the concept of home is largely derived in the experiential world of every one of us from the facticity in which we have been realized as existing. *We cannot derive the concept of home from a definition but rather grow into understanding and using the concept by being in those relationships which are referred to by using the term home.*[68]

In this sense we understand the concept of "running" to mean the conceptions on running evolving from the functional relationships through which we have been in touch with running. Thus, running is a relational concept which evolves eventually from human situations and from the relationship between experiential contents of the action we take.

In other words, we understand our lives through and with the help of the structural factors and the concrete content in them in which our existence has been constituted. Similarly, we understand life (and what life means to us) to be the entity which is thematized via the horizon (point of understanding) of the lifeworld.

---

[64]In Heidegger's text the term is written in Greek.

[65]In Heidegger's text the term is written in Greek.

[66]Heidegger (1978, 61–62).

[67]Sheehan (1978, 228) writes about being, wisdom and understanding as follows: "(T)he closer we become to just being, the closer we come to understanding 'I am who I am.' This is probably not true about everyone, but the runner would agree. He possesses himself in solitude and silence and suffering. He is gradually stripped of desires and attachment to things. As I run, I get closer and closer to requiring nothing more than life supports, air and water and the use of the planet. I surrender something greater than my will. – Such moments do not come easily or for the asking."

[68]Rauhala (1993, 96). Italics TK.

The constitution of existence is about (a) man's constitution in one's bodily facticity and (b) the constitution of man's awareness of those concepts that evolve in situations in which one is factually realized. Life derives its meaning only so that an individual lives one's life by being-in-the-world. People always live their lives in certain relationships and as members of certain cultures at a particular moment of time.

When seen in this way, running and its environment as a time-consuming situation that produces individually concrete content, will to a corresponding extent begin to take shape as a factor that constitutes our lifeworld and existence.

> When Dasein faces the world, Dasein cannot alter its facticity or the basic structure of it, rather they are inevitably included in the realization of one's existence. In other words, the existence is constituted – also in its consciousness – in such a form that these prevailing terms of its being in the world presuppose. Thus, existence is a term used about such a real person who is constituted as a realization of one's potential on the basis of one's terms of being. In his fundamental ontology Heidegger is ultimately analysing what is the structure of the constitution, i.e. how we could comprehend it. He thinks that in its realization existence in a way "takes into account" all the prevailing phenomena, situations and their relations which then serve, expressed in other terms, as conditions of this existence. Recognized in the realization of existence, the existentiale named *Sorge* refers to the inevitability of taking the world into account.[69]

From the point of view of a running exercise also conceptual understanding, the conceptual possession of the running situation, of the lived body is important to a runner, because it thematizes a runner to focus one's sight inwards and to listen to one's own body. Reading texts, which give us a viewpoint for focusing attention to ourselves and our own bodies, is of importance. Methodical self-reflection may serve as a motivation for practicing in a way that is constructive to our own lifeworlds. A too heavy or wrongly performed exercise may be harmful to the body and mind. For example, an enthusiast may reach for a better and better running time, run wearing a wrist watch and forcibly – without listening to the messages of one's own body – make the performance to be quicker. Adopting competitive structures to perform the exercise does not serve the purpose, which in this case can be seen to be good physical condition and better health. The compulsivity of reaching better results may cause some stress.

At present it is perhaps more typical to run wearing a heart rate monitor rather than a wrist watch. My running diary contains the following notes on a 10-mile exercise on 30 April 2004:

> Is it so that a heart rate monitor produces an experience out of a lived experience, Erfahrung out of Erlebnis? I feel quite OK when running at a normal pace. Running rolls nicely, as simple as that. The monitor shows the rate of 140 – the strain is conceptualized in the heart rate of 140. The strain of the exercise gets recognized consciously. Does this matter? What if the heart rate (pace) were high or low? When desired, it is possible to utilize your understanding to slow down, for example, if your purpose is not to run fast (or to run faster if the idea were to run at a higher heart rate). Yet in some way the heart rate, strain and running pace can be estimated without a monitor, too. On the other hand, it is perhaps easier to let

---

[69]Rauhala (1993, 101).

your will rest on the monitor for a certain period of time than to keep the corresponding estimated pace the same. Thus, the monitor serves as a chase rabbit that drives you to better performance.

I benefited from a heart rate monitor, because it helped me understand that I was running too fast, thus with too high a heart rate. When I dropped the heart rate to the range of 130–150, the quality of my running improved markedly. I was able to run longer distances and running felt comfortable, which in turn increased my motivation to run again.

Lately I have been using the heart rate monitor only every now and then. It may be possible that the monitor becomes your master. It is somewhat the same situation with a wrist watch when you constantly focus on better and better performance. As a result, you may lose joy from running, and it may turn into mere performance. This may be necessary and understandable for competitive athletes who may not do well without some kind of target setting. Yet to a typical enthusiast this kind of a pattern is (or may turn out to be) catastrophic. You may end up developing a mental obstacle to running because of the certain target you have set to yourself as your body and mind have to be in a certain kind of state. If you don't feel sufficiently well, you may end up skipping the exercise, because you don't have the strength to set yourself to a certain kind of bodily and mental effort. And, as you are not always strong, skipping the exercise is possible in such a situation (it is understandable and even recommendable).

J.P. Roos comments on his attitude towards his running career in the light of his motives and failures: "I have focused my mind far too much on competitions, and the failures in them have affected my motivation far too much. I should have put more emphasis on plain running and the experiential variation I have lived through with it."[70] Today his primary goal is good, solid and pleasant running[71]:

> My firm starting point is definitely the idea that I will no longer attend a marathon to compete and don't set myself any target time, rather I will pay attention to listening to my body and focus on such successful and solid runs (and skiing events) in which towards the end I feel at least as good or even better than the beginning. This is not as easy as you may imagine, but whenever I rarely succeed in doing this, the feeling is really rewarding. As a byproduct, you may end up beating some of your fellow runners or at least towards the end passing some of those struck by fatigue before the finish line. The same evening you will still have the energy to do this and that instead of just lying in bed, beaten by fatigue and nausea. I have also calmed down my exercises to some extent: no more tough intervals or fast steady-state runs rather comfortable long runs, flexible fitting of the exercise to other schedules, bearing long breaks in exercising if other more important things turn up: in short, both exercising and attending in competitions is to take place in a more relaxed atmosphere. The topmost thing is the pleasure gained through some effort and moderate sacrifice and in such a way that it is not taken away from other kind of enjoyment. I believe I could warmly recommend this principle to be followed in other areas in life, too.[72]

A similar attitude is depicted in my running diary as follows[73]:

> I started to run right from my front door. I run 50 m along Kaupinkatu street, and then cross over Koljontie way, ending up in the 1.8-mile exercise track at Kauppi park maintained even in winter for pedestrians. The 10-foot wide path dives into the forest towards lake

---

[70]Roos (1995), chapter 18.

[71]Roos (1995), chapter 14.

[72]Roos (1995), chapter 19.

[73]20.8.2003.

Näsijärvi and starts with a gentle climb, followed by a long slide which ends next to a water purification plant, from where it takes a steep turn to the left with a steep climb.

At the beginning I run slowly on purpose in order to avoid the unpleasant feeling that is followed by too fast a pace at the beginning. It is particularly unpleasant in long runs when you realize that the running is not going that well and there's still a long distance ahead to cover. I make an effort to run in such a way that it feels pleasant. Maybe in competitive sports, when you are getting prepared for a competition, you gain more motivation to run hard regardless of the fatigue and lactic acid. But, when running without a short-term goal rather having the intention to do it for the rest of my life, I cannot see any other option but to understand running from the starting point that running feels good and pleasant. If some day I came across the desire to take everything out of me, I could, of course, do that. What I mean is that if you set yourself goals that are too high e.g. in terms of improving the running time, you may be struck by mental obstacles. The threshold to exercising becomes too high because you ought to do well. Therefore, I would much prefer to set myself goals that are too low rather than too high. What is essential is the continuity of the exercise.

From experience I can tell that it is a good idea to let the body warm up. The warm-up takes about 10 min. I have the feeling that my running starts to go at ease first after 40–45 min, and one of my running companions shares the feeling.

When running uphill, I shorten my steps considerably and consciously breathe strongly to ensure sufficient oxygen intake. Fatigued I continue to go uphill for a while even after the end of it. If you let the effort required by uphill running ease right when you reach the top, the rhythm of running gets interrupted, because the uphill running causes lactic acid build-up in your legs, which does not end right at the top of the hill. I continue running similarly with slightly longer steps sensing the state of my legs and eventually return to the normal running rhythm.

After a good half a mile, I reach a vantage point with a broad view over the lake. The view varies tremendously over the seasons. A particularly memorable moment there dates back to an evening run at around 7 PM in summer 2002. The sun was setting and gilded the lake, the air was placid, and there were boats on the lake. I noticed how lucky I was having the opportunity to run in such an environment. It is as if I had my home and summer cottage in the same location, and clean water in the lake. Overwhelmed by the feeling I rolled down the slope towards the lake shore and made a conscious effort to breathe strongly. The track follows the lake shore for a good half a mile, after which there is the toughest climb of the track, some 300 yards in length. The climb requires a lot of concentration. Oddly enough, the first climbs are the toughest ones, and the third, fourth and fifth time feel lighter.

The case in which relaxed exercising turns competitive can be called a fall that is due to the gravity of das Man, i.e. we unreflectively apply the structure of competitive sports to our own action. We can free ourselves from this vicious circle,[74] for example, by "conscience" (refers to a process in which an individual finds a connection to one's deeper essence), since conscience calls for self as das Man back to be one's own self (recollection of one's own possibilities to be a human being, Wiederholung). This, again, calls for conscious concentration to listen to oneself through releasement/letting-be. An individual has to be determined when striving for authenticity.

---

[74]Means doing things like other people do, thinking like other people think, a.s.o.

3.3 Martin Heidegger's Fundamental Ontological Philosophy

In other words, the analysis of bodilyness can be connected to the analysis of Dasein's existential being-in-the-world in the way described above[75] with the conceptual pair of unauthentic and authentic being. I have presented an interpretation about this connection named the existential-ontological experience of opening up of being. I mean that (a) an event has existential impact on a human, (b) man's experience about the way of being of reality (and on changing it). An existential-ontological event thus simultaneously refers to both a human and the reality. In philosophical analysis these two directions of happening can be studied separately, yet experientially they are one. As I see it, this is about Dasein becoming authentic.

In this way I connect something that has been subjectively experienced to the process of Dasein's being-in-the-world; the formal analysis is enlivened by the experiences of the lived body. This is why the analysis of long-distance running is extended to cover man's existence as a human being as well and is not only limited to considering running a mere physical exercise (which is largely the way it has been seen).

Similarly, the analysis of bodilyness can be connected to the analysis of Dasein's existential being-in-the-world with the following thematic question: how does the sportive self-understanding arise from bodily being in the world? The sportive self-understanding is about conscious understanding of our own capacity to move, which can be developed and controlled by ourselves. This can be analysed, as done further in this book, by means of the concept of active-passive process. One of its elements is that an individual can consciously expose oneself to such a connection to the world which has a favourable impact on the development of sportive self-understanding, contributing to the improvement of self-understanding in general (in the sense of the constitution of reality). In other words, how does an individual understand oneself as an exercising and running Dasein? How can we with the help of long-distance running add to not only the sportive understanding but the overall understanding of being in the world in general (unauthentic and authentic being)? In continuation, we will take a more detailed look at Heidegger's philosophy.

---

[75]By authentic being I understand Heidegger to mean that we experience the world and our existence as the place of realization as personal and the most profound way of being-in-the-world. What this means experientially cannot be conceptually expressed. This is something that every one of us has to experience ourselves in the process of taking our own paths. Moreover, as I recall Heidegger himself putting it, *Being and Time* is not only a book but rather a path that each and everyone of us has to take.

Chapter 4
Long-Distance Running as the Subject of the Study

At the core of this study is the running exercise. This relationship is thematized as a research object in order to see how an exercise is constituted (see Sect. 6.4); the starting point for the constitution is the intentional relationship between body and world. The first stage is the description of a running exercise. In the method's subsequent stage the features and experiences included in the description are analysed. The target is to uncover the central properties and the essence (the essence has to be understood as a necessary entity of those properties that make a phenomenon what it is and without which it no longer would be what it is). In phenomenology uncovering the essence is an intuitive process in which the researcher uses reflective thinking. The target is *Wesenchau*, seeing the essence. The question is always about a personal process in which all three elements (research method, subject and researcher) are interwoven.[1] The research ends in interpreting hermeneutical essences seen as the experiential cores of a running exercise.[2] The purpose and existential meaning of the hermeneutical stage is bringing the essences back to human reality.

In Heidegger's terms, the subject is a running Dasein which can be seen to include all "egos". As a starting point, the subject is an "ego" as running in the world.

With this I refer to the idea that each individual ultimately understands oneself as an "ego", since that is the form in which an individual reflectively comprehends oneself. An individual, again, is a broader and more versatile entity than the ego, which becomes understood through a variety of experiences that enlighten the nature of the self. Experiences also tell an individual about the dimensions and levels of consciousness that one has other than those revealed by the everyday self-aware ego. Experiences both "dismantle" and "rebuild" the ego, which in this way gets

---
[1] Klemola (1998, 167).
[2] See Klemola (1998, 163–170).

constituted in a new way. The "ego" covers both me as a Dasein doing this research and other "egos" as presented in literature and spoken descriptions of running. This topic is dealt with in the end of this study, e.g., in Sect. 9.3.

The goal is to uncover the content and the essential nature of running. The purpose of reaching for the essences is to allow us to become aware of the nature of our experiences on a conceptual level. By possessing this awareness we will improve our understanding of ourselves and the world.

Improved self-understanding will allow us to direct our action in a more adequate way. Sara Heinämaa comments on Merleau-Ponty's phenomenological project with regard to trying to capture phenomena in their essence by stating that "essentials are not – the ultimate targets of philosophical work rather only means by which we can take distance to our experiences, move from the actual to the potential and in this way become aware of our interests and connections".[3] I understand "taking distance to our experiences" as a process which would help us understand and make us aware of what we have experienced and place it in correct proportions in our lives. "Moving from the actual to the potential" I understand to refer to the broadening of self-understanding and the perspective of one's own action. This way we can also take hold of the potential which thus could become the actual.

When an attempt is made in phenomenology to find the essences, we resort to a mental experiment in which we vary the subject freely in imagination. Various properties are added to and/or removed from the phenomenon in order to see what the essential properties of it are. This usage of phenomenology is known in literature as "essential phenomenology", or "eidetic phenomenology",[4] but I have also come across the term "eidetic reduction". Spiegelberg[5] writes that "variation in the imagination is the necessary condition for determining what is or is not of the essence of a phenomenon". The mental experiment is thus seen as a necessary condition in evaluating the phenomenon. But, have I understood it correctly if I think that with cognitive mental processes I can draw some final conclusions of a phenomenon? (Shouldn't we at least think that the evaluator should possess life experience to the extent that one could imagine a variety of states of affairs about the research subject in a relevant way? Maybe this is just trivial pondering – perhaps it is seen as a self-evident starting point that a phenomenologist is an average subject who is capable of thinking and who possesses some life experience.) But, what is the validity of the eidetic approach in terms of free variation in the imagination as described above? For example, what possibilities are there or how advanced thinking is needed in order to understand merely by thinking that riding a bicycle is possible? I myself made a mental experiment in which I imagined the situation before the two-wheel vehicle, and I came to the conclusion that I wouldn't have had any chance to understand the constitutive meaning of movement for staying upright. Practical experience tells us that nothing stays upright on the basis of two spots.

---

[3]Heinämaa (2000a, b, 167).

[4]Spiegelberg (1975, 62).

[5]Spiegelberg (1975, 63).

What does the insight need to be like so that we understand a vehicle staying upright in connection with motion? If we cannot do this by phenomenological thinking, according to the idea of eidetic phenomenology we have to exclude the possibility of moving a bicycle in upright position. Or, should we think that if the researcher saw it this way, one is making bad phenomenology (because one cannot imagine a being that is capable of moving and staying upright on two points). With regard to this idea Spiegelberg[6] writes that when striving to see the essence the "essential insight will not lead us to indulging in empty abstractions but to shuttling back and forth between the concrete and the abstract". In other words, a phenomenologist should in practice (if "concrete" in the Spiegelberg quote means the ontic touch between the researcher and the subject) study the properties of the bicycle. But in order to do this the researcher should have at least the idea of the possibility of being able to stay in upright position when moving. And, if something is seen as impossible, an attempt is barely made to try it out in practice.

Bringing the essence discovered through analysis back to human reality calls for understanding and an intuitive approach to the subject by the researcher. In the analysis an experience is objectified when made the subject of the study. The intentional correlate[7] is "an experience as such as one recalls it". The intensity of the experience has an impact on how vividly and how well the recollection that serves as the basis for the analysis succeeds.

I strongly feel that the more personal the researcher's relation is to the subject, the more adequate are also the interpretations and results presented on the phenomenon. Then the research is based on literary sources and personal experience that is used to support the literary material. There is a dialogical relationship between the two, i.e., they hermeneutically promote the researcher's conceptual understanding of the subject. By conceptual understanding I mean the significance and status that experiences obtain when interpreted and understood intersubjectively in a cultural environment. The research process, which comprises description, analysis and interpretation, is constantly accompanied with the self-reflection of the participating researcher. As an example of applying something personal in research we could use the awareness of motion (internal experience of the lived body) which can be activated by a physical exercise. A physical exercise as a process is a methodical means to develop this internal experience to a more sensitive and "deeper" direction.[8]

To gain the best possible analysis, understanding and interpretation of the research subject calls for good experience, understanding and intuitive approach from the researcher. Then it is only beneficial if the researcher has personal experience about the sport in question.

The reason why people are attracted to long-distance running, as I see it, is dependent on its meditative elements. Long-distance running would not be long-distance running without the experiences of tranquility and becoming a whole.

---

[6] Spiegelberg (1975, 63).
[7] The subject to which consciousness is oriented.
[8] See Klemola (2004).

We could call them significant essences to distinguish them from the essences present in running that determine running in a technical sense.

A runner himself, psychiatrist Thaddeus Kostrubala has used running therapy as a treatment for mental illnesses. In his book *The Joy of Running* he says that a running therapist has been trained to understand matters that take place in our inner selves. He has to be a runner himself and moreover, he has to be a good therapist who is capable of joining these two parts as a functioning entity. In other words, Kostrubala is a participating physical exercise therapist.

Crucial for this research is the analysis and interpretation of experiences of physical exercise – and since I happen to have experience on long-distance running, I bring more relevance to the research with the "method of participatory philosophy of exercise".[9] My own experiences are thus part of the research material.[10] The experiences are – and preferably so – in a dialogical relationship with the literary sources of running traditions. One central target is to gain a meaningful interpretation of the lived experience. In this way, leaning on my personal experience, I will make an attempt to analyse the essence of a running exercise.

The goal of the research is to get a hold of the concrete, real subject. There is nothing new about the idea. Wilhelm Dilthey, for example, wanted to study the whole human being in one's versatility as a knowing, desiring, feeling and observing being.[11] One of the central properties of participatory philosophy is the interconnection of experiential and conceptual sides, since first together they submit the meaning to one another.[12]

We can think that man's relationship with the world is the more versatile the more often one is in touch with the world. The philosophical research that approaches its target externally is then an activity of a philosopher who has only a conscious/rational relationship to the research subject. Her understanding emerges conceptually (the participatory research of the philosophy of physical exercise does not diminish the significance of the conceptual).

It is essential and important to underline the fundamental insight that a description of a phenomenon can never generate an experience that is identical to one's own personal experience. For example, reading a description about placing a hand on a burning hotplate can never generate an experience that is identical with placing one's hand on the hotplate. This experience would tell what the occurrence actually

---

[9]The participatory philosophy of physical exercise is a new trend in the occidental academic philosophical tradition. There are not many philosophers who approach their research subject from this point of view. This is probably due to the fact that there are only a few researchers who are both philosophers and exercise the sport they investigate and very few of those who additionally have personal experience on perennial traditions of physical exercise.

[10]See Klemola (1998, 163). On the same page he also writes "the central goal in phenomenology is to get close to human experience and to describe its most essential properties. Therefore it is only natural that when doing phenomenological research on physical exercise, the researcher should have own experience from the phenomenon he is analyzing."

[11]Dilthey (1982, 288).

[12]Varto (1990, 46).

means from the bodily human perspective. When a human touches the world with one's body, it is an event that takes place at a different level than when consciousness 'touches' concepts.

As a Finn and Ouluite, grown up in the north, I find Sheehan's description of running in winter most appealing.

> It is beautiful and real and a delight. The snow crunches underfoot. The pure light of the sun flashes off the white surface, the sky is high and blue. The air is dry and clean in my lungs. My senses are filled with these realities, with the sound of my breathing, the soft noise of my passage. I am living time and I am living space. The time and space Blake described, when a pulsation of an artery is equal to six thousand years and where a space no bigger than a globule of man's blood opens into eternity.[13]

It is a different matter to run in the nature or to fight your way with full energy to an opening in the ice than read about them on your easy chair. When a human is concretely in nature as in these examples, her touch to the world is different than when sitting on an easy chair. The description of a non-participatory philosopher of an athletic phenomenon cannot generate a description that is similar to the description made by a participatory philosopher, because the latter is both mentally and with one's body part of the described phenomenon.

As the research is also based on my own experience, I use the participatory philosophical method in my work. With the help of the personal experiences of a physical exercise enthusiast I possess a pre-understanding of the ontology of the research subject. This allows me to adequately (in some sense of the word) analyse and interpret my research subject. From the viewpoint of participatory philosophy, philosophy and personal exercise are inseparable and two necessary elements for understanding and experiencing the same entity.

Participatory research on the philosophy of physical exercise is a new field in the research of exercise (at least in the occidental philosophical tradition). In connection with his notions about psychotherapy Lauri Rauhala[14] writes that "it is somewhat rare in humanist sciences for a researcher to set one's existence as a situational homeostasis. So far, psychotherapy is the only kind of research in which the researcher sets himself as a subject under observation here called for." This also relates to the question what kind of relationship the researcher has with his own mind. In an exercise process an attempt is made to take control over one's mind. As the exercise takes place in an individual area, the broadening of the horizon of consciousness has to take place via the only thing that each and every one of us has as personal experience, the body.

Thaddeus Kostrubala sees running as a kind of natural psychotherapy. The question is not so much about the therapist's personal properties rather the improved health and organization that long-distance running brings into our existence. He sees running to contain a property that opens up our inner gates. Kostrubala talks

---

[13]Sheehan (1978, 242).

[14]Lauri Rauhala (1993, 116).

about "internal running", which is the outcome of exercise. The central factors are adequate duration and correct attitude of the runner.[15]

According to Spiegelberg[16] the original purpose of phenomenology was

> a direct investigation of the phenomena. Its peculiar thrust was to get away from the primacy of theories, of concepts and symbols, to immediate contact with the intuited data of experience. – To phenomenology the primary stimulus of philosophy is what *is* and *appears*, not what anyone thinks or says about it. Yet, phenomenology wants to be more than a mere return to the things, as free as possible from conceptual presuppositions.[17]

According to him approaching phenomena through texts only is "meta-phenomenology". It is not the proper kind of phenomenology.[18] He writes that "if the philosophical study of the texts is meta-phenomenology, then a study of their history is meta-meta-phenomenology. In this sense, and studied in this spirit, the historical way to phenomenology can become a flight from the phenomena".[19] For example, the description of a type of experience can be approached by means of text analysis. In this case the original question, the immediate experience is transmitted as a conceptualized and interpreted experience in textual form, and so the original touch to the phenomenon and its accuracy become thinner and thinner. In other words, the more layers there are between the original experience and the subject who reads about it in textual form, the harder it is to obtain an adequate interpretation about the original experience.[20]

---

[15] Pekola (2001a, 55–56). See Sect. 7.1 where flow is discussed.

[16] Spiegelberg (1975, 15).

[17] Using the participatory method to do research on physical exercise is a clear statement in favour of the phenomenological method. This being the case, as I see it, the researcher is interested in both sporty events and in what they refer to. With this I refer especially to those experiences which have an impact on an individual's means to understand and experience the world. In humans these experiences touch the level from which I see the ethical and aesthetic to emerge – to me these are ultimately one and the same thing. What they come down to are existential-ontological events. The intentional correlate of a researcher is an ideal being the essence of which one tries to uncover by personal and intersubjective means. In case the researcher has personal experiences about the intentional correlate, its significance is, as I see it, no longer merely conceptual, rather experientially real (not only the content of consciousness), when the experience itself takes place. At this single moment the researcher does not, of course, perform an analysis on what is happening in one's consciousness. This is done only afterwards, and only then can we say the significance to be again conceptual by nature. The meaningful act of an experience at the very moment of its occurrence, its significance and perceptual content are, however, factually united in the researcher. Thus, the significances of one's experiences are then experienced personally in the entity of one's own being. Thus, what is meaningful and important is time and its nature as a process: what is happening and how conscious is the researcher's consciousness about itself? This is an important matter and worth emphasising, because the analysis constructed from the viewpoint of the ego is not necessarily valid for altered states of consciousness. As the analysis on this level is problematic and difficult, I will no longer discuss it in connection with this research. See Koski (2000, 38).

[18] Spiegelberg (1975, 20–21).

[19] Spiegelberg (1975, 22).

[20] Koski (2000, 43–44).

As phenomenological research is largely dependent on the researcher's own intuitive ability to approach the research subject, a question and problem may arise about its subjectivity and objectivity. What is subjective and what is not? How can an individual subject verify something objectively? The verification takes place through the tools shaped in the course of cultural evolution. The culture is a result of human activities and in this sense subjective. If there had not been anything in common to all and in that sense "objective" in the conception of the world between individual subjects, how could the emergence of cultural scientific apparatuses have been possible? Subjective turns into objective (or to that direction) only by being in contact with other subjects and their corresponding experiences. And, as Spiegelberg writes,[21] "all objective experience is really intersubjective experience, i.e., a selection from subjective experiences. This makes subjective experience even more indispensable".[22]

Rauhala[23] writes in his book *Humanist Psychology* that

> the fundamental insight promoted by hermeneutical thinking of research functioning within-the-world scuttles the myth of "value free" science in which the researcher were a neutral observer, totally separate from the researcher's subject. To a researcher being within-the-world means operating through one's life situation. We cannot step outside those relationships to which we have committed ourselves when we have come to existence. Even as researchers we are these relationships. When we study human relations, also the research done at that time is a human relation. When we study thinking, the research done at that time is a thinking activity, etc.

In this sense humans are doomed to be within-the-world, since we are born into a world from which there is no escape but death (or by making experience thinner through abstraction, which leads to losing something essential). All subjects are constituted by this common and shared within-the-world structure. The subjects have their differences but also their features in common. There is always a researching subject in question. "Objects are subject-related".[24] Every subjective research always takes place in a within-the-world context common to all of us. This and the presubjectivity of the body enable us to reach also other than merely random results.

---

[21] Spiegelberg (1975, 78)

[22] Another issue is what is the status of the objective as such, such as the relation between the rotation of the Sun and the Earth, for example. There was a time when the Sun was considered to orbit the Earth. I understand objectivity in this kind of a situation to be based on people's common experience about the Sun orbiting the Earth (i.e. the objective fact is that everyone feels the Sun orbits the Earth). The Sun's movement in relation to the Earth is part of the universal structure. By status I mean that the human experience does not reveal the astronomically correct relationship of the Sun to the Earth. It would be more justified to speak about experiential objectivity which provides us an opportunity to improve the status of the objective experience as well (i.e. the fact that it's the Earth that orbits the Sun). We must go beyond subjective subjectivity and consciously exercise reflective thinking and research in order to gain objective subjectivity. See Spiegelberg (1975, 78).

[23] Rauhala (1991, 118).

[24] Spiegelberg (1975, 78).

What is important is **my** body, since the existence of my body is an inseparable part of my consciousness. When I am in the world, everything that happens, happens experientially to me. This is why generally speaking it is very difficult to transmit experiences conceptually to other people, because anyhow it is not the kind of experience that each and every individual "ego" once lived through.

When the ideas about objectivity, subjectivity, personal experience and intersubjectivity are combined, we can state that when a phenomenologist starts to look for something meaningful to say, he cannot resort merely to his own experiences. When he is trying to find something in common, as a theoretical and practical guideline he has to resort to something in common to people, something intersubjective, which can be called – as we are talking about human sciences – objectivity.

Reaching for full objectivity is an ideal. In practice, however, individuals reach the targeted ideals to a varying extent. Yet we must bear in mind that even if we resorted solely to using our own experiences as the source material, it wouldn't result in an entirely subjective research.. This is because of the presubject that comprises each and every human being. It is a structure that is characteristic of the human genre, and it forms the edge conditions to human experience. In other words, the experiences of an individual cannot be entirely unique (i.e. subjective). Sara Heinämaa[25] writes that

> ultimately objectivity means what we are capable of sharing despite the differences between us. Owing to the differences it may mean what is seen or understood *together* with other – different – people. When seen in this way, objectivity does not fade away or pass the individual differences rather presupposes them.

---

[25]Heinämaa (2000a, 157).

Chapter 5
Running as a Way of Life

Running, especially long distances, is often seen as a way of life which organises and dictates runners' lives. In this situation running has been seen to improve the quality of life, but it has not necessarily been thematized from the viewpoint of constituting the self. Timo Klemola thematizes physical exercise as projects of victory, health, expression and the self. By projects of the self Klemola[1] refers to "all those traditions of physical exercise with which man investigates himself". Man uses physical exercise to study his potential of being and tries to realize out of the potential the ones that Heidegger calls the *authentic* self.

Jarmo Pippola writes about the inner essence of physical exercise. In the Finnish runner's magazine Juoksija he strongly and deeply personally describes his own relationship with running. For him "the meaning of running, motion is something else than a swetty run and performance. The question is about a way of life, art, or poetry of physical exercise".[2] As the performance oriented attitude in running changes along with the experiences gained, it may result in a more crystallized and clear idea of running in relation to one's life. He conceptualizes his running as follows: "I have been created to live and to move. When I run and move, I feel alive. The mere idea of being on the way somewhere with the sensation of beauty and ease of stepping, without pain or pressure, brings joy to my heart. This is what I want to experience for the rest of my life".[3]

Roos defines the concept of a way of life in a way that suits the nature of my study. A way of life

> refers to regular, meaningful activities and choices that fulfil our everyday lives: work, consumption, living, spare time, family life. A way of life is often focused to some dominant property (family-orientation, work, physical exercise). It is more appropriate to

---

[1] Klemola (1998, 63).

[2] Pippola (2002, 12).

[3] Pippola (2002, 12).

© Springer International Publishing Switzerland 2015
T. Koski, *The Phenomenology and the Philosophy of Running*,
DOI 10.1007/978-3-319-15597-5_5

say, however, that a way of life is an accumulation of some properties. When we say that jogging is a way of life, we mean that jogging is interconnected with many other things: certain kind of schedule, diet, certain forms of socializing, disciplinary behaviour, target-orientedness. Thus, a way of life is an entity, a system as a contrast to unorganized and contradictory life. – The question is about something repetitive and slowly changing, while on the other hand a way of life is largely dictated by such internalized, incarnated choices that we cannot control ourselves.[4]

"Incarnated choices" show that the body has its own autonomy which in everyday activities forms a practice, a way of action we consider to work well and we take for granted, and it is not reflected when entered into.

When the idea of incarnated choices is broadened a little and seen in the context of running, we can claim that it would be almost impossible (or at least in vain) to consciously ask oneself to run step by step. This is simply not done and there is no need to it. When I monitor my running more closely, it is difficult to ask your foot to take a step and to step. The steps follow one another in such a quick rhythm that giving orders feels almost impossible – the same problem is familiar in playing the guitar, for example. Personally I have noticed that the only means to have an influence on the running pace and strength is to adopt a certain kind of attitude.[5] For example, I consciously decide to run faster. This idea reaches over the whole body, not just the legs. Thus, "the legs begin to run" faster despite my inability to give them clear commands. What is it actually that is taking place here? The only way I can see this is that being-in-the-world has been realized in such situations where the body as a presubject has via continuous repetitions learned to follow its own rules without any exact concepts from consciousness. Man has throughout times learned various bodily means of being-in-the-world, of which the suitable one is chosen at each and every moment.[6] Attitude is both a momentary way of action and something that reaches towards the outcome and that is not trying to nor cannot itself describe the process providing the outcome.

What do I do and what happens when I focus my mind on running faster? What if the outcome were a slower pace instead? Would I be able to conceptually understand that I strive for faster pace in a wrong way and with a wrong attitude, and still did it differently? It seems impossible that: I want to run faster and while trying this, the opposite happens. What would happen in such a case? My body would not be able to realize something that I consciously strive for. But since this is not possible, is it because my body and my mind are essentially one and the same and my understanding about the world true in some profound way? Why this – slowing of the pace while desiring to run faster – is not possible? Or, would it be possible to the mentally ill, for example? Thus, when we want to run faster, we do not give

---

[4]Roos (1989, 9).

[5]What is an attitude? Is it a feeling? A Finnish dictionary paraphrases it as a way of thinking or as a point of view.

[6]In Heidegger's terms this is Dasein's pre-ontological understanding (of Being) – also the existentiale "care" tries to describe this quality of Dasein.

ourselves a conceptual command to do so but rather apply an adopted way of action instead. Then again, there is conceptual content also in the way of action. How about animals? In danger they run fast to preserve their lives (or freeze).

The feedback coming from my legs and the whole body is similar to what I'm consciously giving to my running body (and what is ultimately realized by willpower). The feedback can be, for example, a sensation of fatigue, weakness and lack of perseverance which is conceptualized as the weakness of legs, lactic acid formation and restrained oxygen intake.

The approach is rather such that when I run, I run and don't think of running (cf. Wittgenstein's idea of bodily certainty discussed earlier). When we learn to run, it becomes and innate way of action which does not need the support of consciousness in order to preserve its identity.

A way of life can be seen as a process and a consciously made choice.[7] What is at stake, is an articulated intentional relationship to something that is considered important. What this relationship is in different situations depends on the content of the lifeworld of the person who makes the choice, on her personal preferences. It can be, for example, a project set via the ideals of competitive sports focused on winning and increasingly better performance, or striving towards a good and healthy life.[8]

Roos[9] writes that

> those who run a marathon have adopted running as a way of life at least some time before the marathon. I don't know how many marathons such persons usually run – but I'm inclined to believe that a great majority of them are such who pretty much adjust their lives in terms of running, find the rhythm to it through running and take running into account wherever they are, and use more time in running than to many other things –. But it is hard to say what the significance of running is to man's entire life.

Physical exercise can also be seen as competition by nature, which allows us to view the situation through Heidegger's concept of das Man which overwhelms an individual through the project of winning. From a runner's point of view, how an exercise is understood and adopted is important. How the meaning of the exercise gets settled to the individual, is essential. The way in which consciousness is focused on the ideal that is in the background of the exercise and how focused one is when doing the exercise have a crucial effect.[10] This is the most important thing to understand from the point of view of the content of the exercise. Running derives its nature from how consciously one takes it.

Running – as any other kind of physical exercise – means exposing oneself. Generally speaking, man exists ontologically in the world as exposed. Taking conscious action means exposing oneself consciously in connection to the world (even in cases where an individual would not recognize this). In running one

---

[7] Roos (1989, 11).
[8] See Klemola (1998).
[9] Roos (1989, 49).
[10] See Herrigel (1987, 87).

is exposed, for example, to the possibility of pain through injury. Staying home means exposing oneself to the situations at home. In a long term, when we do our exercises by listening to our own bodies, the exercise strengthens us, whereas with a physically passive person who stays at home the predisposition to fall ill increases.

To the question whether physical exercise can be seen as a way of life Roos[11] replies both affirmatively and negatively: *"Physical exercise is not a way of life as such rather merely one area in which lifestyle is expressed, realized in practice.* Physical exercise can simultaneously be part of a variety of lifestyles."

When running is intensive and the runner is devoted to it, it is considered a significant and meaningful way of being. When running is one of the issues of focal interest, its impact reaches over to other parts of life as well. This idea can be formulated using Hegel's concept of "expressive totality". The question is about totality and the dialectics between its most important parts or moments. The totality affects its parts and vice versa. Expressive totality derives its characteristics through its most important constitutor. The characteristics of totality thus reach over to other parts as well. If running is an important or the most important part of it, from the point of view of life as a whole it affects the other parts of an individual's life. Sheehan[12] thinks that

> the athlete doesn't go on a diet and start training. He starts training and finds he is eating the right things at the right time. In just such a way other things fall into place. His sleep habits adjust. He automatically rests after eating and practices on an empty stomach. He warms up thoroughly and is satisfied with progress however slow. He has discovered fitness and the fine line between peak performance and disaster. He becomes alert to his body signals.

In running it is important to see how one's mind is oriented towards running, as an important part of one's life. The ideal of leading a good life where regular exercise plays a major role may have occurred to a runner's mind. This being the case it is essential how fully one is dedicated to running. The ideal is then seen as a goal worth striving for, because it constitutes the motivation for the exercise. Another important aspect, concentrating on the running exercise and running itself, constitutes the experiential foundation of the exercise which, again, is conceptualized in the (pre-)understanding of the practising person. The conceptual and the experiential are in a reciprocal relationship to one another. The experiential modifies the ideal that lies behind the exercise, which in turn articulates the experiential.[13]

Thus, it is essential how we take the exercise, the intensity of which depends on the way the ideal of the exercise has been internalized. A phenomenologist would pay attention to the goal behind the exercise, making an attempt to find the purpose of running. All in all, to put it briefly, we are looking for an answer to the question what is the means of physical exercise, as presented to consciousness, as its internal movement?

---

[11] Roos (1989, 17).
[12] Sheehan (1978, 56–57).
[13] Koski (2000, 151–152).

This way of being embedded in consciousness is a goal set for one's actions by the person herself with an attempt to achieve it. Eventually, in the course of running this is also realized as a coherent internal experience. The essence lies in the intentional correlate of the exercise. Thus, we could ask, what is the way of being of the ideal of the physical activity and how does it structure the exercise? Analysing this in running itself is, of course, useless. This is something we can forget, 'drop out' and instead we can fully concentrate on running – when the legs are moving and the miles pass, the intentional correlate is not the same as the ultimate goal of the exercise.[14] Any time we run, we concentrate on running only in the way we come to think about it before the run. During the run it is not of importance to think about one's way of life – that is an option, of course, but the important issue is the performance itself and that you do not get tripped by potholes or get hit by a car, etc.

Man's being is paradoxically twofold: on one hand you are what you are, and on the other you are not what you are. In the latter case a human is seen through one's arrival, where a human reaching out towards the future is a project realising its potentials. In terms of way of life the essence of the intentional correlate can be presented as follows: it is an intuitive idea of (mental and physical) well-being thematised by the pre-understanding.[15]

When running as a way of life reaches importance, it has been seen to increase quality of life. This does not yet mean, however, that it was thematized from the point of view of constituting the self. This has to do with whose point of view running is seen from; from one's own or das Man's.

When physical exercise or some methodically performed exercise plays a central role in one's lifestyle, the lifestyle essentially becomes part of the exercise. This is known as asceticism which in ancient Greece stood for regular, disciplinary exercise. Thus, discovering one's true being calls for asceticism, which is a discipline. In Asian yoga and zen-budo traditions it is both about physical exercise and exercising of the self. A way of life is often known as a "way".

If running is seen as a way and a means for spiritual growth, it becomes a challenging project. In the Japanese budo tradition one of the ways to describe "way" is to use the concepts of *shu*, *ha*, and *ri*. Shu refers to a beginner and ri means the highest level where the target striven for has been reached. In the budo tradition the master's level is the highest. In terms of running this would mean having control and knowledge of all the different aspects related to running. By this I mean, for example, finding a suitable running technique for oneself, the right kind of attitude, understanding about the equipment, understanding the significance of dietary and resting needs and their use in exercising, sufficient breaks needed especially in recovering from injuries and for healing, the significance of running on social relationships and to sum up: controlling one's mind and sense of situation. From the runner, whether a novice or a master, stamina, dedication, determination,

---

[14] Koski (2000, 152).

[15] Koski (2000, 153).

and self-control are called for. The same is true when the runner adopts a similar attitude in her way of life. At this point one understands that it is not possible to achieve something that changes the runner and her life without rigorous attempts that lasts for years (the monks of Mount Hiei discussed later in this book serve as an example). During this process it is also possible to experience a kind of spiritual insight or a series of them which allow a runner to better understand one's existence and take her further in the skill of "running".[16]

Good progress in exercising changes one's way into non-way, since the ideal of a way is a way which is not a way, i.e., a means of exercise that is no longer an exercise. By this I mean an exercise that has become a way of life. It has become a solid part of our being such as eating, sleeping and drinking. The same principle is seen when Herrigel[17] writes about artless art. For example, when we have practised some sport for a very long time, doing the exercises over the years is adopted as an organic part of one's being and becomes our other nature.[18]

> An exercise as a way of life goes further than considering an exercise as a performance made in the exercise location. There is no difference whatsoever between the exercise location and everyday world. By this I mean that the same concentrated and focused attitude that – (a runner, TK) has in an exercise, should follow him or her in everyday life as well. – Through concentration and due to concentration we become one with what we are doing. An exercise does not solely mean exercising some particular skill rather ultimately practising to take possession of the ability that forms the basis for all of our skills. An exercise broadens to cover the entire life of a human being, which is the real place and goal of the exercise.[19]

D.T. Suzuki[20] depicts this in poetic beauty in the prologue of Herrigel's work:

> When a man reaches this stage of 'spiritual' development, he is a Zen artist of life. He does not need, like the painter, a canvas, brushes, and paints; nor does he require, like the archer, the bow and arrow and target, and other paraphernalia. He has his limbs, body, head, and other parts. His Zen-life expresses itself by means of all these 'tools' which are important to its manifestation. His hands and feet are the brushes and the whole universe is the canvas on which he depicts his life for seventy, eighty, or even ninety years.

Suzuki's quotation reveals aesthetically the significance of the human body to life. I wish to remind here about the common nominator behind Zen and Merleau-Ponty: the relationship between human body and mind. One of the most apt descriptions about human existence is an answer to a student's question about the essence of Zen: The Zen master replies "I eat when hungry, I sleep when tired".[21]

Lifestyle is an entity of connections in which the runner's experiences get set in the entity. Lifestyle verifies it and provides it its final meaning. What is essential is how the experiences and their meanings are absorbed to the "practical wisdom", the

---

[16] See Chiba (1989).
[17] Herrigel (1987, 18).
[18] See Suzuki (1973, 152).
[19] Koski (2000, 147).
[20] Herrigel (1987, 7–8).
[21] Herrigel (1987, 8).

"fronesis".[22] Life connection, life as totality is the sphere an individual has and in which her being takes place.

For this study the essential concepts are a runner and running, which through phenomenological argumentation raise the question: what does running mean?

Asking a question is an intentional act. Again, the intentional correlate of an intentional act is running as it is set as the subject of the study. In phenomenology a distinction is made between the entity that is being intended (noema) and the entity as it is intended (noesis, as given to consciousness).

In a phenomenological study the subject is the way in which entity is given (in this study: the way of being in the sense how a runner is realized as a runner, what running is like in practice), not the entity as such. For example, the ability of a child to move is not seen in an abstract sense. Rather, what is at stake is the movement of the child in the situations in which her moving existence is realized. I call this realization of movement, which always takes place in a concrete situation, the "meaning of movement" just as Heidegger asks in his book "Being and time" for the meaning (Sinn) of Being. Thus, what is man's way of being as a runner?[23] This analysis reveals the mind of running.

---

[22] With the help of practical wisdom people try to reach goals that they consider correct and worth striving for. Aristotle uses the term *fronesis* about it (The Cambridge Dictionary of Philosophy 1995, 44). Simo Knuuttila writes in his explanations to Aristotelian ethics of Nikomakhos that "in a specific situation practical wisdom calculates with what kind of action the entity of life benefits the most. It provides a concrete shape for the desire that is focused on leading a good life –." (Aristotles 1989, 209.)

[23] Wisnewski (2007, 43) points out that "what it means to understand what runners do is to understand how their bodies express themselves in the world – and how their bodies intermingle with the world around them".

Chapter 6
Viewpoints to a Long-Distance Runner

6.1 The "They", Authentic Being and Inauthentic Being

Heidegger describes being the "they" as follows:

> We take pleasure and enjoy ourselves as *they* [*man*] take pleasure; we read, see, and judge about literature and art as *they* see and judge; likewise we shrink back from the 'great mass' as *they* shrink back; we find 'shocking' what *they* find shocking. The "they", which is nothing definite, and which all are – prescribes the kind of Being of everydayness.[1]

In other words, Heidegger describes man's way of being in the world as an acting and thinking ego constituted by being social. "I" have to be of a certain kind because everyone expects it and because that is how I am supposed to behave and be. The they-self is not the kind of being that has arisen from an individual's own needs but rather a convention in a cultural context. The they-self exists in an inauthentic sense.

What is good, meaningful and sensible about being social is, of course, problematic and difficult to determine. In this context, however, it is sufficient to claim that authentic being does not refer to spontaneous, uninhibited self-expression that ignores all social norms. An authentic being is not "an elephant in a social glass cabinet".

Inauthenticity may become experienced as unfitting and uncomfortable to the Dasein itself. Sometimes the situation can be so unfavourable from Dasein's point of view that one does not even recognize the existence of the "they". When an individual's relation to oneself is silent in this way, the meaningful, personal relationship to the world is missing and has not been realized. In such a situation being the "they" feels normal and natural.

---

[1] Heidegger (1978, 164).

Dasein has two modes of being, authentic and inauthentic.² *"Authentic Being-one's-Self does not rest upon an exceptional condition of the subject, a condition that has been detached from the 'they'; it is rather an existentiell modification of the 'they' – of the 'they' as an essential e x i s t e n t i a l e".*³ Thus, the "they" is an original part of human. Dasein, a fundamental constituent of being a human. Authentic-Being-one's-Self is, again, something that evolves from das Man. This is what the term "modification" used by Heidegger refers to. Thus, authenticity is something that is achieved. It is a modification, an experiential-functional metamorphosis from the viewpoint of an individual. As Heidegger claims above, the Authentic-Being-one's-Self isn't anything such that is kept in captivity and then released. I would say it is a potential.

Ego-specificity (emergence and existence of the ego) is a prerequisite for authenticity and inauthenticity. Dasein has to be first the I to itself before it is capable of becoming aware of its own inauthenticity so that, boosted by anxiety and consciousness, it can reach an initial connection with authenticity. The emergence of self-awareness and the ego are thus related to inauthenticity.

An inauthentic Dasein has as the "they" become dispersed to the "they" from which it has to recognize itself.⁴

George Sheehan⁵ describes in his book how he is connected with running under social pressure. In his case running changed everything that used to be there, and running made it possible for him to start the project of being in his own way from a clean slate.⁶ He writes as follows:

> Why I began running is no longer important. It is enough that it generated a desire to run. Then the running itself took over. Running became a self-renewing compulsion. The more I ran, the more I wanted to run. One reason was energy. – I came to know my body and I enjoy it. Things that previously exhausted me were no longer an effort. Where once I fell asleep in front of the TV set, I was up roaming the house looking for things to do. I was living on a different level of performance.⁷

As part of this process he claims he has discovered and accepted himself.⁸ In addition he says:

> Running made me free. It rid me of concern for the opinion of others. Dispensed me from rules and regulations imposed from outside. – It stripped off those layers of programmed

---

²Heidegger (1978, 68).

³Heidegger (1978, 168).

⁴Heidegger (1978, 167).

⁵Sheehan (1978, 27).

⁶"Running let me start from scratch" (Sheehan 1978, 27). On page 62 of the book there is a picture in which Sheehan is crawling out of a hatching egg.

⁷Sheehan (1978, 202). Rob Schultheis (Murphy and White 1995, 123) writes about some instances through which he discovered an entirely new touch to himself and experienced himself as the kind of a person who he should always have been like. To him those presented the best possible version about himself.

⁸Sheehan (1978, 202).

6.1 The "They", Authentic Being and Inauthentic Being

activity and thinking. Developed new priorities about eating and sleeping and what to do with leisure time. Running changed my attitude about work and play. About whom I really liked and who really liked me. Running let me see my twenty-four-hour day in a new light and my lifestyle from a different point of view, from the inside instead of out.[9]

In the case of Sheehan discovering one's own 'thing' has literally been a turning point in his life. This is probably due to the fact that he began to run at the age of 45 after having felt that he was not in a good enough shape and was therefore looking for a new direction in his life. For him the new direction was the direction of youth and the experiences in his youth, when life was still full of opportunities and when the "they" has not yet taken the upper hand and become a self-evident, imperceptible means of experience.[10]

The "they" is a means of experience ingrown in Dasein. In order to go beyond that, it must be defeated and replaced by an experiential horizon that originates from the security of one's own being. This is exactly what Sheehan went through.

For Dasein there is no activity which in itself is authentic or inauthentic as such. What is essential is the mind or the quality of the being in which we are. Heidegger[11] writes that "we must be careful not to confuse ontico-existentiell characterization with ontologico-existential Interpretation –". I understand this so that when looking at the actions of a single human being, an outside observer will find it difficult to say whether the activity is authentic or inauthentic by nature. The question is about Dasein itself – the authentic being is apodictically verified. Dasein can be hiding from itself and its authenticity,[12] but we cannot always identify this judging by the activity itself or by watching it happen.

Authentic being is about surpassing inauthenticity. The authentic self is a self that has taken possession of oneself. This is a conscious project and calls for exercise and willpower.

Steiner[13] interprets the significance of das Man similarly with me: "There must be inauthenticity and 'theyness', – so that Dasein, thus made aware of its loss of self, can strive to return to authentic being." However, I don't share Steiner's view that the question is about *returning* to an authentic being that a child has had once. It does not make sense to regard the state of innocence that a child had before falling to being das Man as a state of authenticity. As I see it, authentic being comprises consciousness of the fact that there is an authentic being in question – and this experience is the proof of itself. In a way a child is in the state of inauthenticity before the fall, yet not in such a way that will get realized when a human being

---

[9]Sheehan (1978, 27).

[10]Sheehan (1978, 6, 27–30).

[11]Heidegger (1978, 229).

[12]"This phenomenon of Dasein's fleeing *in the face of itself* and in the face of its authenticity –." Heidegger (1978, 229).

[13]Steiner (1987, 96).

evolves via inauthenticity. Also Moran[14] finds that "indeed in order to be authentic we must first of all be inauthentic".

Inauthenticity is a consequence of falling. The foundation of falling is man's being-in-the-world. Merleau-Ponty and Heidegger both share the viewpoint that a human being is essentially someone who is realized *in the world* – the world and the human being realized in it is, of course, a self-evident starting point.[15] It is the irrevocable starting point of each and every newborn child, a starting point which we later become aware of. Heidegger writes that Dasein "has fallen into the world, which itself belongs to its Being".[16]

I understand Heidegger's idea about the human fallen into the world in a genetic sense[17] as follows: the human being born to the world evolves into a self-conscious person, understands beings and makes up concepts on that basis. In this process

> the human being is inevitably separated and alienated from being[18] into an entity that belongs to being, which as part of being has the capacity to understand being. The self-conscious human being also has the ability to understand that she belongs to being. Alienation (Entäusserung) is an irrevocable consequence of becoming self-conscious, because awareness of the world and of the self as a subject arises from understanding. This is why the direct connection to being is said to be vanishing. On one hand the conceptual possession of the world reveals something about the world, but on the other hand it simultaneously tends to cover the experiential connection between being and the self.[19]

Becoming self-conscious means that you turn into a self that is for yourself. This presupposes the ability to surpass your former being (ecstasy).

I[20] have written, that

> becoming being to oneself presupposes a human touch to the world and human interaction. Ecstasy is possible on one hand due to the concreteness of the world, and on the other due to the intentional basic human structure. By concreteness of the world I mean that in addition to human beings there are also other entities from whom we can receive experiential knowledge. It is also essential that a human being is part of the being which has a contacting surface to other entities. In addition, we can still claim that a human being is a self-conscious entity belonging to the being, which due to the ecstasity of consciousness is conscious of

---

[14] Moran (2000, 242).

[15] There are also other starting points for understanding the basics and the essence of human existence. We can understand this, for example, as an eternal and unchanged soul for which joining the bodily form is just an intermediate step towards the final spiritual and immaterial fulfillment and merging with the absolute.

[16] Heidegger (1978, 220).

[17] A genetic, scientific method the purpose of which is to investigate the emergence and development of the research subject, a historical method.

[18] Everything that exists as it is, is called being. For example, in Mahayana Buddhism, one of the forms of which is Zen, people talk about "tathata" which means being "as it is, without definitions, comparisons or division –" (Gothóni et al. 1990, 61).

[19] Koski (2000, 51).

[20] Koski (2000, 67–68).

6.1 The "They", Authentic Being and Inauthentic Being

this being the case. I understand Merleau-Ponty[21] to refer to the same when he writes about a human being as a "project" in which the world is projected as a human being to itself.

The process can be described as a chiasmatic[22] whole which comprises the world (that has taken hold of itself with the help of human self-awareness) and the human body (as a self-conscious body and as a personal relationship of understanding).

> When we take a closer look at the being, we can identify several levels in it. The first one is what I call "the basic level", which we can express using the phrase "the being is". The being is everything that exists as it is. But when we take a closer look at the being, we can notice that in the being there is some entity which calls the being a being. In this case it is me, who thinks so while writing. The object does not exist as such as an object that is of significance to the human being, because as soon as the being is named a being, this being will by itself break up into a relationship between the being and the being in itself (a conscious subject as the nominator of the being). If I think of a human being in my place as a general being, we can say that in the being there is an entity which as a self-conscious being is capable of perceiving the relationship between itself and the entity, being, where a man is one of the two parts. The being has been split. Using a Taoist expression, Tao has been split, and a subject and an object are born. At the emergence of a self-conscious human, the being is split to the ego and the world. The being has been split to an object and a subject despite the fact that it still is one entity. Ontologically the being does not get split because everything that there is in the being is being and belongs to the being. Talking about getting split is an experiential oral expression, which then also allows the harmonization of the being which one can strive for by exercise.[23]

"The human being is a self-conscious being which is capable of independent action and defining oneself".[24] the "phenomenon of Dasein's fleeing *in the face of itself* and in the face of its authenticity". This being that has become self-conscious, Dasein, is according to Heidegger[25] in motion towards authentic being "if Dasein specifically brings itself back to itself from its lostness in the 'they'". As the above-mentioned original connection to the world is lost when Dasein becomes self-conscious, the Dasein, using Heidegger's terminology, undergoes a fall. In everyday life the fall exposes itself at its clearest by Dasein's realization as the "they". Heidegger[26] writes that "in falling, nothing other than our potentiality-for-Being-in world is the issue, even if in the mode of inauthenticity. – (A)*uthentic existence* is not something which floats above falling everydayness; existentially, it is only a modified way in which such everydayness is seized upon."

The fall begins when a subject and an object emerge. My interpretation of Heidegger's idea is that the fall takes place in Dasein's life all the time (if and

---

[21] Merleau-Ponty (1986, 430).

[22] A chiasmatic pattern is, for example, a situation where I touch my left arm with my right arm, thus simultaneously touching and being touched. The subject-object relationship is like a line drawn in water.

[23] Koski (2000, 184–185).

[24] Koski (2000, 122).

[25] Heidegger (1978, 312).

[26] Heidegger (1978, 224).

when it is crossed), and not just once at the birth of the subject and the object. In the subject there is the simultaneous potential for the presence of authentic and inauthentic being. Heidegger sees authentic being as an existential modification of everydayness, which means that authentic being emerges or exposes itself from inauthenticity. In other words, Dasein's evolution towards authenticity goes necessarily and solely via inauthenticity. Before being able to surpass one's inauthenticity, the human being has to become a self-conscious entity, the first self-reflective form of which is constituted by the "they". The birth, falling into existence, this entirely haphazard and ontologically impudent event (because it occurs to every single 'self' and does not ask for a permission), realizes (makes up, constitutes) an individual first as an inauthentic being. In the original form of consciousness into which a child is born the characteristic property is the autogenesis of the ego to inauthenticity.

Falling and living as fallen is the essence of the "they". According to Steiner this has nothing to do with falling in a theological sense and contains no moral judgment.[27] A human being always grows to be fallen, this is the human fate. The born and evolving human being grows and evolves via the "they". Steiner[28] quotes Heidegger's writing about falling as follows: "It is not a *Verfall* 'from a purer and higher *primal status*'. – Existentially, it is only a modified way in which such everydayness is seized upon."

It is not adequate to claim that Dasein would fall in a certain type of action. When Dasein exists as fallen, it is originally in a genetic sense inauthentic. When Dasein is inauthentic, its being exists in the mode of fallenness.

Steiner's interpretation is that as a result of falling

> Being-in-the-world has lost itself inertly (but absolutely inevitably) in what is at its disposal, in what is merely 'there'. But this loss generates a fertile dissatisfaction. It opens busy empty *Dasein* to the vertigo of the uncanny. In its dizziness, *Dasein* hungers and wills beyond itself. – Desire and hope are the reaching-forward of care. Thus care underlies and necessitates 'the possibility of being-free'. – Authentic being is, therefore, a *being-towards-death* –.[29]

Death and being-towards-death cannot be shrugged off, surpassed or forgotten by Dasein, because it is something that every one of us will inevitably face one day (this reminds me of my childhood and my mother's statement that nothing in life but death is a must). Is it truly so that first being-towards-death will turn the inner existential eye of Dasein towards the self, which could be – or is it – the first wedge that has an impact on the quality of existence as the "they"?

When we die, who is it that dies? Is it the inauthentic Dasein? Does Heidegger refer to an individual's clinical death or to the death of the ego of the inauthentic Dasein? If he meant the clinical death, it could be seen to function as an existential trigger towards authenticity. On the other hand, by death Heidegger may refer to that of the ego, the deconstruction. Also this is to an individual, Dasein, a leap to

---

[27] See Steiner (1987, 94).
[28] Steiner (1987, 95–96).
[29] Steiner (1987, 97–99).

6.1 The "They", Authentic Being and Inauthentic Being

the unknown and a potentially terrifying thing, because it means crossing over what is familiar to our conscious selves or metamorphosis, turning into something else, a kind of death.

A similar tenor can be heard in the ideas of Master Eckhard when he writes about experiences that go down to the roots of existence in which the basis of worldly understanding is lost and being thrown to an existential pitch is experienced. A terrifying experience can also be the thunder-like gently crushing silence (and especially in the case of the Christian Eckhard who rests his belief in a personal, speaking God) which faces man in situations where one's mind and body are favourable and open to the world.

Here I understand the matter so that when Dasein moves from inauthenticity to authenticity, the ego 'dies', gets deconstructed. When this happens, i.e. when a transition to authenticity is ongoing, Dasein will understand the illusionary being of the ego – and the ego is then exposed as the aggregate of experiences.[30] This is the moment when Dasein learns that its essence rests upon the relationship between an individual and the world.

Finally, the clinical death of the authentic Dasein means the loss of the collection of experiences and memories that have been attached to one ontic being (in a bodily-mental human being). What I am trying to point out here is that Heidegger's analysis is the analysis of the inauthentic Dasein. Articulated through the ego, the inauthentic Dasein is a worldly project which one has to surpass in order to reach authenticity. Just as we can abandon the ladders after a climb, Heidegger's analysis comes to an end or is no longer needed after the realization of authenticity.

The foundation of the transition (from inauthentic to authentic being) lies in the fundamental tone of Dasein's being. The target is an experiential relationship to the world, which is presented in Dasein, becomes experienced in Dasein, as a comprehensive experience aware of itself. This is the kind of state of being that is being striven for in the different spiritual and self-disciplinary traditions round the world. 'Call of conscience', discussed in more detail later in this book, can be seen as one of the important initiators of change.

---

[30] Ego in Buddhism, the concept of an ego, in the sense of consciousness of one's self, is seen as composed of nonvalid factors, as delusion. The concept of an ego arises when the dichotomizing intellect (the sixth sense, shadayatana) is confused into presupposing a dualism between I and *not*-I (or other). As a result we think and act as though we were entities separated from everything else, over against a world that lies outside of us. Thus the idea of an *I* becomes fixed in our subconscious, a self which produces thought processes like "I hate this, I love that; this is yours, this is mine." Nurtured by such conceptions, we reach the point where the *I* or ego dominates the mind; it attacks everything that threatens its dominance and is attracted to everything that seems to extend its power. Enmity, desire, and alienation, which culminate in suffering, are the ineluctable results of this outlook, which in Zen is cut through by the practise of zazen (sitting zen-meditation, TK). Thus in the course of Zen training under a roshi, who leads people on the path to enlightenment (satori, kensho), the dominance of the ego illusion over the practitioner's thinking and aspirations is gradually overcome. (*The Encyclopedia of Eastern Philosophy and Religion* 1989, 98.)

6.2 Authenticity and Inauthenticity of Running

Becoming authentic means becoming more perfect and whole as oneself. Dasein is a project embedded with possibilities. Due to its nature, Dasein itself can have an impact on the direction of its life. Heidegger[31] writes that "in each case Dasein *is* its possibility, and it 'has' this possibility, but not just as a property [eigenschaftlich], as something present-at-hand would. And because Dasein is in each case essentially its own possibility, it *can*, in its very Being, 'choose' itself and win itself; it can also lose itself and never win itself; or only 'seem' to do so." In other words, reaching ourselves, acquiring this ability of being, always calls for setting ourselves into an appropriate kind of relationship with the world as a prerequisite for taking the action of reaching ourselves and realizing our own potential. Sheehan points out that "jogging or whatever our sport is, then, is the way we move from actuality toward our potential, toward becoming all we can be".[32]

From the viewpoint of running, I see becoming authentic as a process in which a human can choose to be a running individual, and so choose one physical form of exercise in order to be in touch with the world. In addition, running can be used as an exercise in searching for and in achieving authenticity. Authenticity and inauthenticity can also be looked at from the viewpoint of the body, and by this I do not mean the dualistic approach, because mind and body are two different attributes of the human entity, inseparable from one another without the death of a human. What I mean by this is that if running damages your body, also your mind is damaged (as per its own characteristics).

A wrongly performed running exercise may damage your body. This may happen especially when the runner has a clear idea about the target of the exercises. For example, in competitive sports striving for the top form may prevent a runner from noticing and listening to the messages the body is giving during and after a too heavy exercise, the damage of which is then compensated for by medical means. As a consequence, the body may not have the strength and be able to reach the goals that were once set consciously. The runner will come to face fatigue, illnesses and injuries. The factors that contribute to setting an athlete to the position of an object and to the state of reification are many. I have pondered about this in my doctoral[33] thesis, which I quote in the following:

> The question about the relationship of the essence of physical exercise to that of competitive and top-level sports is very problematic and many-sided. In competitive and top-level sports the target is, according to its own logic, to reach maximal performance, which is understandable. The problem lies in the logic of competitive sports which has become an autonomous structure by itself across nations and individual athletes. This is the logic you must conform to, if you desire to go to the top. Consequently, all the support given to the athlete is focused solely and primarily on this very idea, and so is the athlete as

---

[31] Heidegger (1978, 68).
[32] Sheehan (1978, 69).
[33] Koski (2000, 17).

well. Sports psychology, for example, concentrates on trimming the athlete's mental engine to an 'optimal stroke'.[34] All this is an outcome of complex historical factors in society, institutionalized and hegemonized structures that generate an atmosphere that is in favour of competitive sports. A young athlete – or anyone in fact – may find it difficult to adjust the targets of her top-ranking sports career with growing as a balanced personality. Experiences from physical exercise may, however, help her in seeking for a balance between her goals as a top-level athlete and growing as a personal whole, and so prevent her from being alienated from her own experiences.

This raises the question how to be authentically and inauthentically. Or, is this distinction primarily made by the spiritual and conscious side of Dasein? Could authenticity partly be what Spinoza calls 'good' for one and one's body, while the 'bad' damaging the body is something that generates bodily inauthenticity? J-P Roos has presented a concrete and much more prosaic idea than Spinoza's abstract metaphysical view about the relationship between physical exercise and life possession by dividing people to 'good' and 'bad'. "The good are those who exercise, because their lives are in any case controlled and dictated by good self-discipline, while the bad keep smoking, drinking and eating greasy food, and do not exercise", writes Roos.[35] The basic idea is clearly manifested in both of the cases. Roos personifies the activities that generate good and bad for people, while Spinoza speaks about activities that contribute to an individual becoming a whole and to one's life power (conatus).[36] Getting injured is often the event that reveals the physical limit that should not be exceeded. At the same time it also reveals a faulty and reificated relationship to one's own body, and can act as an eye-opener to seeing the significance of a reasonable exercise.

Next, I will analyze those structures in which Dasein takes a hold of itself and awakens to the thematics of inauthenticity and authenticity.

6.3 Running as "Care"

In a philosophical sense, analyzing it by the means of Heidegger's fundamental ontology, running is one human way of positioning oneself towards the world, which as a means to see oneself and one's environment is about taking the world into account. This is an existentiale, of which Heidegger uses the term "care" (Sorge). Heidegger claims that in some sense it is possible for man to choose the way to be in touch with the world. This is naturally dependent on those situations in which an individual is realized.

---

[34]Liikunta & tiede 3/97, p. 21–26; see also L&T 3/98, p. 13–15.
[35]Roos (1989, 21–22).
[36]Tendency towards self-conservation, conatus sese conservandi (Spinoza 1949, III.7).

Dasein's *closest* way of being is the world in the horizon of conventional everydayness. The world closest to the everyday Dasein is the environment.[37] Being-in-the-world has dispersed into means of being-there: having to do with something, making use of something, undertaking, accomplishing, looking after something, evincing, interrogating, considering, discussing, determining and so on.[38]

Heidegger[39] writes, "because Being-in-the-world belongs essentially to Dasein, its Being towards the world [Sein zur Welt] is essentially concern". For Rauhala[40] "the existentiale of Sorge only represents the necessity of Dasein's relationship with the world".

> The means and quality of human existence are originally always directed and organized as part of the relations represented by one's life situation. Man will turn into something that is determined by the boundaries set by one's life situation. The human existence in a way 'takes into account' or in a numb way understands the terms of one's existence. – Life situation refers to that part of the world to which a certain individual is engaged. Thus, the human being will always be in the world via one's life situation.[41]

There are many kinds of considerations because the question is about the necessity of being in touch with the world. Neglect and loosening one's grip, for example, also have to do with care but in an incomplete mode. Since being towards the world covers all the ways of recognition by Dasein, care covers behaviour that has both positive and negative consequences. In terms of running "Sorge" is thus an example of how a runner can exercise both constructively by listening to one's own body as well as destructively by breaking it.

"Man's *perfektio* – his transformation into that which he can be in Being-free for his ownmost possibilities (projection) – is 'accomplished' by 'care'".[42] Thus, we are in the world together with entities, in touch with them, and we recognize them. As I understand it, the recognition does not mean care as cherishing[43] rather as coexistence, when entities are taken into account more or less consciously. This theme is dealt with in the section *Ready-to-hand and present-at-hand as the dimensions of man's relation to the world*.

> Proximally and for the most part, Dasein understands itself in terms of that which it encounters in the environment and that which it is circumspectively concerned. This understanding is not just a bare taking cognisance of itself, such as accompanies all Dasein's ways of behaving. Understanding signifies one's projecting oneself upon one's current possibility of Being-in-the-world; that is to say, it signifies existing as this possibility.[44]

---

[37] Heidegger (1978, 94).
[38] Heidegger (1978, 83).
[39] Heidegger (1978, 84).
[40] Rauhala (1993, 102).
[41] Rauhala (1991, 20).
[42] Heidegger (1978, 243).
[43] Protective caring, giving strength in a motivated way.
[44] Heidegger (1978, 439).

6.3 Running as "Care"

Heidegger gives the concept of understanding his own meaning. To him understanding represents the primitive strength of getting by in the world, which is not a result of reflection. Similarly, Dasein takes gravity into account in all of its actions without having first theoretically taken it into possession.[45] Rauhala[46] explicates the concept as follows:

> When Dasein – this truly undefined momentum of possibilities of human existence – faces its terms of being in its life situation, the realizing human existence 'understands' these terms and becomes real by means enabled by the structural patterns of reality. For Dasein this 'understanding' does not mean conscious understanding rather precomprehension (*Vorverständnis*). –. Heidegger also uses the expression 'preontological understanding of Being' (*das vorontologische Seinsverständnis*) in order to refer to the same kind of understanding.

I see this to mean that Heidegger's concept of understanding is an articulation of humans and the world being made of the same 'stuff' – and so describes how man and the world fit together. When I use the term understanding (elsewhere than in direct quotes), I'm using it in a conventional sense, and when I want to refer to Heidegger's idea of understanding, I use the term "preontological understanding of Being".

Understanding means being always somewhere and in a certain kind of mental state. We are always in relation to something, and this being-in-relation-somewhere-to-something is determined by our understanding of being-in-the-world. This means understanding the self in the existential readiness-to-hand, revealed as a project (Entwurf). When Dasein finally understands (if ever it understands) its selfness (as a concrete, meaningful feeling in all of its existential authenticity), the existential project is over. The oppressive and bitter 'backing of the oars' reveals its own insignificant importance. One cannot reach the goal without "vanity". Heidegger[47] expresses the beginning of this existential project as follows: "If in care we have arrived at Dasein's primordial state of Being, then this must also be the basis for conceptualising that understanding of Being which lies in care; that is to say, it must be possible to define the meaning of Being". I will discuss the topic later in chapter "Call of conscience" where "*conscience manifests itself as the call of care*",[48] the basis of the call is Dasein's anxious being-in-the-world. As Heidegger[49] writes, "the call of conscience – that is, conscience itself – has its ontological possibility in the fact that Dasein, in the very basis of its Being, is care". From the viewpoint of authenticity the significance of care lies in "that in the call of conscience care summons Dasein towards its ownmost potentiality-for-Being".[50]

---

[45] See Kupiainen (2003, 15–16).
[46] Rauhala (1990, 112).
[47] Heidegger (1978, 273).
[48] Heidegger (1978, 322).
[49] Heidegger (1978, 322–323).
[50] Heidegger (1978, 365).

In terms of running, the existentiale of care is in practice present for the first time when an individual run begins. I consider the first time to be a runner's conscious and thematic relationship to a running exercise.

The process of running can be seen to start from (1) awakening to the next run, i.e., to the idea of running. This will bring along appropriate, (2) eating and drinking, (3) selection of running clothing and significance of other equipment, (4) warm-ups and stretching, (5) selection of the running terrain – a long or heavy exercise will bring (6) tiredness and fatigue, (7) the social aspect of running (it is different to run alone than when accompanied by someone), (8) and last, finishing the exercise and the feeling after that. In the following I will discuss these issues more thoroughly:

1. What precedes an exercise? When does running actually begin? One way of looking at it is to consider it to start from the thought that thematizes the exercise. This is the moment when we become both mentally and psychophysically tuned to what is coming. The state of tuning will rise when the coming is thematized as being confronted in real life. The coming determines the present, the very moment at hand. The thought about running is one of the essential properties of the exercise. No-one could leave for a run without the thought about running, without the constitutive meaning of the idea of running. Where does the idea arise from?

   - From being conscious that it is, for example, Wednesday, one of your running days. If you want to run with a friend, you typically have to agree on this in advance. The thought can arise also by other means, such as
   - The feeling in your body. You may turn out to have a stuffed-up feeling in your body, which awakens the idea about going for a run. You may be in a grumpy mood and feel being out of balance in an unpleasant way. Realizing this may remind you of the fact that already a week has passed from the previous run.
   - The idea of going for a run may also be triggered by the senses. A picture of runners in the morning paper may capture your eyes. Your 'ears' may hear rhythmical sounds, reminding you about the way you step when running. A certain kind of smell, some sweaty piece of clothing for example, may remind you about the running clothing. Some taste may remind you of a certain kind of food or drink you have enjoyed during and/or after the exercise. The sense of touch may also generate the idea of running: wet hands may have a connotation to sweat; climbing the stairs may feel too heavy in the thighs, reminding you about an uphill run. These experiences and awakenings which are not related to a conscious decision to go for a run can be called ontic experiences that prepare you to become conscious about running. These are the experiences that thematize your consciousness.

   Consciousness enabled by ecstasy will take a hold of the forthcoming exercise in a temporal sense. The possession will make your state of mind tuned. At this

6.3 Running as "Care"

starting point the runner is in anticipation.[51] The runner hastens in advance to be in connection with her forthcoming factual self when running.

2. The next phase are the preparations made before getting dressed for the exercise, the most important being eating and drinking. The longer the exercise the more accurately you must plan the moment when you eat. Having a lacto-vegetarian diet, I am in the habit of enjoying a meal rich in carbohydrates 3–4 h before the run. If for some reason I end up eating too close to the beginning of the exercise, I would feel uncomfortable, heavy and swollen. In that case especially the beginning, the first 5 km of the exercise, feels tedious, uncomfortable and unpleasant to carry through. The desired light feeling is missing.

   During a period of time when I wanted to lose some weight, I chose to run for an hour or an hour and half at noon with an empty stomach, having drank only some water, juice or black coffee without sugar in the morning. This required me to keep a slow pace during the exercise. After the exercise I enjoyed a milk shake with berries, fruit, soy flour, sesame paste. After that, the exhaustion that took over my body required me to take a half-an-hour nap.

3. A bodily, physical activity, dressing up for the exercise is where the idea of running is concretized. I see this as a rite which prepares you for the run and as a situation in which you ultimately decide whether or not to start the run. The more demanding the circumstances the more time it takes to get prepared. In the winter, you need to evaluate what kind of clothing is appropriate for the weather, select the location of the exercise (for example by avoiding open terrain in a harsh wind), do your warm-ups longer and more thoroughly, or running a longer distance may necessitate grabbing a bottle of water along. I myself have come to notice that the longer and the heavier the exercise, the more concentrated and conscious I am when dressing up and doing the warm-ups. With the intention of making a 30 km run, I may have a loaded, adrenaline-rich itchy feeling, which is not present when leaving for a one-hour exercise. The dressing rite thus prepares the runner psycho-physically to the exercise.

4. Warm-ups and stretching are both important, ritualistic activities which help you get prepared for the run. Marko Vapa writes that "the warm-ups make you mentally prepared for the exercise, rise your body temperature, and make your body relaxed, consequently leading to a more economical performance".[52]

5. The running terrain or environment is principally always similar. Your feet touch the ground, your body feels the sun, wind, rain, or frost, and small objects like leaves and tiny branches may fall against your face from the trees. In a sublime environment it is easier to make your mind tuned to be more sensitive and more receptive to the world. However, what is essential are the experiences you gain during your run. (At least my own) experience has proven that even if the circumstances were always similar, the experiences keep changing. In other

---

[51] See Heidegger (1978, e.g. 306, 349–350, 353–354).
[52] Vapa (2001, p. 5/10).

words, the empirical factors do not guarantee a regular generation of similar experiences.

Sometimes the touch of the world (the ontic touch) can be very concrete and overwhelming. This is what happened to me on 9 October, 2002[53]:

> Three rounds around my regular 3-km training path. Then, around 8 PM I went for a swim in the nearby lake. The northerly wind was harsh but it didn't feel as cold as it was, since the higher pace I kept during the third round had worked as planned making me, owing to the increased body heat, better able to withstand the wind. I moved quickly into the water, wearing my running shorts and a woolen cap on my head. After some strokes I took away the cap and made a quick dive, and then put the cap back and got very quickly out of the water. The harsh wind felt cold against wet skin. Next, a quick dry-off. I had no trouble putting on a dry shirt and a jacket, but pulling the pants up the wet legs proved more of a challenge, and then I faced a similar frustration when pulling on the socks. My fingers totally numb, I had to tie the shoe laces with the help of my eyesight. Then, I realized that the bicycle key was in the pocket of the running jacket only after I had already squeezed all the running clothing inside the bag. I spent some desperate moments looking for the key, and having found it, it was another struggle to push it in the keyhole without a chance to feel it with my numb fingers. I turned the bicycle sideways toward the lamp post in order to see where to push the key. Then, I quickly put the gloves on and rode home. I twisted my fingers against the palm so that they need not be separately located in their own departments, and was so forced to riding the bicycle with my fingers in that position. Finally at home, when the sense of feeling was returning to my hands, the pain was so overwhelming that I couldn't do anything but stand there silent in the porch and breathe deeply. My wife came to me asking "what's wrong?" The pain was so hard that I did not want to answer her rather used all of my energy to myself. This inferno took probably some 5 min to pass. When I finally managed to tell her that I had taken a swim after the exercise, my wife just said that "there's no sense whatsoever in those doings of yours". Only later did I comment on that by asking her "did you really think that I've done this just for the fun of it?".[54]

This kind of touches with nature remind us of our bodilyness and vulnerability, how we are in touch with the world and how we are bound with multiple ties to the products of our culture. I could have perished, had I not had the opportunity to put on some warm clothes and had I failed to reach the shelter of my home. But on the other hand, had I been a stone-age man, I would probably not have taken a swim in that weather either. Although the circumstances were somewhat unpleasant, I found experiencing my body strongly a valuable experience somehow. People should be thankful for their bodies. This is what the angels think in the motion picture *Wings of desire* by Wim Wenders. They are jealous to people about their bodies.

What a great pleasure it is on a cold autumn morning to scrub numbed hands against each other and to buy a cup of hot coffee from a street corner kiosk, drink it with both hands and to feel the lovely warmth floating into my body! In order to live a full life, one must be able to fully experience it in all of its sensory concreteness.

---

[53]Running diary.

[54]Instead of desiring to go through the pain!

6. Having run for a long time, or when the exercise is short but heavy, the runner may need to consciously concentrate on things that would otherwise happen automatically. The long distance or strain makes you numb and you may lose the relaxed feeling, after which running becomes stiff and forced. Good understanding of your own body, "the bodily understanding", will help you to more quickly notice when your running technique turns forced and to fix it (if possible).

The unity of the body and mind seems to have disappeared from situations where your legs no longer obey you. Although from an intellectual point of view we could consider the unity to be missing, experientially it is still clearly exposed. I remember how in my first ever marathon, which I ran alone in 1999, my stepping began to feel insecure at about 33 km. I was trying to concentrate on my legs and so to get rid of the fatigue, stiffness and insecurity I felt in them. It was really difficult to try to concentrate on this idea, as if it was trying to slip away from my consciousness. A conscious control of your thoughts requires some strength. When looking at it afterwards, the memory of repeating to myself "stay focused, stay focused" makes me smile gently at myself.

When your legs are having trouble to run relaxed, it is difficult for you to take hold of the idea of asking them to do so. In other words, as it is hard for your 'legs' to surpass a forced running technique, your effort to consciously try to direct your legs may prove difficult. The tight coupling/intertwinement of the mind and body is exposed again. Or, it is perhaps too much to talk about coupling because it contains a connotation to the dualistic expression, as if there were two separate entities embracing one another. Would we be able to accurately say which part of us is the body and which is the mind?

6.4 Prerequisites of Physical Exercise

A self-evident *primary prerequisite* is the existence of the world as the 'home' of man's Being. Using Heidegger's own expression, living in this 'home' is caring. It means living with those tasks and people which being there is facing in its situations. Care can appear in diverse forms, for example as something that destroys nature or preserves it.

This is the most fundamental of all prerequisites, something that makes the touch between man and the world possible (the ontic touch). This is also what a runner is actively and consciously seeking for and aiming at, even if one was not aware of the significance of the ontic touch. There is no need for that since running takes priority. Thus, the ontic touch is the basic, factual way of being-in-the-world, which contains all such forms of touch which a human being is physically participating in. The criterion for defining something as ontic is that the touch is perceivable by senses.[55]

What is the nature of the ontic touch if we are touching an imaginary object? If it manages to cause a "bodily change" (state of fear, for example), I consider it ontic in a secondary sense, because it causes an individual's own, innate ontic touch (the stomach is aching, one does not feel well, etc).

Second prerequisite: the sportive basis of humans rests on being an ecstatic being with an innate ability to move (operative intentionality). This ability is mostly exposed as an axiomatic fact of being, because one has "grown into it" since birth. When someone, whether a child or an adult, wants to have an object, one does not analyse her ability to go to the object rather does it naturally. Only when the ability to move is limited, the ability to get the desired object with the help of one's own actions is thematized as problematic.

Third prerequisite: In running, or in any sportive activity, there is always a drive to actively seek a touch between the body, mind and the world. As a prerequisite of seeking for this touch and physical activity there is always the presence of a certain kind of feeling or mood (Stimmung). This is what makes us prepared for facing the requirements brought by the touch, such as a heavy exercise, unpleasantness introduced by bad weather, and so on. Without being in an appropriate kind of mood about the exercise in advance, it is difficult for you to orientate to performing it. This is especially evident, for example, when you have given up performing an exercise which calls for motivation and directed your attention elsewhere (for example, the running conditions are bad, and your spouse is having a meeting which requires you to stay home as a babysitter), but then all of a sudden you hear from your wife that a meeting has been cancelled and that "you can go and make that 30 km run, the longest one in a month". The feeling that you used to have and then gave away, your determination to doing the exercise, may prove to be difficult to restore (so that you do the exercise after all). Also Roos[56] has pondered about the weather conditions in his web book. According to Roos

> It is more worthwhile for a runner to adjust one's exercises to the weather than to follow one's training regime rigorously. It would be silly not to make use of perfect conditions for a long run, or on the other hand to try to do it in heavy rain only because your regime tells you to do so. That is (i.e. the flexible mindset, TK) what builds up your character –.

Sticking stubbornly to your training regime may eventually turn into a stress factor which kills the joy of running and your motivation. In running, as well as elsewhere in life, it would be beneficial for you to keep your mind open and to avoid slipping into a functional role with too tight boundaries structured by the ego. This is well

---

[55] Koski (2000), 81–87.

[56] Roos (1995), Chapter 12.

suited with the idea that you must not take yourself (that is to say, your ego) too seriously. Several years ago I discovered from my consciousness the idea that "it is not good for you if your ego is what is preventing your development".[57] As Roos puts it[58]:

> In other words, the running regime is easily adjustable based on the weather, and you are allowed to run when the conditions are favourable. Or, you can run less when the weather is bad, run a lot during the weekends when possible, or take a week's break or go to a pub as you wish to do so, when running simply is not possible.

Even though the feelings, impressions or other movements of our minds come and go, some of them are more tightly coupled with being a human. This is what happens when we are determined, in ways described above, thematized by a thought or a feeling. When a feeling gets a runner attuned, the feeling and the idea that it represents will become a power that controls your attitude, which is more real and "fleshly" than random thoughts. If you have given up the thought that involves engagement and if you have to get attuned again, gaining it back would require a more full-bloodied and more bodily mental effort and control than random thoughts, which have a lower status in relation to engagement.

Fourth prerequisite: desire, will, willpower

> A physical exercise has an impact on the human being as a whole. As a bodily exercise it also serves as a mental one – for example, physical and mental effort can both be seen to call for a similar act of will, since in both cases the question is about conscious actions and the intention to do so. Thinking is, for example, something that you do consciously even when lying in bed, yet something that calls for an effort. Thinking is similarly consciously present when, for example, when you have to make a bench press possible in a bodily sense. By exercising your ability to withstand the mental effort in connection with a sportive activity you are also developing your spiritual strength and will.[59]

Will is, in fact, present in all of our doings. Often we only use it so that we are not even aware of what we are doing – especially when it is easy and does not require much of an effort. Again, if we did not want what we are doing, for example lifting an arm, nothing would happen. The Japanese philosopher Kitaro Nishida considers will a fundamental factor which unites the body and the mind.[60] Klemola quotes his thoughts as follows:

> The power of the mind and the power of the body are simultaneously present in will, or are inseparable from one another. They are one and the same thing. By exercising one we also exercise the other. Different bodily exercises such as sport in its different forms can be considered extending the area of will to the area of the body. This is done by broadening your consciousness about the inner state of the body but also by experimenting

---

[57] Relates to the idea that one would not regard one's ego as the criterion for oneself or one's true self.

[58] Roos (1995), Chapter 12.

[59] Koski (2000, 176–177).

[60] Nishida (1987, 120–123); see Klemola (2004, 116–121).

with the relationship between your body and the gravity directed to it. The velocity, power, performance as well as inertness all call for special use of willpower.[61]

A runner has to have a desire, a will to run. Willpower is resorted to when the runner is not motivated to run. In such situations willpower may get its fuel, for example, from the ideal set by the runner to oneself. An experience about power also gives willpower.

This ideal worth reaching for that a runner wishes to achieve, possesses as a forerunner a property which cannot be achieved otherwise than in an exercise happening "now". The power and motivation to ourselves are thus sought from what we are not at that moment – the search takes place via the "ideal-self". The ideal-self is non-existent in the sense of being not-yet-realized. It is not entirely non-existent because it already contains something that has been achieved and is already in some way similar to the runner. With the help of exercise the existential status of the ideal will change eventually, as the runner becomes more and more like the ideal. A runner may desire to position one's factual self together with the ideal self, which in some cases is also realized. The only way to realize the ideal is to see it in the process of coming. In other words, Dasein must be able to see itself as exercising, as a runner who is going towards a goal with engagement. Dasein must be able to see that it is possible to reach the goal with the help of exercise. If you fail to see this, the exercise as a process is lost. Rushing once in a fury does not help you to reach the goal. First by understanding the process it is possible for you to realize a concrete, long-lasting training regime in which the self turns via the ideal self into a new self, a self that has reached the ideal.

Sometimes the running exercise also has to be thematized via will. This is when the desire does not suffice. In such a situation the willpower helps you surpass the gap in the continuum of exercising inflicted by lack of desire and passion. Willpower has to do with the understanding that you know a long-lasting exercise to bring into your life. Good running experiences also inspire and make you desire more exercise.

Will can be utilized in many ways. When I run slowly, I can let my will rest in its own space. But when my aim is to practice more rigorously, for example by lifting up my heart beat to 160 per minute, I am forced to consciously use my will. When I know that I'm about to begin a rough climb, my whole being is overwhelmed with a nervous sort of slightly unpleasant and itchy feeling. At this point I feel electrified and prepare myself to a strong effort of will and physical strain. I can feel my breathing become faster and the energy level to increase. What is it, in fact, that is happening here? In my consciousness the climb and my own performance place themselves as intentional objects. I will get attuned to the desired mental state via this orientation of consciousness, and I am ready to face the challenge set by the terrain. Thus, I am capable of having an impact on my mood. In this way I will take in advance the possession of an occasion in my immediate proximity. This requires that I have thought about the nature of the exercise in advance – of course sometimes

---

[61] Klemola (2004, 118).

6.4 Prerequisites of Physical Exercise

what happens is that even though the target has been to run a very light exercise, the feeling in my body makes me work harder than was my original intention. As a result of focusing my consciousness the reduction of everything else takes place. Usually this happens spontaneously, by which I mean that I am not consciously making the reduction, but rather the situation does it for me. I myself just simply get adjusted to the requirement set by the situation, by taking care of it as I see adequate. I am taking notice of the coming terrain with the intensity thematized by my will. Because the event is very intensive by nature, no other thing "fits" then in my consciousness or there is no room for anything else. The approaching extra effort has taken over my whole being. I'm not thinking about the past or the future, rather all of my interest is focused on that very moment and the heaviness of the climb.

It is possible to use various means to attune your will and bodily power, hence your willpower. One of them is to think of a situation in which you notice, when riding a bicycle, that all of a sudden you are about to collide with an obstacle. Your body will get attuned to the event in an instant, preparing you to accept the forthcoming collision. A voluntary generation of this kind of an experience will free resources to a runner.

Consciousness is exposed in running in two different modes.

1. It can be as it is, in itself. This being the case, the thoughts wander spontaneously from one association to another. Our minds are operating as they please.
2. Consciousness can be consciously focused. Roughly speaking, this can be divided in three different ways:

    (a) consciousness may be focused on monitoring the terrain and the environment. When the terrain is rough, your eyes must be concentrated (in order to avoid injury) on selecting suitable positions for placing your feet.
    (b) A runner may consciously focus one's sight inwards and concentrate on listening to what is happening in herself during the exercise.
    (c) A runner may only run, letting her consciousness rest relaxed in itself. This is related to the phenomenon of flow.

The last point (c) is a union between the two modes, but it can also be seen as a third mode. Although consciousness is allowed to be as spontaneous as it is on its own, it does not consist of an accidental chain of associations rather stays calm and placid. As comes to focusing the consciousness, although it is not thematized, it is not consciously focused rather it has positioned itself in a way that results from the exercise. Consciousness has quieted down on its own and focused itself without conscious focusing.[62]

These prerequisites represent man's ways of being-in-the-world in which the being is exposed. These are aprioric (prior to an experience) forms of being-at-hand – being-at-hand because they are bodily forms that are always present.

---

[62] In Zen exercises this is known as "shikan-taza", see Kapleau (1988, 397).

Typically, those go unnoticed, because an individual is them. In a genetic sense, at birth the human being is focused away from the self, because there is no conscious being to be conscious of. Only after that, after having been ontically in touch with the world, through which your consciousness develops, you can focus your inner sight on yourself and you can discover the aprioric forms in question.

6.5 Uncovering and Covering of the World for a Runner

The conceptual framework in which man and running is analysed in this study is Heidegger's characteristic epistemologic-ontological view on the uncovering of being and Being. It is the way of existence of the world, which is uncovered in man's bodily being-in-the-world. The uncovering happens in situations of caring.

Reality and its nature are always revealed to man in one way or another, the way being dependent on the being-in-the-world of each individual. By the term "uncovering the reality" I refer to all those physical and mental impressions, ideas and conceptual systems that emerge as a result of interaction between man and the world.[63] The question is about all those events that exist in some way and can be experienced by man as a bodily and thinking being.[64] The uncovering of reality is a metaphysical view about the way in which a being exists and acts. This is the perspective which will form the framework for human action. This perspective defines the boundaries where from man's experiential horizon will widen and open up.

Reality is revealed to man in its directness without a rational intent. Heidegger speaks about *Aletheia*,[65] which means uncovering the truth (Unverborgenheit) as it takes place in the touch between man and reality. Juha Varto interprets Heidegger so that truth "is not a relationship rather the means in which reality expresses itself",[66] but which can only appear in a relationship. Thomas Sheehan[67] writes that the entities are self-revealing (alethes) only to the extent that they correlate with the human, uncovering (aletheuein) and primarily practical proactive actions. As a comment to Sheehan's text I cannot but claim that physical exercise is a human and practical form of action par excellence.

The authenticity and inauthenticity of running are shaped up on the basis of the relationship an individual has in relation to the world as a runner. This is related to Dasein's worldliness and to how (1) it is covering and uncovering the world in its being and to how (2) the world is covered and uncovered to Dasein

---

[63]Touch refers to the relation between the body and the world, which takes priority. Interaction means social interaction between people.

[64]Koski (2000, 53).

[65]Heidegger (1978, 262–273). See also Gelassenheit (Heidegger 1988).

[66]Varto (1992, 63).

[67]Sheehan (1998, 40).

6.5 Uncovering and Covering of the World for a Runner

(which is dependent on Dasein's being-in-the-world and touch to the world). Heidegger writes that "to Dasein's Being and its potentiality-for-Being as Being-in-the-world, disclosedness and uncovering belong essentially".[68]

These are fundamental things which lay the foundation for the entire human existence. One of Dasein's structural properties is the ability to uncover the being – yet at the same time this uncovering is also a covering by nature. In order to possess the ability to uncover one must be open to existence. All of this means that Dasein has the ability to sense and understand being. But since Dasein is not a God rather an incarnated, bodily being, the uncovering of beings encountered in the world is always uncovering to some individual Dasein depending on the touch relationship and point of view characteristic of it. Uncovering is thus always incomplete and means covering as well. In this respect Dasein is also "closed". In continuation, this theme is clarified further when I discuss it in relation to running.

Running means an active touch to the world. Through the touch a runner will personally get a hold of the part of the world that is characteristic of this relationship. Concrete bodily action reveals new aspects of the world. This uncovering lays a foundation for receiving feedback about our own being-in-the-world, and consequently for realization as an inauthentic or authentic being. As a bodily being a human is always only in one location at a time. Dasein will only get a hold of the part of the world where one is located as a dimensional entity. The rest of the world is "closed". Heidegger[69] says, "but only in so far as Dasein has been disclosed has it also been closed off; and only in so far as entities within-the-world have been uncovered along with Dasein, have such entities, as possible encounterable within-the-world, been covered up (hidden) or disguised."

Man's touch to the world inevitably covers some aspect of the world. But because covering is possible, so is uncovering, respectively.[70] Dasein goes via the route of covering and uncovering at the same time.

Using the metaphor of the road and a walker, we could think that one foot uncovers and the other one covers. Alternatively this can be seen so that covering means narrowing of the existential horizon, which inevitably follows when one is focused on something, thus covering and uncovering result from a kind of division of labour. Dasein is always in one situation at a time only, wherefore care is bound to one situation only or is part of it. Dasein can take notice of beings enabled and opened up by one situation only. But isn't the case in this 'division of labour' also that there are different grades, i.e. better and worse divisions, some of which make one authentic and others that do the opposite? Single-mindedness narrows the horizon of the world of Dasein and limits the amount of the present-at-hand.

---

[68] Heidegger (1978, 270–27).

[69] Heidegger (1978, 265).

[70] "To Dasein's state of Being belongs *projection* – disclosive Being towards its potentiality-for-Being. (But, TK) *Dasein is essentially falling, its state of Being is such that it is in 'untruth'.*" (Heidegger 1978, 264.)

When an individual has a relationship with something, uncovering and covering takes place. From the viewpoint of a bodily being we can state that when an individual is located in a situation, she is in that location and nowhere else. Here we open up the relations between the self and the world, and not those in which we are not at that moment. In running, for example, only relationships to running can be uncovered. The uncovering takes place in touch, which cannot exist if we are not factually realized in running. Running uncovers levels related to running but covers something where we are not at that moment. For example, sitting on the sofa uncovers sitting-on-the-sofa and covers levels related to running. We can choose ourselves what opportunities of a project we want to open up. Heidegger puts it this way: "Our Being alongside entities within-the-world is concern, and this is Being which uncovers. – Dasein expresses itself [spricht sich aus]: it expresses *itself* as Being-towards entities – a Being-towards which uncovers. – The assertion which is expressed is about something, and in what it is about [in ihrem Worüber] it contains the uncoveredness of these entities".[71] Rauhala explicates the idea as follows:

> In fateful existential selections and/or in selections that we make ourselves we solve the means and quality of our existence either as momentarily changing or as relatively stable. In this way we realize ourselves as reading, sitting, opening the door, studying, teaching, or as a teacher, spouse, father, mother, etc. In all these selections, whether as actors or targets, there are always other possibilities that are excluded. We will always be realized in a relationship with the world in a way that is somehow special –.[72]

The way we have to become realized and the opening of the horizon (the context of understanding) is so close to ourselves that it typically passes us unnoticed or typically we never come to think of it.[73]

In this process of realization the being is uncovered as it is, and uncovering is always actually present. Outside of uncovering, the world is a potential sphere, which is always in the process of becoming. Heidegger writes that "Dasein (has, TK) always something still *outstanding*, which, as a potentiality-for-Being for Dasein itself, has not yet become 'actual'. – Such a lack of totality signifies that there is something still outstanding in one's potentiality-for-Being".[74] This is probably what Heidegger means when he writes that the being of Dasein is always about being ahead of itself.[75] In other words, it is possible to reach the goals, the wishes may be fulfilled, life has always something to offer, every day is a new day, and the potentials of Dasein can be realized. "It is essential to the basic constitution

---

[71] Heidegger (1978, 266).

[72] Rauhala (1990, 113).

[73] Rauhala (1990, 114). But, "the structure of a life situation can be changed (with regard to experiential topics, TK) so that it leads to mental states that give inspiration or motivate new ideas. Controlled alteration of the structure of a life situation naturally presupposes mental activity." (Rauhala 1990, 119.)

[74] Heidegger (1978, 279).

[75] Heidegger (1978, 279–280).

of Dasein that there is *constantly something still to be settled* [*eine ständige Unabgeschlossenheit*]".[76] First at death Dasein will reach its entirety (when it is closed existentially).

6.6 The Distant Is Far and Near

Covering and uncovering have to do with Dasein's ability to reach a target that is outside the immediate reach from itself, generally the ability to take possession of something in a distance. As it is self-evident that the main point in running is moving from one place to another, it also serves as the exercising factor of an exercise. This is the "ontic friction", which is exercising the body and mind as running.

One of the properties of Dasein's way of being-in-the-world is "cancelling remoteness" – in other words one of Dasein's means of realization in the world is to exist by cancelling remoteness.[77] For example, the goal and finishing point of running are located somewhere and are always in relation to Dasein. The body cannot be "here" and "yonder" simultaneously. As Heidegger[78] puts it:

> The 'yonder' belongs definitely to something encountered within-the-*world*. 'Here' and 'yonder' are possible only in a 'there' – that is to say, only if there is an entity which has made a disclosure of spatiality as the Being of the 'there'. – Only for an entity which is existentially cleared in this way does that which is present-at-hand become accessible in the light or hidden in the dark.

"Being-in-the-world has a spatiality of its own, characterized by the phenomena of de-severance and directionality".[79] Running is about cancelling the distance in a concrete way. Only such a being that is being realized in the world, "here", can cancel remoteness. A Being which would be situated everywhere at the same time, could never be "here".[80]

Dasein's "spatiality shows the characters of *de-severance* and *directionality*", writes Heidegger.[81] In other words: the body is a centre through which the world as a space derives its meaning. Directionality is coupled with the concept of remoteness,

---

[76] Heidegger (1978, 279).

[77] Heidegger (1978, 139–140).

[78] Heidegger (1978, 171).

[79] Heidegger (1978, 346).

[80] "'De-severing' amounts to making the farness vanish – that is, making the remoteness of something disappear, bringing it close. Dasein is essentially de-severant: it lets any entity be encountered close by as the entity which it is. De-severance discovers remoteness –. Proximally and for the most part, de-severing is a circumspective bringing-close – bringing something close by, in the sense of procuring it, putting it in readiness, having it to hand. But certain ways in which entities are discovered in a purely cognitive manner also have the character of bringing them close. *In Dasein there lies an essential tendency towards closeness.*" (Heidegger 1978, 139–140.)

[81] Heidegger (1978, 138).

which contains a means of being far that cancels remoteness. This is a consequence of a bodily property – the body is always spread out to the environment via the senses, so something that is reached by all senses will come close. For example, a distant view transmitted by vision comes close because experientially the distant view enters the "body" and is experienced there.

In running something that is further away is reached by running, and brought close. The exercising dimension of running is based on reaching something that is further away. What is essential is taking possession of the remote by means of bodily action. Running is the most simple and most original human means of moving fast. When there are no accessories bringing the remote present in an instance, the ontic touch between a runner and the world is at its biggest. The better a technical device such as a car is used for reducing the distance, the less reaching the remote exercises the individual and the less the journey is ready-to-hand.

The ecstasity of Dasein serves as a starting point for understanding this analysis. The directionality of a bodily-sensing human being is ecstatic by nature due to the structure of Dasein's existence. A human being is continuously exceeding oneself. Taking a step or moving a finger is ecstatic. Looking at the stars is ecstatic, which can be emphasized using a telescope. In a way the Internet has tremendously emphasized the ecstasity of humans. In other words, the bodily performance has been increased.

I wonder if we could playfully call this kind of expansion of human ecstasity ontological doping? Ecstasity can be divided into a bodily and a mental aspect. To clarify what I intend to say, I quote myself[82]: A concrete prerequisite for ecstasy is

> that a human being is connected to the world through her senses. The senses transmit to preconsciousness/consciousness the matter that makes self-consciousness and thus ecstasy possible. The senses are the means of the human body to project a human being to the world, and so get connected with it. – In order 'to step out of ourselves' with each of the senses, the prerequisite for man is that the world as an object of touch is reachable by all the senses. Because the senses are different, their touch to the world is different and takes place as if from different perspectives, enabling the touch to the world at many levels simultaneously. As an analogy, senses can epistemologically be compared to five humans each of whom is approaching the same object from their own perspective. Together these perceptions make up a more realistic idea of the object than if there was only one viewer in question. The more senses are involved in the relationship of man with the world, the more experiential touch we are receiving from as many ways of being in the world, respectively. We can think that the human experiential horizon to the world is the broader and the more open, the more senses are involved in the creation and opening of an experiential horizon. The broader the horizon of senses, the more versatile and the more holistic conception may form up for us about reality, which is represented in our consciousness according to its fundamental nature.

Here we must emphasize that the question is about the body as an entity that synthesizes the senses, and not about senses as such. Only by being articulated by the body the information produced by the senses shall gain the meaning that they have.

---

[82] Koski (2000, 68–69).

6.6 The Distant Is Far and Near

Our senses transmit to us the part of the world where conscious experiences about the entanglement between us and the world emerge from (for example, what is remote comes close to us via vision and with the help of that we "move" far away, respectively).[83]

When something that is remote comes close with the help of technical devices, what is close may become more distant, and the within-the-world readiness-to-hand may alter. When this happens, the within-the-world readiness-to-hand is reduced, and presence-at-hand is in the increase, respectively. We must look at this from the viewpoint of the body. (For example, paying the bills on the Internet does not require you to visit the bank concretely. This kind of use of the body is left out, which reduces physical activity, or utilitarian exercise.) On the other hand presence-at-hand will become more like readiness-to-hand (e.g. we gain a video and voice contact to a target on the other side of the world) part of the lifeworld (not tangible rather something ready-to-hand through sight and hearing as well as conceptually). This is one spatial modification which gives a structure to human existence.

This can also be understood with the help of the concept of "bodily division of labour". It can be divided to active and passive body. The distant that is coming close and the close that becomes more distant will change the work division to a more passive direction. This kind of evolution is often triggered by technical inventions such as the phone. Typically, an actively exercising person has the motivation to be active in a bodily sense. A regularly exercising runner is committed to running. An individual engaged and devoted to one's activities is continuously occupied by running.

"Coming-close" speaks for the ability of humans to move in the world. The distant comes close owing to your own bodily action. This reveals the functionality of the body and health of humans, the significance of which is emphasized when we look at it from the point of view of running which has been experienced as significant and important. Recognizing the issue as an important structural factor in your existence contains a clear demand for looking after your health.

This structure of running, in the form of the distant coming close, comprises a runner's relationship with the environment. I have learned to understand that most runners prefer to run in nature. Good-quality air is important for breathing. When a runner is forced to exercise in an environment where air quality is poor (air contains dust raised by traffic, exhaust fumes and industrial emissions), a runner may become conscious of nature in a new way. This shows that a runner's relationship with nature is by no means insignificant. The significance of nature will become concretely important and it may expand to cover a runner's entire world-relationship, and not only an exercise factor related to the running environment. In other words, a newly experienced nature relationship may help a runner change the attitude that she has towards the world. In general, running may produce an existential state yielding

---

[83]Perhaps I shouldn't say this, but could this be considered a kind of preliminary stage for the existential experience in which we are united with everything and in which we find our existential home in the world?

one's mind to rest, so supporting the runner. The space, time, body, mind and senses melt into one aesthetic-ethical life-supporting entity, as proven by Sheehan's experiences described in the following:

> It is beautiful and real and a delight. The snow crunches underfoot. The pure light of the sun flashes off the white surface, the sky is high and blue. The air is dry and clean in my lungs. My senses are filled with these realities, with the sound of my breathing, the soft noise of my passage. I am living time and I am living space. The time and space Blake described, when a pulsation of an artery is equal to 6000 years and where a space no bigger than a globule of man's blood opens into eternity.[84]

Nature conditions concern those practising outside in a different way compared to those who practise indoors. A runner may feel the wind on her face, the sun may feel scorching and make the exercise feel heavy and sweaty to carry through. Outdoors, a specific kind of ontic touch prevails between the world and a runner, generating corresponding bodily-conscious experiences. One's own existence is present, which brings a runner closer to the world, consciously or unconsciously, and brings the unity of oneness of the body and mind clearly present. Sheehan writes about running in the autumn:

> Cross-country is free running at its best. Just me and the land. Me and that crisp air. Me and the leaves underfoot. Me and the silent hills. That's cross-country. Just me and the breathing and the leaves crunching underfoot on those silent hills. – Everything around me is dead or dying and I feel reborn. I am at my best.[85]

The touch brought in by running is intensive by nature, which introduces the tendency that prevents a runner from falling into the pale mood of everydayness. An active relationship with the world breaks up the everyday elements that draw one's mind towards inauthenticity. Sheehan writes about this, putting emphasis on the rebirth of the body and mind:

> There on a country road – I discover the total universe, the natural and the supernatural that wise men speculate about. It is a life, a world, a universe that begins on the other side of sweat and exhaustion. I am purified by that sweat. I am baptized in my own water. I move again through a new Eden. – I am saturated with the goodness of the world, filled with the sight and the sound and the smell and the feel of the land through which I run.[86]

---

[84]Sheehan (1978, 242).

[85]Sheehan (1978, 177).

[86]Sheehan (1978, 246–247). Timo Klemola (2004, 293) writes quoting Charles Laughlin (see references Klemola 2004, 298–299) about "comtemplative experience in which the entire field of perceptions can be seen as one single field, either limited or limitless, spatial or spaceless and in which consciousness cannot be separated from the monad (alteration, TK) of perceptions, nor this monad from consciousness. Consciousness can be experienced as one, inseparable phenomenon, even as a limitless space, as a living, energetic flow of existence. The question is about the alteration of the tuning of our whole existence where not only the categories between senses break apart rather than the cognitive categories as well. – (I)n reflection we can describe it as a state in which the concepts of classical truth, goodness and beauty melt into one experiential presence. The question is about an internal touch in which both the toucher and the touched are exposed as inseparable elements of the same mystery."

The intensive nature of running is emphasized in utmost conditions such as practising in winter. A freezing wind forces you to become conscious of the unprotected parts of your body. Running in winter causes (at least to me) a particular "sauna-like" experience which brings me back to my childhood memories. I can recall how I used to spend long times with my friends skiing and gliding down the hills, which was a sweaty thing to do, making the clothes alternately get soaked with sweat and then eventually dry up again. The air was constantly filled with the presence of a warm, humid and gently sweet smell.

Ecstasy may thus expand to the past and generate a strong and live connection with something that has been experienced earlier. At the same time this experience will solidify my existence, introducing an experience of a compact existence.

6.7 Repetition

A running exercise provides affects, experiences that bring us pleasure, calling for repeating the exercise. An essential part of a running exercise is rhythm and repetition, which together as "temporal actions strengthen the training element of an exercise –".[87] Running is, at least at the beginning and especially when the person is in a poor condition or when her target is maximal performance, a heavy physical exercise "when the bodily touch to the world requires a lot of physical strength and stamina. This external touch will necessarily generate a strong internal touch, which can be controlled and made to promote achieving the goal sought for".[88]

A runner may have many kinds of goals as the motivator for practising. But, the more intensively and the more you practise, the more experiences that have to do with "big issues" will emerge. These experiences set the runner face to face with fundamental questions such as existence and one's position and significance in relation to it.

If running is about repetition, then "*repeating is handing down explicitly* – that is to say, going back into the possibilities of the Dasein that has-been-there" writes Heidegger.[89] My understanding of Heidegger's concept of repetition is that the same repeated action will set up the same horizon in which Dasein has already been and in which a certain way of being-in-the-world and content has been introduced to it. In this situation you may be capable of taking it with more understanding and you are able to interpret both old and new experiences brought in by repetition. The lack of repetition will also become better understood through pre-understanding. Roos[90] writes about an experience that is familiar to all those who exercise actively. He says: "If for some reason I cannot run for a long time, I become nervous and feel that

---

[87] Koski (2000, 203).
[88] Koski (2000, 203).
[89] Heidegger (1978, 437).
[90] Roos (1989, 68).

something is missing. Are we talking about a physical or a mental dependence, that I cannot tell, but in any case I feel somewhat slack after a couple of days without being able to run (or ski)." Roos[91] writes that running is a routine-based activity where repetition is the key:

> This kind of training typically takes place in the same location, and often on a relatively short track that you tend to go around numerous times. Even if a runner changed the route, her exercise is steady-pace, not too rough nor too relaxed, rather reasonable. Moreover, even if a runner followed a regular training regime which contains all the changes in rhythm or long and short intervals, this exercise would still rather bring more regularity than irregularity to a runner's performance.

As I will come to analyse in later chapters, a physical exercise is an active-passive process in which the active refers to a conscious act when shifting into a training situation. Passive, again, refers to something that is independent of an individual. In a training situation you must only focus on what you are doing. In this sense this is what being essentially means in a training situation: waiting.

When the same performance is repeated over and over again, then the activities that were originally considered physical, will become events "which are not in themselves intelligible".[92] The body has its own autonomy. The body as a presubject synthesizes something that has been perceived by senses and is modified into something qualitatively different. The event can be called a metamorphosis.[93] Here we probably have an event that is similar to that described by Spinoza. In his conception about information *the first kind of knowledge* (opinion or imagination) and *the second kind of knowledge* (reason and knowledge which consist of the common notions we possess and of adequate ideas about the properties of entities) will change *the third kind of knowledge* which he calls intuitive. The third kind of knowledge has to do with understanding everything, the being in its divine context in a profound, existential sense.

I see the significance of the temporality of the body as follows: The ecstatic nature of the body gives and generates through operational intentionality an understanding about time and change. In order to give an opportunity to see running as a process, thus naturally primarily as a concrete, physical activity but also as a forthcoming sphere of action, running must be realized with the help of the body and understanding as a concrete exercise so that running would not be a random activity. Temporality as a structure makes it possible for us to consciously understand the significance of repeated exercises to a runner's personality, health and peace of mind.

---

[91]Roos (1989, 23).

[92]Herrigel (1987, 23).

[93]Sheehan (1978, 94) has come to the same conclusion. He thinks that running roads are a laboratory where the runner's metamorphosis takes place.

6.8 Running, False Devotion, Fanaticism and Dependence

When running is meaningful, a runner is devoted to training. I see devotion[94] as one of the ontological definitions of the human being. To paraphrase the idea, devotion is one of the ontological connections between the runner and the world. Devotion is an active intentional relationship which constitutes the being of a runner. It signifies the desire to make certain concrete choices and concrete actions through them. The level of devotion varies. The more running becomes a "natural" part of one's own way of being, the less there is need for a conscious act of will (mental effort, self-discipline) to make oneself run. Long-term devotion will eventually level down the edges that fight against running in one's ego.

As any human activity, also running can be associated with elements that a runner cannot control. This is related to the entire functional horizon of training which has eventually evolved via a runner's being-in-the-world. Acting in the world is not thoroughly and transparently reflected. In one's own actions there are hidden such factors that have power beyond an individual. In this context a central factor is dependence, which can be related to pleasure or competitive drive, for example, and why not to both of them. Being devoted to running (as something that pleases one's competitive drive and gives pleasure) may gain such an emphasis that it conceals other areas of a runner's life. Heidegger[95] sees the structure described above as follows:

> In hankering, Being-already-alongside – takes priority. – Dasein's hankering as it falls makes manifest its *addiction* to becoming 'lived' by whatever world it is in. – What one is addicted 'towards' [Das 'Hin-zu' des Hanges] is to let oneself be drawn by the sort of thing for which the addiction hankers. – Dasein has become blind, and puts all possibilities into the service of the addiction.

Roos writes about the addiction related to running as follows[96]:

> Lately there has been more and more discussion about physical exercise as a dependence that can be compared to alcoholism or drug abuse. There is surely some truth to it, and just as all dependencies, also the dependence on physical exercise can be harmful to you, even to your health. The human body cannot withstand continuous strain, no matter whether related to your pastime or work. This dependence has many other downsides as well: human relationships turning secondary, narrowing of your life, wasting all of your energy on the sidetrack of keeping fit.

In a Finnish runner's magazine Juoksija the cross-country skier Kati Pulkkinen[97] writes about her obsessions. She ponders about the reasons why she trained herself to an overstrained state. Excessive training, of course, she answers her own question.

---

[94] I see it ultimately as a desire to continue being in relation with the world – thus as an attempt to preserve one's own existence as being-in-relation (similarly to Spinoza's "conatus").

[95] Heidegger (1978, 240).

[96] Roos (1995), Chapter 11.

[97] Pulkkinen (2001, 8).

The worst thing was the obsessed mind. She just had to get the hours of the training regime fulfilled; making markings to her training diary were a must.

> The heart rate was not increasing anymore, it was difficult to get proper sleep, the muscles were continuously in a bad shape and finally, I got into a vicious circle of stress injuries. In my case also losing weight and my eating habits had their share of the obsessions. I just had to go out and practise in order to consume energy. Thus, I was burning my candle efficiently from both ends. – Fatigue was vented in the form of whining because of excessive training and hunger.[98]

Winning, which is a built-in property of competition and exposed in an athlete as a desire to be the best, also alienated Pulkkinen from herself. The obsession of winning in competition as a strong internal motivation structure built up a wall. The wall was built in between her competitive athletic identity and a reasonable, self-caring athletic identity which was seeking for a balance between the bodily and mental growth. "It was mentally really tough to compete because I had to be the best. Even if I had been the fifth with good performance, I was not satisfied. My self-esteem was fully in line with my placement in a competition that day"[99].

A fanatically training person whose running turns into an addiction, is devoted to running (the relationship comprises running, the environment and the individual). The dependency resulting from this relationship attracts the individual because she is already part of that relationship! Some structural parts of one's own being are constituted in within-the-world factors ready-to-hand. A relationship constituted through the principle of pleasure and/or competitive drive broadens Dasein to the world that is ready-to-hand, and becomes part of itself. This way part of its within-the-world being, which is caring in itself, becomes attractive.

If an inauthentic escape from oneself makes Dasein fall far in its existential state[100] it may turn into a fanaticism which is "'towards this at any price'".[101] The downside here is that Dasein's internal existence can become socially limited – "the urge seeks to crowd out [verdrängen] other possibilities".[102] It will make an attempt to expand its power to cover the potential horizon. In this case Dasein will only see a dependence that is thematized with the help of fanaticism.

> But then Dasein is not – and never is – a 'mere urge' to which other kinds of controlling or guiding behaviour are added from time to time; rather, as a modification of the entirety of Being-in-the-world, it is always care already.[103]

---

[98]Pulkkinen (2001, 8).

[99]Pulkkinen (2001, 8).

[100]See Heidegger (1978, 216–217, 230, 240). In this context Heidegger writes about the frenzy of living, which is related to "being-ahead-of-oneself". Starting from the being-ahead-of-oneself, frenzy attracts Dasein towards inauthenticity. (In my opinion it is difficult to see what Heidegger tries to say here.)

[101]Heidegger (1978, 240).

[102]Heidegger (1978, 240).

[103]Heidegger (1978, 240).

6.9 Ready-to-Hand and Present-at-Hand as the Dimensions of Human Relationship with the World

The Heideggerian terms ready-to-hand and present-to-hand describe the totality of how humans face the world or how they encounter one another. To use a dualistic way of putting it, a human being and the world are face to face with one another all the time. In reality a human being is in the world, so according to the traditional ontology the question is about different parts of the same entity (thus a human being and the world together form the being).

How and on what grounds does a human thematize the entities as encountered? How is the way in which the world and a human encounter one another constituted? It is a different matter to come across with entities that are essentially diverse – a human being exists in a different way than a stone. For example, being faced with a sawdust track is different than facing a forthcoming competition. The runner herself is a real being while the forthcoming competition is only an imaginary and conceptual entity sought after in one's consciousness.

Steiner gives an answer to this, commenting on Heidegger:

> The world comes at us, answers Heidegger, in the form and manner of *things*. But of the obviously innumerable object-entities which *Dasein* encounters, those that will constitute *its* being-in-the-world, are not just *any* things. They are what the Greeks called *pragmata*, 'that is to say, that which one has to do with in one's concernful dealings'.[104]

The entities whose existence is "viewed upon" and taken into account as part of one's own action are ready-to-hand, *zuhanden*. The exterior, something to which one does not have a relationship, is present-at-hand (*vorhanden*).

> It characterizes the matter of theoretic speculation, of scientific study. Thus 'Nature' is *vorhanden* to the physicist, and rocks are *vorhanden* to the geologist. But this is not how a stone-mason or a sculptor meets up with a rock. *His* relationship to stone, the relationship crucial to his *Dasein*, is that of *Zuhandernheit*, of a 'readiness-*to*-hand' (observe the formidable gap which separates *at* from *to* in the two instrumental terms). That which is *zuhanden*, literally 'to-hand', reveals itself to *Dasein*, is taken up by and into *Dasein*, in ways absolutely constitutive of the 'thereness' into which our existence has been thrown, and in which it must accomplish its being.[105]

The ready to hand beings exist for a reason. Their way of being resembles that of tools (Bedeutsamkeit).[106] A human being's own life provides a use at least to the person herself. If the person has "turned under" the prevalence of "running hackery",[107] she might see herself as follows: a runner may see her body as an

---

[104]Steiner (1987, 86–87).

[105]Steiner (1987, 87).

[106]Routila (1970, 89).

[107]Pekka Himanen (2001, 22) quotes in his book "Hacker ethics" Burrell Smith, the designer of Apple Macintosh computer, who in connection with a hacker's definition spoke about the importance of a craftsman's attitude, that is you care about what you are doing. Hackering is not limited to information technology rather everyone who shows passion and care towards one's

intentional correlate and as an existing being. But, on the other hand, the (ontic) being-like reference of the intentional correlate is herself as a living body.

Thematizing oneself as ready-to-hand is something that deviates from all other beings (just as Heidegger thematizes the human being as Dasein, which is at the same time a being that understands one's existence as a being, a being which in its everydayness can be characterized fundamentally as pre-ontological understanding of Being).[108]

Heidegger's analysis of an object/tool can be applied heuristically to the analysis of a runner and her body, when the body is seen as if it were a tool. But, it goes without saying that the body cannot be understood as a thing. My idea has been to ponder about whether it would be possible to disclose with the help of Heidegger's readiness-to-hand and presence-at-hand analysis, at least in a heuristic sense, some new views towards the entity of personally experienced running, how it feels like and how it probably is at the very centre of one's ontic-ontological area and significant in that sense.

Heidegger writes that "we shall call those entities which we encounter in concern '*equipment*'".[109] Ontically, the most ready-to-hand "equipment" (although the body is not literally "used" like a hammer, for example) is the body of Dasein as a presubject. It is this ontic readiness-to-hand of the body where understanding the world can arise from. Although Dasein is-always-already something that understands being, the development to a conscious (ontological) understanding of being takes place on the basis of the being-in-the-world of the bodily Dasein. I share Merleau-Ponty's idea of the body's constitutive meaning as a fundament.

"A totality of equipment" (i.e. the horizon of physical activity) that comes before and is more original than an individual object (in this context a physical exercise, action, moving, a particular kind of sport) is the totality of meaning from which particular equipment (form of physical exercise) get their meaning (as an individual exercise). The identity of a physical exercise is constituted via the mental entity which forms and in which the meaningful horizon of a runner or runners is formed.

---

work is a hacker. Is this one of the forms of Sorge which Heidegger writes about, Sorge as a means of independent "caring of the world"? Similarly thinking, the more consciously a runner cares about her body and an exercise, the more she is as a bodily-mental entity and as a living body exists for herself and for the world, caring as care. Could we think that conscious caring is visible in all activities related to running? In that case it would show in the choice of correct kind of equipment, careful warm-up and so on. Or, is hacker as a concept something that needs to be understood through work, especially normal salaried work? Although a hacker does not have clear distinction between work and free time, should the primary, meaningful starting point be thought through work? Himanen (2001, 22–26) writes about hacking being a common social challenge to protestant ethics. However, as far as I have understood, the answer to the above questions is negative.

[108] See Routila (1970, 82).

[109] Heidegger (1978, 97).

6.9 Ready-to-Hand and Present-at-Hand as the Dimensions of Human...

According to Heidegger,[110] equipment is always "'something in-order-to...'" in essence. The means of this in-order-to relationship are, for example, conduciveness, usability and manipulability, which constitute the equipment entity. "Taken strictly, there 'is' no such thing as *an* equipment".[111] In genetic sense, this totality of equipment has been discovered before any 'individual' item of equipment shows itself.[112] The human being is always born to an existing world, which forms the pre-ontological foundation of meanings for further organisation of systems and equipment entities. To quote the same using Heidegger's own words[113]:

> Whenever a 'there' is disclosed, its whole Being-in-the-world – that is to say, the world, Being-in, and the Self which, as an 'I am', this entity is – is disclosed with equal primordiality. Whenever the world is disclosed, entities within-the-world have been discovered already. The discoveredness of the ready-to-hand and the present-at-hand is based on the disclosedness of the world for if the current totality of involvements is to be freed, this requires that significance be understood beforehand. In understanding significance, concernful Dasein submits itself circumspectively to what it encounters as ready-to-hand. Any discovering of a totality of involvements goes back to a 'for-the-sake-of-which'; and on the understanding of such a 'for-the-sake-of-which' is based in turn the understanding of significance as the disclosedness of the current world.

It is only in an active relationship where the special nature of being ready-to-hand gets uncovered, depicted by Heidegger as follows:

> Equipment can genuinely show itself only in dealings cut to its own measure (hammering with a hammer, for example); but in such dealings an entity of this kind is not *grasped* thematically as an occurring Thing, nor is the equipment-structure known as such even in the using. The hammering does not simply have knowledge about [um] the hammer's character as equipment, but it has appropriated this equipment in a way which could not possibly be more suitable. In dealings such as this, where something is put to use, our concern subordinates itself to the "in-order-to" which is constitutive for the equipment we are amploying at the time; the less we just stare at the hammer-Thing, and the more we seize hold of it and use it, the more primordial does our relationship to it become, and the more unveiledly is it encountered as that which it is – as equipment. The hammering itself uncovers the specific 'manipulability' ["Handlichkeit"] of the hammer.[114]

In other words, when applied to running, we can note that only running itself can uncover the special dimensions related to a running human being and running. The more the body is "used" for running, the better running is adopted. The more you just stare at the thought of running or leaving for a run, the more covered it becomes. The negative side of staring lies in the fact that it creates new (unnecessary) concepts and metaphysics of running which covers the essence of the matter, i.e. running itself.

---

[110]Heidegger (1978, 97).

[111]Heidegger (1978, 97).

[112]Heidegger (1978, 98).

[113]Heidegger (1978, 343–344).

[114]Heidegger (1978, 98).

In running a runner understands oneself as running. The body is an object-like pragmatic being which in the analysis is thematized as the performer. Although in a factual sense it is difficult to make a distinction between the body and mind, it seems relevant to raise the body on the level of analysis as a dimensional being to a performing "thing", because it is the body that in a certain sense performs the run – one's mind cannot run. (In this context it seems to be almost impossible to avoid getting into using dualistic expressions. The meaning of the matter must be seen according to the perspective: approaching either from the viewpoint of the mind or the body. It is difficult to write about the matter because there is always the danger of reduction or the possibility to reduce one at the expense of the other or to be blamed for tautology in the attempt to avoid the dualistic mind-body expressions.)

The meaning of running is revealed only by running in a running environment. Analogically to this Heidegger writes that "in the assertion 'the hammer is too heavy', what is discovered for sight is not a 'meaning', but an entity in the way that it is ready-to-hand".[115] The statement "running is a monotonous, boring and numbing hobby", does not reveal the meaning of running (or the meaning of the relationship between a human being and a running exercise), rather just the way of being of a running exercise that is true for the speaker. The statement expresses the speaker's own mindset about the understanding of the matter by which it is exposed to the person herself. The levels of running are not revealed especially to those without any running experience, rather are covered due to one's own way of being-in-the-world. The matters are revealed to Dasein through the way how the world is ready-to-hand. If they are not ready-to-hand, they are exposed only in one's awareness but not as bodily performed by oneself.

As I see it, a runner's relationship to her body is typically that of fostering and caring, because the relationship is fundamentally about partnership with concern.[116] It is important for a runner to be strong and in good health and to keep fit.

An example from cycling: I'm riding with a friend of mine on a narrow country road when he suddenly shouts a warning "a car". At that moment the car as present-at-hand, or potentially ready-to-hand becomes actually ready-to-hand in an instant. The understanding of the significance of the environment is the reason for taking the car into account in terms of safety. In this situation speech or a concept may guide your action, since when cycling in this kind of a situation, you show caring concern towards your environment. A cyclist as a bodily entity is an organic part of the world ready-to-hand, and your understanding about the injury risk brings the world ready-to-hand present in such a way that mere simulation of the same situation (e.g. when lying on the sofa at home) cannot generate.[117]

---

[115] Heidegger (1978, 196).

[116] In page 370 he states, that "when fully conceived, the care-structure includes the phenomenon of Selfhood. This phenomenon is clarified by Interpreting the meaning of care; and it is as care that Dasein's totality of Being has been defined."

[117] "By reason of this *with-like* [*mithaften*] Being-in-the-world, the world is always the one that I share with Others. The world of Dasein is a with-world [Mitwelt]. Being-in is *Being-with* Others.

The significance of the personal aspect is well exposed in the following descriptions.

I asked Jorma Peussa,[118] a friend of mine, to write about his running experiences. This is how he describes the early stages of his running hobby:

> For the first 38 years of my life I did not do any kind of physical exercise. My hobbies had more to do with drinking beer and smoking. Now I'm almost 43. Five years ago, at the darkest winter period I found it difficult to fall asleep in the evenings and, consequently, very difficult to get up from the bed in the morning. I had a constant flu and my back was aching. The doctor could not name any illness to explain my condition. He only made a discrete suggestion that someone doing light office work should do at least some kind of physical exercise in order to stay in good health. Since I felt obliged to change my lifestyle somehow, the idea was to discover a physical exercise that would make sense to me. There was no sport from the youth that I could have restarted, and none of the ball games appealed to me. The idea of going to a gym sounded repulsive. The only thing that I could think of was jogging. Or, that's how I called it then. I don't use that word any longer. Today, I call myself a runner.
>
> The first running attempts 5 years ago were quite a challenge. Jogging turned into walking only after a couple of hundred metres. The experience made me angry; I could not bare such wretchedness in myself. So, I set myself a target. I chose one silver birch not far from home and decided to run there from home without stopping. It was only the third attempt that finally proved successful. I had, however, reached the first target and gotten my reward. I had beaten the inner loser in myself, which plead for mercy and asked me to stop running. The next target was to reach a rock a little further away. That is how it got started. Eventually the distances grew. The pain I used to feel had been replaced by joy and warmth. My legs, my lungs, and the rest of my body were getting accustomed to physical exercise and sent the message about good feeling instead of pain and fatigue that used to be the case. I was totally hooked. The mental pleasure about my capability and strength introduced by muscular exercise were like a drug to me.

This process description wraps up the theoretical tools discussed earlier and someone's personal experiences into a clear entity. The theoretical tools are: uncovering and covering, running as an intentional correlate, running ready-to-hand and present-at-hand, the themes of desire and will, the significance of the constitution of the body for being-in-the-world, conceptualizing experiences as joy, as the capability to "exceed the ego" ("the inner loser in myself, which plead for mercy and asked me to stop running") with the help of something discovered deeper in one's own being.

Another good example is George Sheehan's description about his running and about its relationship to his life. He says that originally he used to run "by instinct".[119] "He started to run at the age of 45 because he felt he wasn't 'functioning' as cardiologist, husband and father".[120] Eventually, over the years he comes to the conclusion that he is running only because it as a truly physical form

---

Their Being-in-themselves within-the-world is Dasein-with [Mit-dasein]. Heidegger (1978, 154–155).

[118]Peussa (2003).

[119]Sheehan (1978, 70).

[120]Sheehan (1978, 6).

of exercise simply is the right one for him. "My true aim now is a state of fitness prior to and unrelated to sickness or disease. My true task, to live at my authentic level. My true goal, to reach my original splendor. Run for my life. You had better to believe it".[121]

With these words Sheehan has given a versatile and detailed analysis about his running lifestyle. The focus of practising has shifted towards an angle that takes life into account as a whole. For him running has become more "spiritual" in the sense that he thematizes running via the perennial ideals.

The ontic touch is triggering touches with the world that are different and in my opinion more profound than "the theoretical touch". Heidegger[122] agrees with me. He asks: "Why does Being get 'conceived' 'proximally' in terms of the present-at-hand *and not* in terms of the ready-to-hand, which indeed lies *closer* to us?" Being ready-to-hand is important to Dasein in the sense that this is via which the theoretical orientation towards the world and its possession by being present-at-hand become possible. Being ready-to-hand becomes possible along with Dasein's birth to the world, via which the world as a location of being has opened up to it.

Heidegger[123] writes that "whenever the world is disclosed, entities within the world have been discovered already. The discoveredness of the ready-to-hand and the present-at-hand is based on the disclosedness of the world for if the current totality of involvements is to be freed, this requires that significance be understood beforehand." The last sentence means that the realization of the ready-to-hand as readiness-to-hand is only possible by coming to the world, after which the bodily, ontic being in the world creates pre-understanding towards the ready-to-hand. This analysis may seem useless with regard to running. Maybe it is, but the point here is articulation of the foundation of human existence, making an important self-evident idea consciously as transparent as possible. This creates understanding about what is the significance of the personal touch to all factors related to running. When the runner has as good an experience as possible of the different aspects of running, also her understanding about the ontic experiential quality is at its best. In addition to this we will have a good reason to become conceptually more familiar with running, which means learning about the experiential descriptions of other runners and theoretical studies in general.

Environment – the location where man is realized in his own sphere (i.e. within-the-world) – becomes present solely through the ready-to-hand because no world or state as such exists for man in the sense of feeling and experiencing. This is the personal feeling "to ourselves", which ontologically speaking has the primary experiential status. Anyone can imagine what it would feel like if we did not have a touch to the world. In fact we could not even imagine the situation, because there would be no substance which could turn into ideas (except for our bodies from which we could have substance to be able to be conscious). But, in general, without

---

[121] Sheehan (1978, 70).

[122] Heidegger (1978, 487).

[123] Heidegger (1978, 343–344).

6.9 Ready-to-Hand and Present-at-Hand as the Dimensions of Human...

a touch to the world there wouldn't exist any humans as a bodily, dimensional being, thus as a human being, without the world and the touch to it.

The simple and obvious issue of touch to the world is an extremely important starting point and foundation when looking at human existence. What is essential and important is not primarily the scientific structure of the world rather (1) how it is related to the bodily-mental being in the world of the human being, and (2) what is the relationship of the readiness-to-hand of entities in the world with the human being.[124]

In the following, Heidegger writes on a general level about the structures described above[125]; about the orientation of every ego to the world as a personal way of being and feeling, i.e., about a runner's ontic relationship with the different elements of running and about the significance of readiness-to-hand of running for the possession of the running environment.

> When one is orientated beforehand towards 'Nature' and 'Objectively' measured distances of Things, one is inclined to pass off such[126] estimates and interpretations of deseverance as 'subjective'. Yet this 'subjectivity' perhaps uncovers the 'Reality' of the world at its

---

[124]See Heidegger (1978, 145–148).

[125]See "The ontic touch is triggering touches with... ."

[126]Heidegger (1978, 140–141) refers to the following text: "De-severing does not necessarily imply any explicit estimation of the farness of something ready-to-hand in relation to Dasein. Above all, remoteness never gets taken as a distance. If farness is to be estimated, this is done relatively to deseverances in which everyday Dasein maintains itself. Though these estimates may be imprecise and variable if we try to compute them, in the everydayness of Dasein they have their *own definiteness* which is thoroughly intelligible. We say that to go over yonder is 'a good walk', 'a stone's throw', or 'as long as it takes to smoke a pipe'. These measures express not only that they are not intended to 'measure' anything but also that the remoteness here estimated belongs to some entity to which one goes with concernful circumspection. But even when we avail ourselves of a fixed measure and say 'it is half an hour to the house', this measure must be taken as an estimate. 'Half an hour' is not thirty minutes, but a duration [Dauer] which has no 'length' at all in the sense of a quantitative stretch. Such a duration is always interpreted in terms of well-accustomed everyday ways in whick we 'make provision' ["Besorgungen"]. Remoteness are estimated proximally by circumspection, even when one is quite familiar with 'officially' calculated measures. Since what is de-severed in such estimates is ready-to-hand, it retains its character as specifically within-the-world. This even implies that the pathways we take towards desevered entities in the course of our dealings will vary in their length from day to day. What is ready-to-hand in the environment is certainly not present-at-hand for an eternal observer exempt from Dasein: but it is encountered in Dasein's circumspectively concernful everydayness. As Dasein goes along its ways, it does not measure off a stretch of space as a corporeal Thing which is present-at-hand; it does not 'devour the kilometres'; bringing-close or de-severance is always a kind of concernful Being towards what is brought close and de-severed. A pathway which is long 'Objectively' can be much shorter than one which is 'Objectively' shorter still but which is perhaps 'hard going' and comes before us as interminably long. *Yet only in thus 'coming before us' is the current world authentically ready-to-hand*. The objective distances of Things present-at-hand do not coincide with the remoteness and closeness of what is ready-to-hand within-the-world. Though we may know these distances exactly, this knowledge still remains blind; it does not have the function of discovering the environment circumspectively and bringing it close; this knowledge is used only in and for a concernful Being which does not measure stretches – a Being towards the world that 'matters' to one [... Sein zu der einen "angehenden" Welt]."

most Real; it has nothing to do with 'subjective' arbitrariness or subjectivistic 'ways of taking' an entity which 'in itself' is otherwise. *The circumspective de-severing of Dasein's everydayness reveals the Being-in-itself of the 'true world' – of that entity which Dasein, as something existing, is already alongside.*[127]

This kind of existential action is taken into body-mental possession in one's own way of being. It describes an intimate and close relationship with (a familiar) environment as opposed, for example, to a jungle that appears as unknown and unreachable; there you would not be able to say that the remaining distance is another 30-min walk. If you claimed the distance to be 10 km as the crow flies, even that would not tell much about the "distance", because the actual pathway you need to walk can be a lot longer and because time is then an important dimension of the pathway. 10 km would bear some relevance when we have some previous knowledge about the area and some former experience about walking in the jungle. When we have taken the environment into possession, we also possess some knowledge that is based on the familiarity about the distance (not in terms of kilometres) – we could claim that the pathway has been conceptualized by your own feet, which means that it is also adopted and understood in your mind, and the remaining distance is already anticipatorily present as understood.

When I think of the run I'm about to make, I think about the distance in terms of the terrain. So, I do not see it merely as an abstract number of kilometres rather as a scene of action which I will actively enter into and participate. If the wind was strong, I would not choose to run around the lake rather take a forest route between two suburbs. To make up my mind which way to go for my run I compare the properties of the terrain and with my mental agility at that moment. Had I decided to run a long distance, I would do it. If I felt heavy when running, I would slow down the pace but would still keep running all the distance. The experience I have gained from the previous exercises has given me some familiarity knowledge about my own body, my mind, about the way I have experienced certain distances in certain circumstances, agile states and terrains. I would make use of this familiarity when thinking about the next run. The familiarity as knowledge is in my body and in my mind. At that moment, in relation to the forthcoming run I prepare to it in advance and I can take it into possession this way.

We can say some distance or time to be like having a smoke, or that it is just a stone's throw away.

> These measures express not only that they are not intended to 'measure' anything but also that the remoteness here estimated belongs to some entity to which one goes with concernful circumspection. –(Exact knowledge, TK) does not have the function of discovering the environment circumspectively and bringing it close; this knowledge is used only in and for a concernful Being which does not measure stretches – a Being towards the world that 'matters' to one.[128]

---

[127] Heidegger (1978, 141).

[128] Heidegger (1978, 141).

6.9 Ready-to-Hand and Present-at-Hand as the Dimensions of Human...

How a concernful Being should be understood? I myself see there the question how Dasein sees the world from the point of view of itself. If the Dasein in case was a smoker, it would be good to measure one's craving for a cigarette with the chances of having moments that suffice for having a smoke. A break as long as having a smoke is a very good operationalization.

Similarly, a runner will take the running environment ready-to-hand bodily into possession. The exercise may take place in various circumstances such as on asphalt, forest track, sawdust track, gravel road, snowy road, slippery terrain, sand, and so on. The weather may also vary. I may decide to go for a run in an inadequately agile state if I was sufficiently motivated – hungry and tired because I want to try out what it feels like. I did this once before a marathon in order to get an idea what the last kilometers of a marathon could feel like. Not so much fun, but the desire to try out and experiment gives you the motivation.

In all the above-mentioned circumstances the runner is within-the-worldly present and in connection with the running conditions ready-to-hand. The more varied conditions you have been running in, the less present-at-hand the running conditions will turn into, and the more comfortable the runner feels in different conditions. Owing to the readiness-to-hand of the running conditions the runner can get prepared for the forthcoming runs.

Being ready-to-hand means being active, a procedure in the environment and participation. When being is passive and nothing is of interest to you, the things are in a bad shape."We were not created to be spectators. Not made to be onlookers. Not born to be bystanders".[129]

Running does not take place in a space, in some anonymous being, rather in a space that is more or less familiar to you.

> *Space is not in the subject, nor is the world in space.* Space is rather 'in' the world in so far as space has been disclosed by that Being-in-the-world which is constitutive for Dasein. Space is not to be found in the subject, nor does the subject observe the world 'as if' that world were in a space; but the 'subject' (Dasein), if well understood ontologically, is spatial.[130]

Being-in-the-world as an opener of the space is a splendid, existential definition. Being-in-the-world opens up the space, because in order to experience the space you have to be in the world into which you must be born. Being-in-the-world opens up the space and makes it a sphere of personal experience, constituted by the incarnated, concrete being. Its foundation lies in coming-to-the-world, which in principle opens up everything to humans. It opens up an existential horizon, which contains the space.

Heidegger analyses that

> when space is discovered non-circumspectively by just looking at it, the environmental regions get neutralized to pure dimensions. Places – and indeed the whole circumspectively oriented totality of places belonging to equipment ready-to-hand – getreduced to a

---

[129]Sheehan (1978, 246).

[130]Heidegger (1978, 146), underlined by TK.

multiplicity of positions for random Things. – The 'world', as a totality of equipment ready-to-hand, becomes spatialized [verräumlicht] to a context of extended Things which are just present-at-hand and no more.[131]

This is what happens when I don't look at the world from my point of view but rather without any relationship to it. When I look at the world from my point of view, caring with concern, there is a relationship between myself and the beings, making them ready-to-hand to me. Without a meaning to me the beings "lack spirit". In this situation they exist independent of me, and I take no interest in them because I don't have any. They become insignificant to me, in one way or another.

For Heidegger, a property of a thing transmitted by the senses reveals, from its being to the caring Dasein that is within-the-worldly present with it, in its readiness-to-hand something that theoretical knowledge can never reach. Steiner[132] quotes Heidegger: " 'The smell communicates the being of this essent far more immediately and truly than any description or inspection could ever do'." The key is the within-the-world relationship of a ready-to-hand being to the bodily, caring Dasein.

When running, a runner is present in her body readiness-to-hand. Readiness-to-hand represents a bodily way of being as an immediate experience in which the body reveals itself to the human. Heidegger[133] emphasizes the practical usability of readiness-to-hand: "No matter how sharply we just *look* [Nur-noch-*hinsehen*] at the 'outward appearance' ["Aussehen"] of Things in whatever form this takes, we cannot discover anything ready-to-hand. If we look at Things just 'theoretically', we can get along without understanding readiness-to-hand." This idea could thus be extended to concern the relationship of the look of someone who does not run to running. As a person with no running experience does not have a positive experience about running, her eyes and mind cannot reveal the readiness-to-hand that opens up to a runner in running. The look of someone who does not run focuses on what she saw only theoretically, merely formed by sense via the concepts about the subject matter. Steiner formulates the conceptualized tendency of this theoretical attitude by stating that already Augustine warned about the Platonic way of emphasizing "seeing" the essence of entities instead of experiencing the essence through full-blown existential dedication and patience. Being, *Sein*, is then always inevitably something that has been imagined, abstracted and allegorized. These visual sights are faulty. They make Being a mere object, an objective thing "somewhere out there". A human being should not be "viewed objectively" this way. Steiner summarizes his thoughts by stating that objective pondering, logical analysis and scientific classification distract us away from genuine ontology towards a merely theoretical conception, away from the immediacy of Being towards a technical analysis of the concept of Being.

---

[131] Heidegger (1978, 147).
[132] Steiner (1987, 45).
[133] Heidegger (1978, 102).

6.9 Ready-to-Hand and Present-at-Hand as the Dimensions of Human... 101

Thus, running is an entity, which is not present-at-hand rather ready-to-hand. An entity is revealed as an entity especially through being ready-to-hand, which in my opinion in its most original form is represented by Being as a body ready-to-hand for oneself. It is reasonable and in this sense intelligible to consider with care the bodily properties and way of being, which make one's body a unique entity. The understanding about this uniqueness is shown in the way in which an individual relates to her own body and how she "handles" it (cf. the side effect of competitive sports to disable one's body through excessive training and doping). It is not being by taking care if the body of an athlete is ruined and ill after the active career.[134]

Dasein as a body is a readiness-to-hand of its own. How could we become aware of this experientially, since as I stated in my doctoral dissertation[135] – one's own body is "too" close to the person herself (as this is the case since birth; an individual grows as a body) in order that we could always understand its significance as an immediately experienced fact. Paradoxically, we can state that if a human being were any further away from her body, she would be too far from it. The body is always present, which is why it becomes self-evident (except for when we fall ill and/or lose our health).

The nature of the readiness-to-hand of one's own body may alter and become conscious as altered (carrying along its past). When an exercise is objectivized in the runner, it is noticed. Improved running properties refer to their producer, the actor. In his analysis Heidegger writes that the work that has been prepared contains a reference to its producer. It is a "constitutive reference", which in the case of a runner becomes apparent in her ability to run. Running properties, which have improved through exercise, refer to the runner's own efforts (and possibly those of the coach). When a matter or an entity is not as desired, it is seen as a deficit, we find its unusability. When running is not succeeding as it should, it bothers us, or putting it in Heidegger's own words, becomes "conspicuous".[136]

When running (action) is not going as it should, we become aware of the deficit and it calls our attention. By becoming conspicuous a deficient ability is in a way useless. In this situation it loses part of its readiness-to-hand. When something that is needed in working out something else is missing, we can talk about lack of readiness-to-hand. In other words, when a certain exercise cannot be performed or one cannot participate a competition, the runner lacks the needed "ability", i.e. the sufficient level of performance. If the focus lies on this aspect, the present-at-hand gets equipped with the mode of "obtrusiveness". When what is not ready-to-hand prevents us from caring, it uncovers the "obstinacy". The function of these modes

---

[134]Playing is a form of readiness-to-hand in its own, characteristic way. It is a praxis of a temporal sequence in which the temporality is lost or which loses it as an experienced world event. It is Erlebnis, in which the subject is one with its making and environment without a conscious experience of oneself as a playing being.

[135]Koski (2000, 80).

[136]Heidegger (1978, 102–103).

is to bring "to the fore the characteristic of presence-at-hand in what is ready-to-hand".[137] When readiness-to-hand is of this kind, "it loses its readiness-to-hand in a certain way".[138]

In other words: When a runner is not satisfied with the outcome of her practising efforts it becomes conspicuous. This may have been caused by an illness or injury which has prevented her from practising, the runner does not have a sufficient health. Exercising is only present but not ready-to-hand. Exercising is not present in a real sense as readiness-to-hand. An illness is a hindrance to exercising and uncovers obstinacy. Being off shape prevents exercising in a obstinacious way. To remove the obstinacy, the runner must have the patience to cure oneself to return to a good shape. Before this is done, the body as readiness-to-hand in a way loses its readiness-to-hand with respect to practising. When one cannot perform an exercise, the body exists in relation to running as presentness-at-hand only, which anyhow contains in itself a reference to its readiness-to-hand (because Dasein is hastening in advance) taken into possession at the beginning of the exercise. The being of a runner is moving between readiness-to- and presentness-at-hand. When running is meaningful, the intention is always to gain maximum readiness-to-hand. Without presentness-at-hand there would not be any understanding about the significance of readiness-to-hand. The significance of readiness-to-hand lies in its functional, concrete nature, which unites Dasein and the world. This bidimensional "dialectics" deepens the runner's understanding of the world and the levels of different opportunities.

In this sense practising adds depth and understanding to one's own experience. When running is not possible due to illness, one understands the significance of health and thus receives feedback on the preobjective/ontic nature of one's own body. An illness shows its place to consciousness as part of the body. Heidegger writes that "even one's *own* Dasein becomes something that it can itself proximally 'come across' only when it *looks away* from 'Experiences' and the 'centre of its actions', or does not as yet 'see' them at all. Dasein finds 'itself' proximally in *what* it does, uses, expects, avoids – in those things environmentally ready-to-hand with which it is proximally *concerned*".[139]

One's own way of being is discovered by discovering those results of action which are objectivized to the world/oneself and which are understood in reflexive repossession. The evolution of Dasein's self-consciousness also necessarily needs this kind of back and forth movement between the self and the world.

A runner discovers herself as a runner through the actions of the objectivized results of her own actions, in other words she discovers the results of the exercises from her own body and mind. She has acted with care (consciously) with the readiness-to-hand of her own body.

---

[137] Heidegger (1978, 104).
[138] Heidegger (1978, 104).
[139] Heidegger (1978, 155).

When one's own being is seen as a process, it can be thematized (thus one is capable of thematizing, is comprehensively and cognitively capable of doing it) as being ready-to-hand. In practice this means that an individual will have the strength to do something for herself. Self-imposed, meaningful action has characteristically a strong motivation. A passive, unmotivated and weak individual floats in her life not caring about her potential. She does not see or care about them.

What is the significance of running ready-to-hand? What is the purpose of running caused by a running body? There can be several purposes, of course, ranging perhaps from the extremes of (1) thematizing one's own body indoctrinized by an objective purpose and (2) seeking one's authentic Being with the help of the ready-to-hand body. The sensibleness of running is revealed only through running, because only in running can running be uncovered as a personal experience of a living body. In this case running as an intentional correlate is realized in the entity of an experiencing subject. After this, we can take this realized experience as a target of reflection and continue developing its proficiency (or refining it, since the target is "something" that is achievable by running).

6.10 The World as Present

Tero Töyrylä writes about his experiences in the 246 km Spartathlon race from Athens to Sparta as follows:

> While Spartathlon takes a lot, it also gives a lot. Above all, it puts me into a situation where I feel that I exist and live strongly, truly and directly, as if I were raw next to the world surrounding me. Compared to this I feel that in my everyday life I'm only somehow vaguely and indirectly in touch with reality.[140]

Do we have to interpret this so that during the race the dominating effect of the ego reduces and the factors calling for authenticity strengthen? And, is it so that in our everyday life the routines, the ordinary things and the dimming and thinning effect of das Man draw the individual towards the fallen state of inauthenticity? That is what Töyrylä seems to be claiming.

At this point it is time to expand the analysis by taking "presence" into account. How does the existing world become present, and what is it that becomes present? According to Heidegger, in being present Dasein faces the world in a situation like "a twinkling of an eye".[141] Reijo Kupiainen, the Finnish translator of Heidegger's *Being and time* commented on the concept of "twinkling of an eye" (Augenblick) claiming that it contains a reference to Aristotle's *kairos*, which means a unique,

---

[140]Töyrylä (2003, 54).

[141]Heidegger (1978, 376).

opportune moment that opens up one's eyes.[142] Rousseau writes about the feeling of existence which seems to be similar to kairos, a powerfully experiential feeling. These events authenticate Dasein. This view is also defended by Pierre Hadot, commented on by Klemola[143] as follows:

> According to Hadot, being present at present is in fact the key to all mental exercises. It releases humans from passions caused by the past or the imagined future. This continuous awareness of the presence can also deepen into a cosmic awareness about the infinite value of every moment as well as allow us to accept every moment of our existence as part of a cosmic, universal law.

Similarly to the above, I define the present to mean the dimension in which something comes experientially so close that it is existential-ontologically present. The question is about feeling the world and entities ready-to-hand, how it is felt by the person experiencing it. The subject experiences and feels the event powerfully as a vivid bodily experience. This presence of the world cannot be separated from the presence of entities, because they are inseparable parts of the same entity that becomes present. The ontological nature of entities becoming present is not revealed by studying the entities and the world like a scientist or a philosopher who studies the entities as being present. Instead, we would rather need a contemplative (Heidegger would speak about thinking and letting-be) method (which is an active-passive process), with the help of which you reveal first your body and then your experiental reality as ready-to-hand intimacy. When this process goes on, the world may become experientially present through internal and external integration. After this awareness and consciousness are in connection also to the world by presence. The experience of being present will bring the world back to you, and it does not need to be ontic world at hand (concretely in our hands). The experience of presence in a way broadens the subject into the connection of entities. Sheehan writes:

> But more than anything, that hour on the road is for ideas and principles, for meditation and contemplation. – Somehow in the relaxation, the letting go, we arrive at a state that Heraclitus described as 'listening to the essence of things'. We open up to the world.[144]

In presence everything comes back to the human being. Or, to be more precise, an individual will transcend to everything, or still more to the point, everything and the human being form an entity in which the human being is only one point-like awareness, which in itself carries awareness about this relationship.

Steiner[145] writes about *Being and time* which ends with questions, one of them being "how is one to think the transcendence from beings to Being?" The above is my answer to the question as well as to another question raised by Steiner, "how is the everyday timelessness of *Dasein* to relate to that authentic temporality

---

[142]Heidegger (2000, 395). Zimmerman (1986, 123, 207) analyses the concept of "kairos" in the New Testament, which he sees to mean "the time of fulfillment" and "redemption here and now".

[143]Klemola (2004, 25), ref. Hadot (1995, 85).

[144]Sheehan (1978, 95).

[145]Steiner (1987, 109).

6.10 The World as Present

which is 'the transcendental horizon of the question of Being' –?" As I see it, in this expression the question is about Heidegger's attempt to solve the variations in Dasein's temporal being between authenticity and inauthenticity. Authentic temporality as a transcendental horizon of the question of Being is Dasein's way of being in which we are as replied-to-the-call-of-being. My understanding is that in presence we are as replied-to-the-call-of-being. All the time through the forthcoming time in this situation is then realized the original, active refreshing of Being which has been received as an ontological gift from the being. Levin[146] writes that "'ecstatic' *sense* of the openness of Being – is an ontological gift – the primordial *Es gibt*". I have written about this[147] issue earlier as follows:

> I understand the "ontological gift" in the sense in which I – have spoken about humans as beings who belong to and understand being. As I see it, the original understanding of Being is a property that belongs to the way of being of the nature realized in the human being. Merleau-Ponty (1986, 216) also writes that the human being as a natural being comprises for example the ability to see, which is a gift from nature.

We have a contradiction also here, since the original authenticity is not the same as the authenticity gained via inauthenticity. The original authenticity (which I myself would not even necessarily call authenticity) is derived ready-made, which is not realized when it is there. The loss is noticed only afterwards. The existential fears aroused by losing it and the unpleasantness of being unreachable is being awakened into only after childhood. Only after this, only then, can we start to reach for authentic being, when Being, "time and space hang heavy on my shoulders".[148]

And then, to go back to the analysis of running, I make a short summary. The starting point of the phenomenological analysis of running is conveniently my own running body. When you look at other people running, you see them as research objects with some 'distance' to the researcher. This 'distance' is missing when you are studying your own running body. Theoretical understanding does not reveal how running as running is to a runner.[149]

Steiner[150] asks in his book, has Being passed totally from human reach, or are there processes and embodiments of experience in which the primal sense of essence

---

[146]Levin (1989, 7).

[147]Koski (2000, 55).

[148]From the song Childlike Faith in Childhood's End by Van Der Graaf Generator.

[149]"Platonic-Cartesian cogitation and the Cartesian foundation of the world's reality in human reflection, are attempts to 'leap through or across the world' (*ein Ueberspringen*) in order to arrive at the non-contingent purity of eternal Ideas or of mathematical functions and certitudes. But this attempted leap from and to abstraction is radically false to the facticity of the world as we encounter it, as we live it." (Steiner 1987, 86.) When we run, something is revealed that does not fit into the scope of a scientist, if the scientist looks at running as an object only. The viewing eye is not able to possess running and fails to understand its concrete weight.

[150]Steiner (1987, 43).

remains vital and, therefore, recapturable? Is there anything left on which late-twentieth-century man can build if he is to seek a homecoming to 'the house of Being'?

When we apply this thought to running we may ask what is the impact of a running exercise to the lifeworld and mental well-being of humans, them becoming a whole, or their existential significance? Also Burfoot[151] asks the same question about human connection to life, and answers it himself: "But what shall we do, I wonder, to keep in touch with ourselves? For me, the answer is that I run. Because it keeps me fully tuned, both physically and mentally."

It is important to articulate an answer to the question what is this "original significance of existence". Is it joy, the delight of living and existence, which means "returning home"? Are these experiential qualities something that come forward through presence? Can we look for returning to "the home of Being", finding it in the active-passive process. In relation to this Sheehan writes:

> Crying starts when we see things as they really are. When we realize with William Blake that everything that lives is holy. When everything is seen to be infinite and we are part of the infinity. Tears come when we are filled with the joy of that vision. When we finally and irrevocably say yes to life. – Yet each of us, if Blake is right, has the faculty of seeing things as they really are. The visionary faculty is a natural gift. But this perception must be cleansed, otherwise we remain in the world of reason and mortality. This cleansing, it seems to me, must start with a cleansing discipline, a purifying effort. And for me, that means running, distance running. Running keeps me at a physical peak and sharpens my senses. It makes me touch and see and hear as if for the first time. – Goodness and truth and beauty suddenly possess me. I am surprised by joy, filled with delight, and there is nothing to do but exult in tears.[152]

As a starting point we can claim that all actively performed exercises and activity is good for humans, because it connects and maintains the relationship of an individual to the foundation of one's existence.

---

[151] Burfoot (2000,7).
[152] Sheehan (1978, 248–249).

Chapter 7
The World Is Running

7.1 Running Experiences

In this chapter I concentrate on describing and analysing the running experience. The purpose of the phenomenological method is to uncover the necessary, essential properties of an experience. The phenomenon under investigation can be varied in consciousness, and consequently it is not limited to lived experience. The horizon of possibilities is extended to concern also other kinds of potential related experiences, either real or imagined, past or forthcoming. In this way an attempt is made to uncover all potential levels from the phenomenon itself.

The event of running is typically described afterwards with the help of reminiscing. Here the aim is to be able to identify from the continuous flow of perceptions related to running the ones that are central, important, significant, essential. How is this done? With the help of pre-understanding brought by running. When a running event is being described, the understanding brought by running already exists in the form of conceptual pre-understanding (which evolves during the description and analysis).

When we start to analyse the description, we must always take notice of the terms and conditions that affect the description. From the viewpoint of research human experience has the problem that always when we talk about experience we are talking about a subjective response, we are dealing with a subjective counterpart, to something that has already happened. In the analysis the experience is objectified when it is done the subject for research. The intentional correlate is "the experience as it is remembered". The intensity of the experience affects on the fact, how lively and adequate the remembering, which is the base for an analysis, succeeds.

The conceptual understanding we have about the phenomenon at the given moment is already present in pre-understanding. Nothing gets experienced in a "void human being" rather only in an always-already-constituted living subject. When being interpreted and grasped, the experience becomes part of the understanding we have at that moment and so forms a pre-understanding for future perceptions.

Individual runs are never alike. What takes place and is experienced once, does not necessarily take place next time. In this sense the definition of the essence of running must be seen in such a way that if the target was to study the essence of running in relation to experiential cores, it is defined as the sum of the runs of all people.

If only the factors determining every run are qualified as the essence of running, i.e. such things that happen every time, the result would be a list of common factors that are of no interest whatsoever (equipment, intensified breathing, increased heart rate, sweating, etc.). There is only one exception to this. As I see it, a runner experiences a pleasant psycho-physical state after every run without exception.

Amby Burfoot has said about the "runner's high" that it occurs rarely, to him only once or twice a year although he runs three to four times a week. Instead, he underlines the runner's mellowness, which is a warm, contended feeling that almost any runner has after almost every single run.[1] "This mellow happiness is one of the immediate rewards of running that keep many of us always looking forward to our next run".[2] He[3] writes about runner's transcendental moments one of which is related to sunrise. About six times a year he begins his run before sunrise. He runs to the east, which allows him to experience his motion to be connected with the motion of the rising sun. This experience fills him with happiness and hope, and he stops to take a breath to admire the miracle of a new day. "Then I am off running again, fully renewed."[4]

Running is not every time an easy and world-embracing experience, but when it goes well, it is close to magical. On 1 July, 2003, I was awakened by a pleasant feeling during my run. After having pondered about this experience I named it as "enchantment". Thus, I ran enchanted.

Had I not done research on running then, I would not have consciously made an attempt to reflect an experience and recollection about the nature of an experience. In other words, my situation at that moment defined the thematization horizon. What had been experienced became grasped (on the basis of pre-ontological understanding of Being).

Peak experiences occur rarely. A major part of a run is characteristically pleasant and refreshing.[5] Sheehan states that if you are after the runner's high, you must run around 6 miles (10 km) daily.[6] On the basis of my own experience the required amount is about 50 km (e.g. three exercises) per week. Experiential sensitivity and openness begin to emerge 1.5–2 h from the start.

---

[1] Burfoot (2000, 15, 80).
[2] Burfoot (2000, 80).
[3] Burfoot (2000, 78).
[4] Burfoot (2000, 78).
[5] See for example Sheehan (1978, 121).
[6] Sheehan (1978, 132).

7.1 Running Experiences

Tapio Pekola[7] writes in the Finnish runner's magazine Juoksija about the mental effects of running. He points out that according to a Canadian study (in 1967) 67 % of runners had experienced runner's high "in which a runner goes through a great delight and an almost omnipotent feeling, as if you were gliding half a metre above the ground".[8] According to the research in question the phenomenon calls for an average of a couple of years of regular running, at least 35 km per week and a minimum of 1 h at a time. Pekola writes, quoting the research, that "mentally the best contribution comes from somewhere beyond 'reasonableness', in the land of Great Ecstasy, the visits to which you wouldn't change for any other experience in your life even afterwards –".[9]

In 1982, Summers studied the runner's high among ordinary runners 30–50 years of age who were getting prepared for their first marathon. The phenomenon occurred at the end of the exercise in 48 % of the cases and 92.6 % of the occurrences fit into one of the following conditions: (1) feeling of mental well-being, which suggests utmost pleasure and self-esteem (37.6 %), (2) physical pleasure connected to a feeling of power and omnipotence, gliding lightness of motion (35.6 %) and (3) languishing, dreaming mental state which was seen as relaxation (26.8 %).[10]

I have a vivid recollection of my first "light" run in Oulu, Finland in 1995. I had been exercising regularly for quite some time when all of a sudden in a regular pace run I was awakened by the sensation of lightness in running. The feeling was so strong that I felt like sitting on a chair, only that the scenery kept changing. Sheehan has had a similar experience: "Down the hill out of Hopkinton and through Ashland and over the gentle slopes to Framingham, I coast along. The running is automatic. I feel nothing but elation of being in this company. The miles pass as if I were watching them out of a train window."[11]

The following is a quote from my running diary about a long exercise (24 Aug 2001, 3–6:20 PM) when I was getting prepared for the Scenic Road Marathon from Punkalaidun to Huittinen in Finland[12]:

> A month earlier I had agreed with Kari Vulli to run together with him. Whenever I'm about to head for a longer run, the atmosphere is a little tense. The preparations, stretching and the like are made more carefully than if I were about to leave for a 10–15 km run. The weather is ideal for a long run, half cloudy, and the temperature around 20°C. I fill my bottle with mixed fruit syrup, with some salt in it. I spend around 10 minutes stretching. As very often is the case, the very first steps feel a bit stiff and forced, and the first couple of kilometers pass on getting accustomed to the pace. The pace turns out to be the regular 10 km per hour, into which it has evolved over the past couple of years.

---

[7] Pekola (1999, 18–19).

[8] Pekola (1999, 19).

[9] Pekola (1999, 19).

[10] It is interesting to ponder about how "different" experiences the physical and mental feelings of pleasure are. Is it possible to make a clear distinction between the two?

[11] Sheehan (1978, 209).

[12] An extract from my running diary.

My body is warm and running is beginning to feel good. The feeling is always pleasant when I begin to sweat. My eyes follow the traffic and the terrain. At times I pay attention to the ground and the unsmoothness on it. At some other moment I keep looking at the horizon, the clouds, the surrounding nature. My breathing rhythm is two steps in and two out.

We keep running abreast as usual and talk about this and that – Kari has the habit of being quite talkative. Then there are long silent periods as well.

The run is progressing nicely, my heart rate being around 140. There's no indication of pain or sore skin anywhere, my Achilles tendons are as if they didn't exist (I hurt my left tendon in everyday activities about a year earlier). I drink a little every 25 minutes.

Around 5:50 PM I feel as if I had received an extra boost of 1,000,000 kilowatts or a turbo engine from somewhere. Everything happened very quickly, as if I had been ripped off to the sphere of pure energy, apart from my ego and my body. This was preceded by the toughest climb of the round. We are running slightly downhill and *the world suddenly quiets down. The world or the existence in a way concentrates around me and becomes tangibly concrete, full-bodied. The experientiality gets concentrated: everything comes close, I touch the world more vividly, or the touch of the self and the world feels vivid.. The feeling of presence is strong, as if everything was in the now.*[13] *It covers everything – not only covers but is everything.* My eyes are focused on one point on the horizon. A hint of a bravely euphoric, *empowered* smile begins to prevail on my face. My consciousness is bright, placid and sharpened. The horizon draws *powerfully* forward, as if there was a strong draft. The pace builds up effortlessly and I let it happen. The steps become longer, my legs feel strong and light. *I'm not running rather I am being run or the run is taking place in me.* My heart rate varies between 153–163. After two kilometres the terrain turns prevalently uphill, the pace slows down and the energy fades away eventually. It is hard to tell how long the extra boost would have carried me on, had the terrain remained level. The rest of the run continues in silence.[14]

Next a description from George Sheehan:

But at first the day floods my senses. The sky is as high as heaven. The bay and the ocean on either side are a deep blue to the horizon. I am framed in the bright whites and the ocean colors that sea and sun and sand possess in the fall. There is a breeze at my back and the sun is warm between my shoulder blades. I am already bathed in pleasant sweat. But now I begin to get beyond this sight and sound, of observing the road ahead and the water to the side. The running alone occupies me. Fills my awareness. I am a steady flow. I am pure involvement. Total concentration. I am comfortable, calm, relaxed, full of running. I could run like this forever. And during all this I narrow my consciousness to the immediate moment. I am moving from time measured to where time stands still. I am giving up past and future for this now. I am leaving the linear time where my footsteps are a metronome, my pulse and respirations are in harmony, and every eight minutes I move my body one mile. And for a while I alternate. Briefly, I return to sweat and movement and sun warm between my shoulder blades, the sight of sea and sky. Then once again I am in the now, the eternal present where literally nothing happens. I am suspended, content with the nothing. And the peace that comes with it. And that perhaps is the essence of the running experience for me, and any number of different experiences for other people. The lack of anxiety, the complete acceptance, the letting go and the faith that all will be well. In running I feel free. I have no other goal, no other reward. The running is its own reason for being. And I run with no threat of failure. In fact, with no threat of success. There can be no consequences

---

[13] See Murphy and White (1995, 47–48).

[14] Similar experiences are also found from the descriptions and interpretations of other runners.

7.1 Running Experiences

to make me worry or doubt. I am secure whatever happens. And in that security I reach a wholeness that I find nowhere else.[15]

Finding rhythm and speed. Making adjustments for wind and hills, for heat and humidity. Attending to the sensations from feet and joints and muscles. I am a thinking animal using my brain instead of my mind. Then, quite mysteriously, I am in the second wind. Like a jet suddenly settling into cruising speed after the surging of the takeoff, my running becomes easy, automatic. I had become play. And I have moved from animal to being a pleasureseeking adult. A castaway enjoying what he can. But that euphoria, that glow passess. The running asks for effort. It is no longer easy. The next quarter hour will demand more and more. I will be tempted to turn and head back to town. Being human, it seems, is more than enjoyment, more than pleasure. Life is also pain. And because of that, it is perplexity, essential and continual perplexity. Some of that perplexity clears when I reach the third wind. The second wind is physiological and has to do with the heart and blood vessels and core temperature. The third wind, which comes after half an hour, is psychological and has to do with the mind and the spirit, with joy and peace, with faith and hope, with unity and certainty. Sometimes, this state, this awareness comes at the best part of my running. I am at the crest of my hill, looking down on my river and seeing in the distance my town, where people are right now working and sustaining life, theirs and mine. And now that hill becomes every hill, the river every river, the town every town, and the people all humanity. And in those moments there is a light and joy and understanding. For a time, however brief, there is no confusion. I seem to see the way things really are. I am in the Kingdom. Just once, I have gone beyond this. My running became my offering. A dozen years of training and discipline, hours upon hours of perfecting the art and purifying the artiss, came to this: — 'Absolute certainty; beyond reason. Joy. Peace.' We begin in the body and end in the vision.[16]

Next, Sheehan describes a competitive situation (in which the significance of the social situation gets revealed). One's own body and mind get settled in an ascetic state which is similar to what fighters in different spiritual disciplines have used in self-exploration for thousands of years. In this exercise the physical-psychological pressure and strain is so hard that the grip of the ego on itself gets loosened. The ego does not in a way have the strength to keep itself as a whole, and something that is more original and profound than the ego appears.

And we go down that last stretch head and head, each demanding the other do more. Each giving until there is no more to give. Until there is nothing left but the "I".[17] I am beyond pain and guilt. I am where I have never been or seen or touched in daily life. In those final yards, I am near the state described by the dying patients of Dr. Elizabeth Kübler-Ross, of floating out of the body and having a feeling of peace and wholeness. I feel – the total peace.[18]

Sheehan writes also about another peak experience where he shadowed a tough runner in a 2-mile run:

I reached a state of blessedness that I have rarely equaled. I was for those minutes completely absorbed in what I was doing. I was in what has been described as a cocoon

---

[15] Sheehan (1978, 251).

[16] Sheehan (1978, 253–254).

[17] Sheehan talks about the "I" which, as I understand it, is not the ego.

[18] Sheehan (1978, 196).

of concentration, absolutely involved, fully engaged in running. Not racing or winning but simply running. Everything was harmony and grace. Everything was pure. Effort had become effortless. – And so it went. I felt incredibly fresh the whole race. And latter it seemed to have been run without reference to real time or real space. Space and time had narrowed down to him and me and the running. It was almost as if I had taken some hallucinatory drug that altered my perceptions. Then there were only two laps to go. I gunned past him, increasing my lead with every stride. And finished still fresh in 10:53. So there it was, my personal best by following the leader. Letting him do the work. Letting him pull me through that air. Letting him establish the pace. And all the while letting myself go. Letting myself get inside the running and become the running itself. Letting my body do what it does best.[19]

And still one more quotation:

The first half hour of my run is for my body. The last half hour, for my soul. In the beginning the road is a miracle of solitude and escape. In the end it is a miracle of discovery and joy. Throughout, it brings an understanding of what Blake meant when he says, "Energy is eternal delight". – I move beyond ambition and envy, beyond pleasure and diversion. In those miles downhill, I have a new vision of myself and the universe. The running is easy, automatic, yet full of power, strength, precision. A tremendous energy pours through my body. I am whole and holy. The universe is whole and holy and full of meaning. In the passion of this running, truth is being carried, as the poet says, alive into my heart. So in those final miles meditation becomes contemplation. What has been a measuring of things becomes an awareness of the sacred. The road now becomes sacred ground –. There are cars and traffic, noise and exhaust, but I am past sight and sound, past this disturbance. I know or, better, I experience the whole of what Blake said.[20]

7.2 The Buddhist Marathon Monks of Mount Hiei

7.2.1 *Running Exercise as Bodily Enforcement and Meditation*

The history of humankind proves that experiences constituting an individual can be methodologically reached for (this is exercising the primordial understanding of Being). In this situation the relation par excellence between a running exercise and meditation becomes the subject. One of my assumptions related to this relationship is that regular, long-lasting rhythmic breathing has a harmonizing impact on the psycho-physical entity of an individual. Marko Vapa whom I quoted in the introduction saw that the effective factor is the change in the state of consciousness caused by rhythmic and monotonous movement. I personally see that it is especially the long-lasting regulated rhythmic breathing (to which the regularity of running brings a clear pace) that contributes to the harmonization. From the viewpoint of

---

[19]Sheehan (1978, 174–175). A two-mile run in 10 min 53 s corresponds to the pace of 3 min 23 s per kilometre.
[20]Sheehan (1978, 225–227).

an individual the question is about the experiences caused by an exercise, such as a change in the time horizon, changes in the states of consciousness and the meditative states generated by running.

Later I will approach this subject with the help of Heidegger using the notion "the call of conscience" and responding to the call as a starting point. In other words, can running tune a runner so that one can hear the call of conscience? In my opinion this is possible. Also Sheehan[21] writes that "I have found my specific pattern, heard the voice that calls me, found my art, my medium to experience and interpret life."

Conscience calls in silence and from silence – silence can be kindled in a runner. One of the mental ways of being is to be silent. The mind has the capability of quieting itself. In practice this means that when the noise and mental "babbling" stops, one's mind quiets down. Many kinds of experiential states can appear from silence, the existential ones being the most addressing, such as call of conscience, for example. One of the levels is that running brings a runner closer to the world. A physical exercise opens up one's mind and one's body for vitality and joy, for example. This serves as a harmonizing factor if, for instance, otherwise one would be overwhelmed by the grey anonymity of everydayness, in a mental state which is filled with powerlessness and lack of vision.

Before dealing with the monks a few words about perennial philosophy because it joins (1) the concept of authenticity found in Heidegger's philosophy (for example to be gained via the call of conscience), (2) running and (3) a historical running tradition reaching for wisdom.

Perennial philosophy focuses on investigating the fundamental questions of human existence. As self-exploratory by nature humans have made attempts to answer these questions also by means of physical exercises. Exercising and sports have often been seen to be part of a good life and as ways to it.[22]

Through the disciplines of the perennial tradition we can ask the question how humans can reach for vitality and grow up mentally with the help of bodily exercises.

Some words about understanding and its development: What I wish to bring out is the bodily-mental transformation generated by exercise (which occurs the better the more their is weight on meditation, as is the case with the monks of Mount Hiei). The impact of this is related to the relationship between passions and the human being. The body (or mind, whoever can ultimately make a distinction between them) of a person who has undergone a transformation is in a way neutral to passions, as if with a duck from the back of which the water of passion drifted away. The "hooks" cast by passions and cravings are no longer bitten by people – I see this as development of the primordial understanding of Being. The relationship of powerful emotions to a person like this "can be interpreted phenomenologically so that passions no longer have a 'mental adhesive surface' –. They can no longer

---

[21]Sheehan (1978, 126).
[22]See Koski (2000, 48), Kauppi (1978, 7).

"take a grip on" a human as they used to. In this sense they are meaningless, since they have no adhesive surface."[23] This have to do with the bodily aspect of understanding. The idea is that one cannot neutralize passions through sense rather only use willpower if one wishes to overcome a passion. In bodily understanding the call of passion is simply not of interest, it is unimportant. In this situation the pleasure brought by passion is even more enjoyable, because passion is not the master but the servant. This idea is closely related to the concept of wu-wei, the undone act, in Taoist philosophy. When acts get done as articulated by wu-wei, they are easier to do – in case there are powerful passions related to the nature of the act, they shape up the making process through the psyche of the actor.[24] Edwards[25] draws a parallel between wu-wei ("non-action") with flow, runner's high and being "in the zone".

7.2.2 Tendai-Buddhist Monastery at Mount Hiei in Japan[26]

In addition to the traditional meditation the monks exercise themselves also physically, and are therefore known as marathon monks. Their goal is to reach satori, enlightenment.[27]

In the course of 7 years the exercise they need to go through[28] is a 1,000 day marathon totalling at 38,632 km (or 46,572 km in the more demanding form):

- **1st to 3rd year:** the exercise is 100 running days a year, 30 km (40 km) per day, 54 km once a year
- **4th to 5th year:** 200 running days a year, 30 km (40 km) per day, 54 km once a year
- **6th year:** 100 running days a year, 60 km per day

---

[23] Koski (2000, 113).

[24] Ks. Koski (2000, 106, 224).

[25] Edwards (2002, 3). Edwards, Steven: Experiencing the Meaning of Exercise. *Indo-Pacific Journal of Phenomenology*, Volume 2, Edition 2 September 2002. http://www.ipjp.org/september2002/Edwards,pdf.pdf. Viitattu 10.5.2004.

[26] Philosophical texts concerning running and religion see Fry (2007, 57–69) and Moreland (2007, 151–160).

[27] Murphy and White (1995, 107) write that the accurate structure of an athletic performance, which organizes our being, mind and energy in a concentrated manner, can evoke our spiritual depths similarly to living in a monastery. In the case of the Buddhist monks of Mount Hiei we have them both: physical exercise and monastery life.

[28] The Finnish long-distance runner, four-time Olympic champion Lasse Viren has told to those intending to be top-class runners to reserve 7 years for it plus the time that is required to get prepared for the next Olympic games (Saari 1979, 214). Thus, the foundation for exercising your body at the top level is built in 7 years!

- **7th year:** 200 running days a year, of which 100 first days 84 km per day, and the other 100 with 30 km (40 km) per day, and once 54 km.[29]

The first 30–40 km, which is started around 1:30 AM, is done in 5.5–7.5 h (including rituals that last from 10 s to a couple of minutes at 255 different locations). Since the trails are in a poor shape and dangerous especially in winter time and in darkness, older monks do not encourage the novices to run too fast. After the wandering (which is mostly walking[30]), after they have eaten, washed themselves and done their meditation, there is a 1-h rest around noon. The monks go to bed around 8–9 PM. The wake-up call is at midnight, after which the monks go through an hour-long common ritual. After a light meal the monks start their exercise.[31]

After 700 days the monks take part in a 9-day long meditation period (dooiri), during which they do not sleep, rest, eat or drink.[32] The only thing they are allowed to do is to rinse their mouths with water once a day from the fifth day onwards – with which they prevent the mouth from drying. Anyhow, after rinsing the water must be spitted out.[33] Two colleagues are watching over so that the dooiri goes as ordained.

---

[29] Stevens (1988, 71).

[30] In the pictures of the book all monks are walking. However, this does not mean that they would not jog lightly occasionally. At the end of the exercise the monks may use a long stick, which also refers to walking pace.

Aristotle has been claimed to have been walking when he was teaching (and so to have founded the "peripathetic school"). This gives me the opportunity to make an awkward transition to the following quadruplet: philosophy, walking, relaxation of mind, meditativity, and consequently to refer to a net quote from Sinikka (2004): "This well-known philosopher [Aristotle, TK], was quite a walker. He had realized that walking promotes both thinking and the emergence of fine philosophical ideas. – Walking around is different by nature than running which aims at significantly improved physical performance, for example, because in the latter the main point is a tough physical performance and maximization of oxygen intake. Walking around is more philosophical. First, you make an attempt to find a suitable pace. As soon as walking begins to heat up your body, it relaxes the muscles and significantly increases the oxygen level in your circulation. Having found a suitable walking pace any interrupting ideas will disappear from your mind, your ability to concentrate will sharpen up and you will notice that you are capable of creating new, fresh ideas and solutions in your mind. – After a couple of weeks of getting accustomed to it, daily walking around becomes as necessary to you as food and drink. As soon as I have returned from my daily walk, I feel refreshed, pouring with new ideas. Even more excellent spheres can be expected, since those who have advanced in their circle walking philosophy have told about having discovered the meditative ecstasy of long walks that have turned into wandering."

[31] Stevens (1988, 64–67).

[32] Actual time without sleep, rest, food and something to drink is 7.5 days, 182 h (Stevens 1988, 75).

[33] Stevens (1988, 71–72).

According to Stevens, at the end of dooiri one's mind has been "stripped off" from everything – good, bad, or neutral – and existence is uncovered crystal clear.[34] This exercise deconstructs the ego.

After having recovered from this the monks will start the exercise of the remaining 300 days, of which the 7th year 84 km exercise done on 100 subsequent days is the hardest. The monks typically spend 16–18 h per day doing this.[35] The monks are assisted in wandering by a pusher who changes daily. His task is to conveniently push the monks using a stuffed stick and reduce the strain by as much as a half. In addition, there is a group of supporters who take care of other needs of the monks such as making of food, clothing and other basic things.[36]

But why does a monk "run"? Stevens sees this as an attempt to reach one's true self, one's own nature, i.e. Buddha nature because of both oneself and others. Although the monks are totally committed to the exercise, they take every day as if it were their last.[37] What this really is all about can only be uncovered by running, not in mental terms; as I have often stated, with the help of your intelligence you cannot generate experiences that cover an individual as a whole.

At some point of the exercise the monk "wakes up from the egocentric dream". The monk has come in touch with compassion and "transcendental wisdom". When wandering across villages and towns he feels compassion towards other people and shines with joy. He does not make a distinction between helping himself and others. He has reached the balance.[38]

In the end the monk will feel having become one with Mount Hiei. This means worshiping and praising the nature with the whole mind and body.[39] This experience extends to all being. The joy of the exercise has been found. Every being, plant, or stone on the trail is born again every day. Everything is flourishing with the miracle and joy of life. All beings shine like gems, and this is no metaphor rather a lived experience. It is both a visual observation and an experiential joy about the existence of all beings.[40] Experience has a totally reconstructing impact on human existence. Nature and other human beings, for example, are not seen as separate from the self, because man is everything else, and everything else is man. Consequently, everything else is not objectified, but rather treated according to each one's own value and nature. Nature is not an object that can be treated like an object, because by mistreating nature man mistreats himself. By treating other people as objects a

---

[34] Stevens (1988, 76).

[35] Stevens (1988, 77).

[36] Stevens (1988, 81–83).

[37] Stevens (1988, 93–94).

[38] Stevens (1988, 94).

[39] Stevens (1988, 58).

[40] See Stevens (1988, 94). One monk describes his experience on page 94 as follows: "Gratitude for the teaching of the enlightened ones, gratitude for the wonders of nature, gratitude for the charity of human beings, gratitude for the opportunity to practice – gratitude, not asceticism, is the principle of the 1,000-day kaihoogyoo." Kaihoogyoo means a 1,000-day exercise.

7.2 The Buddhist Marathon Monks of Mount Hiei

human being begins to grow in herself some nihilism which will become a force from inside alienating herself from life and other people.

Monk Hakozaki who had had a long experience on exercising told the novices that if they saw the exercise as torture of the body or subjection of the flesh, they would destroy the exercise. The purpose of the exercise is to discover the joy of life.[41] Another monk, monk Sakai once said that his exercise "is to live wholeheartedly, with gratitude and without regret".[42] The exercise does not have a beginning or an end. When the exercise and everyday activities are one, this is the true Buddhism.[43]

An occidental runner Cudahy shares similar experiences. He is saying that the longer he runs, the more he is one with the surrounding nature. Artificiality of the society is pealed off, and only the plain, simple essence of a natural being is left.[44]

Cudahy has, for example, run through the 435 km Pennine Way trail, and claims having felt then a cosmic unity with nature and mankind. He also tells that he had never before experienced such a pure and simple joy. Such moments not only give us answers to questions like why we do different things rather also to why we live altogether.[45]

---

[41] Stevens (1988, 106).

[42] Stevens (1988, 131).

[43] Stevens (1988, 131)

[44] Cudahy (1989, 2–3).

[45] Cudahy (1989, vii).

Chapter 8
Experiential Cores

Running as a long exercise impacts the runner's consciousness by making changes to it. I refer to this change when discussing the deconstruction of the ego. As a result of the changes to consciousness caused by running, a runner can undergo important experiences which I have named as "experiential cores" in this chapter. The foundation of these cores (dualistically stating: bodily and mental foundation) is discussed in Chap. 9. From the viewpoint of the consciousness of a runner and the ego, the location of Chaps. 8 and 9 should be swapped, but I wish to conclude the book with my own statements on consciousness, especially with regard to "the call of conscience" and "active-passive process". As regards consciousness and the ego I find consciousness more fundamental. In the active-passive process I will make an attempt to make the authentic self and the metaphysical concept of call of conscience more understandable to those who are not familiar with Heidegger's philosophy. In the active-passive process I will both make an attempt to articulate my own ideas about Heidegger's call of conscience and to make my interpretation of it. In the analysis of the active-passive process I will present one way to relate to practising and to how we can gain at achieving something that cannot be reached through rational thinking. I will present a concrete way to strive for a more whole human being and to open up what can happen in a long running exercise. Personally I do not find Heidegger's diffuse way of thinking and presenting his ideas very pleasing, nor do I believe it to provide much of a reason for action for many other people as well.

The experiential cores presented in the following are about having an intuition of essences (Wesenschau, eidetic intuition) of running in the sense that they exist as potential. Thus, they do not occur in every single run.[1] If, however, the theoretical interest is to map and investigate the meaningful experiences related to running, they are meaningful. They have a meaning from the viewpoint of human existence and the constitution of feeling the existence.

8.1 Disappearance of the Contradiction Between the Subject and Object

When running takes place "on its own", where "I don't run but I'm being run or running takes place in me", we can state that there is the disappearance of a certain barrier. Maybe the best way of putting this is to say that "running takes place", because the experience is different than the experience of the everyday ego. The quality of an experience is egoless, although it is the runner who experiences it. The quality of the experience is that the happening of running is one of the happenings in the world. It is as if there was a phenomenon in the world that is called running, but the conscious experiential location of running is not the ego rather the consciousness that originates from the oneness of the runner and the world.

The traditional interpretation for this is that the border between the conscious self (ego) and the world disappears. In other words, a long-lasting physical exercise has a deconstructing impact on the ego.

Disappearance of the conflict between the subject and the object is a traditional, old and a bit stiff philosophical expression. Yet, it directs understanding towards the correct direction. The question is about the disappearance of an egologic-social "curtain" that makes our being more difficult. Experientially this is an experience of oneness,[2] in which existence just takes place and feels beautiful and lovely.

In addition, in a long-lasting run I see a unification in which the Heideggerian meditative thinking is combined with the physical power of the body. Admittedly, Heidegger himself deals with and suggests reaching for meditative thinking solely on a rational, conscious level. Combining the bodily aspect to the meditative thinking has been analysed by David M. Levin, who in his thinking makes a combination of Heidegger, Merleau-Ponty, psychoanalysis and Asian traditions.

I articulate the disappearance of the conflict between the subject and the object with the traditional phenomenological manner, as I see it: Ego is reduced without a consciously made reduction. Thus, the question is not about a traditional epoché

---

[1] To be precise, it is biased to talk about the experiential cores or essences of *running*, because they may appear in connection with any long-lasting exercise.

[2] The explorer Richard Byrd, who spent months in the arctic region, living in cold and primitive conditions, describes his experience one evening as follows: "Here were the imponderable processes and forces of the cosmos, harmonious and soundless. Harmony, that was it! That was what came out of the silence – a gentle rhythm, the strain of a perfect chord –. In that instant I could feel no doubt of man's oneness with the universe." (Murphy and White 1995, 33.)

(method of reduction), but since the ego gets reduced – and does so radically – it is meaningful to claim that some sort of an "existential-ontological epoché" takes place. The conscious goal of this does not necessarily need to be the ego, rather it is sufficient to set continuing the run as the only goal. (Reduction of the ego can also be the goal, but this has no meaning from the viewpoint of reduction, because it happens if it ever happens – the fundamental nature of the presubject comes before the intention.) There is no other goal, nor a need for one (although reduction is focused on the ego when it happens). The ego cannot perform an existential-ontological reduction, because it is the ego that makes the reduction when it makes the reduction. In this case the ego (as a conscious action) cannot reduce itself. If it tries to do that, the reduction will only enforce ego's consciousness of its self-reducing nature. After the occurrence of existential-ontological reduction what is left is only a consciousness that is not egological by nature (sometimes this is an ecstatic existential experience of oneness, sometimes not). When the subject-object setup is removed, we may experience the original affinity between us and the reality.

8.2 Calming Down One's Mind, Quietness

In running it is possible to experience quietness – one's mind and the world quiets down. When the inner talk one has going on in one's mind ceases due to an exercise, the mind quietens. There is an "intuitive experience of the immediacy of the reality without the categories of rational thinking".[3] As a metaphor to this we can talk about a pond, the surface of which calms down. When it is no longer stirred and disturbed, the surface calms down and we can see the bottom. This means that when the ego during the exercise loses the grip of itself, something else that is more than the ego may appear. When the mind quietens, something more real may realize. The senses transmit (according to their ecstatic nature, which they have "from the forces of nature") to the mind's an experience about quietness of the world, which thus adopts the definition of quietness to itself. The senses allow the emotion to reach the world, which thus adopts the mental attribute of quietness. The senses transmit subjectivity outside according to their ecstatic nature. The quietness is experienced in the world, because it is difficult for the mind to see its own quietness. In order for the quietness to be seen, the prerequisite is thematizing one's mind to be monitored by itself. Without active orientation of mind to itself, the world as spontaneously experienced will adopt attributes of mind to itself.

---

[3] Koski (2000, 149).

Quieting down is a "call of conscience". However, because the conscience is not talking with the help of concepts, it is difficult to "hear". On the other hand the call penetrates the human being so thoroughly that it is impossible not to hear it. The power of the call is so strong that it will inevitably be experienced and consciously noticed.

8.2.1 Meditative Thinking and Releasement[4]

Expressed in Heidegger's terminology, this is a state of mind that has been analysed above ("disappearance of the conflict between the subject and the object" and "quietening of mind, quietness"). A running experience can also be looked at from the viewpoint of Heidegger's concepts of meditative thinking and releasement. Steiner[5] writes about meditative thinking or "mind-seeking thinking":

> When thought is present in the inmost of man, it involves far more than 'mind' or 'brain' –. It implicates what the great mystic Meister Eckhart called *das Seelenfünklein*, 'the little spark or live ember of the soul', and which Heidegger will call 'heart'. – At its most penetrating, the exercise of thought is one of grateful acquiescence in Being. Inevitably, jubilantly, such acquiescence is a giving of thanks. For that which has been placed in our custody –.[6]

When we run, the world is not defined and no attempt is made to take it under control or to exploit it. When we run, it is sufficient that we just run. No more, no less. A long-lasting running exercise can be considered meditative thinking. During the exercise the world is allowed to be what it is. What is essential is the exercise itself and concentrating on what we are doing. In this way the world is left to be as it is. In Heidegger's terms this is called "letting being be as it is" (Gelassenheit zu den Dingen). In this situation there is a chance to see being as it is and not as we wish or imagine it to be. When this happens, it will concern the "existential understanding of Being" of an individual as an experiential happening of a living body. To put it another way, the contradiction between the subject and the object is overcome by the removal of the consciousness of the ego. Something more profound than the everyday consciousness will emerge.

---

[4] Releasement = Gelassenheit, letting be, cf. detachment of mental assertiveness. The connection between these concepts could be such that releasement takes place with the help of meditative or mind-seeking thinking. Some light to this concept may be shed with the concept of "mind-seeking thinking".

[5] Steiner (1987, 125–126).

[6] Steiner interprets meditative thinking as gratitude ("grateful acquiescence in Being"). See Sect. 8.7.

8.3 Attunement

In this context we are not talking about states-of-mind (*Befindlichkeit*),[7] which is one of the fundamental existentials.[8] Attunement is related to mood (Stimmung), which is an ontologic-ontic example of state-of-mind. Attunement means growth in the intensity and activity of one's mind (consciousness) to an experientially conscious level, and in the bodily sense as well. In this state the entire being of the runner is intensive and energetic.

The meaning that Heidegger gave to the existentiale state-of-mind forms a pre-understanding and foundation for the ontologic-ontic meaning of the term attunement used here.

"A state-of-mind is a basic existential way in which Dasein is its 'there'.[9]" By emphasising that having a state-of-mind is an existentiale, in which Dasein finds itself "here" (Da), I want to bring into focus the ability Dasein has through attunement for affecting the experiential intensity of being "here". I understand attunement as personal Sorge. While care describes Dasein's relation to the world, attunement is focused on a markedly smaller target in which Dasein positions itself as a self-conscious being distinguishable from other beings.

When applied to running, this means that according to Heidegger a runner is always in some sort of mood. For Dasein a mood is always about understanding its own being, not in a conscious sense rather in the sense of preontological understanding of Being. "If we Interpret understanding as a fundamental *existentiale*, this indicates that this phenomenon is conceived as a basic mode of Dasein's *Being*".[10] "Every understanding has its mood. Every state-of-mind is one in which one understands."[11] Is it a mood if there is only an experience of being in one's mind or if there is an "empty" moment which one comes to notice only when awakening from it? The answer is probably positive, since one's mind is always in some kind of sensing state, thus is always in some way in some kind of qualitative state.

The mood and its nature determine the orientation of the exercise and whether a conscious attempt is made to focus the exercise on something (e.g., towards the direction of authenticity implicitly appreciated by Heidegger).

---

[7] State-of-mind is a human way of being (ontological structure), which "enables" moods. State-of-mind is the structure which provides the moods to manifest themselves. In other words, state-of-mind enables understanding through a mood. Heidegger has probably come up with the idea of state-of-mind (Befindlichkeit) as one of the ways of realization from his perception that mind always seems to be in some kind of state – cf. to the concept of mood (Stimmung). "The fact that moods can deteriorate – and change over means simply that in every case Dasein always has some mood –." (Heidegger 1978, 173.)

[8] Heidegger (1978, 172–173).

[9] Heidegger (1978, 178).

[10] Heidegger (1978, 182).

[11] Heidegger (1978, 385).

Moods and affects as fear, anxiety, hope, joy, enthusiasm, gaiety, satiety, sadness and melancholy "are founded existentially upon one's having been".[12] I understand one's having been to mean that the touch between Dasein and the world generates a mood, which in its own way in accordance with its characteristics tells something about the nature of this touch. The ability and possibility to this is an indication of understanding of Being. It in a way provides a cue, and is a project within the framework of which Dasein's being progresses and provides the horizon that orientates Being. In Heidegger's words, "the understanding has in itself the existential structure which we call 'projection'".[13] The understanding, which is sketching by nature, sketches out the being of Dasein towards what it is for.[14]

Since moods are based on one's having been, and one exists in a body or as a body, it is possible to have an impact through the body to moods and their emergence. It is a well-known fact that through exercise it is possible to have an impact on one's own psycho-physical being, and here the question is about action that takes place via the body and mind, i.e. about attunement. Long-distance running as a bodily activity is one way of attunement,[15] of mind-seeking thinking and of movement that falls into Gelassenheit zu den Dingen. When a runner is consciously set for an exercise, the grade of attunement increases, making a person receptive. This will broaden the bodily-mental experiential horizon of an individual. In this way the reality has a wider surface or band to "enter into" a human being. In other words, mind-seeking thinking will have a better chance of realization.

The elevating grade of attunement refers to the sharpened and active experiential state of mind that prevails in the runner. Compared to a normal state it is energetic and vital, and feels as if it gave additional antennae for sensing the touch of one's self and the world. Although I have not come across this theme even in the works of Heidegger, I still see it as good expression to describe the altered experiential relationship generated by settling for running. One bodybuilder once described in a television documentary the relationship of his own exercising to his mental agility by claiming that "bodybuilding keeps me alert". Sheehan[16] says that

> running keeps me at a physical peak and sharpens my senses. It makes me touch and see and hear as if for the first time. Through it, I get past the first barrier to true emotions, the lack of integration with the body. Into it, I escape from the pettiness and triviality of everyday life. And, once inside, stop the daily pendulum perpetually oscillating between distraction and boredom.

For example, in the Zen-Buddhist tradition one of the primary targets of an exercise is to experientially discover the profoundness in everyday life, and not to escape from it.

---

[12] Heidegger (1978, 395).

[13] Heidegger (1978, 184–185).

[14] Heidegger (1978, 185).

[15] See Heidegger (1978, 172). See also Klemola (1998, 86–87).

[16] Sheehan (1978, 249).

What is behind the impact of the existential-ontological touch triggered by attunement remains a mystery. As Michael Levin puts it, it is an "ontological gift". Since a long run allows a human being to enter a receptive state, the latent essences may realize.

Running is preserved in the body and the body carries the impact of running in itself. This is possible due to the temporal nature of the body (for which thus exstasis lays the foundation). Sheehan[17] writes, that true, running does not fill my day. But it influences the rest of what I do and how I do it. Klemola[18] describes his rock climbing experience as follows:

> This experience is present not only on the rocky wall or by the camp fire at the foot of the rock. It is an experience that your body carries along for a long time, even for several days. I have described it as electric because after the climbing, sometimes several days after it, you can feel in your body the intensive stream of life, an inner vibration the pulse of which you can feel at the tip of your fingers and which allows you to see the same life that I experience in myself, flowing through everything around me.

The body remains attuned even though the exercise itself is over. The body and mind are tuned, altered and different than in everyday life. The experiential horizon is present in an opened-up state. Then, all of a sudden, some essence may realize.

8.4 Presence

For a modern man it is an existential problem that the experience of presence is missing. The hectic rhythm of life shatters one's personal lifeworld. One of my acquaintances has said that it is extremely hard to live either in the past or in the future. This means that one cannot stop or rest mentally and just live in this moment trusting that things shall get done and that hurrying does not help either. When an individual does have some time just to be there, the hectic rhythm that has emerged and grown inside one's body and mind, drags one away from the calmness of Being. This restlessness and uneasiness cannot be easily overcome with the help of a rational intention, because the hectic way of being builds up some kind of a psychic-physical structure that is shaping our way of life, for example. So, the question cannot be solved with the rational will or intellect (you may compare this with the desire to be spontaneous). The existential experience of presence that becomes real in long-distance running can help to break this negative spiral because it rearranges one's structures of understanding of Being.

Presence is the intensity of an experience. It means being open to the world without repression or without the fear of becoming repressed. In this situation the world does not get thematized from the ego rather from the *relationship* between the world and human being. Presence is about the opening of the human being to

---

[17]Sheehan (1978, 81).
[18]Klemola (1998, 170).

the world (or about the opening of the relationship between the human being and the world), when everything is "at the moment", which is a presence that embraces everything to itself. It is a full abundance of Being, which wraps together the past and the future to the present moment. Although the experience is accompanied with some kind of sense of time, timelessness is paradoxically emphasized in it.

In a heightened sense of presence, the experiential nature of the world seems to concentrate around us – it is like a warm existential blanket which surrounds an individual everywhere like water. Even though I have written about the similarity between people and their experiences, which is based on the body as a presubject, it is truly heart-stirring to notice other runners describe their feelings in almost identical strains. Sheehan's[19] description about space and a blanket wrapped around himself: "I run in complete touch with myself. I can tell you the wind speed, the temperature, the humidity and whether I'm on a grade and how steep it is. **I take the universe around me and wrap myself in it and become one with it**, moving at a pace that makes me part of it."[20] In this situation the experiential horizon opens up, and the "sensual channels" provide more content than earlier (probably causing the sensation of concentration of the experience).

In my opinion presence has similarities to Heidegger's concept recollection (Wiederholung). We could think that recollection brings present and near (sic!), brings into presence what has been forgotten. What is Heidegger's idea about the intensive nature of recollection I cannot evaluate. "What has been forgotten, is our bodily experience of the connection to the being", writes Klemola.[21]

8.5 Power

When I described my preparations for the Scenic Route Marathon, I wrote about an empowering smile which was a spontaneous exterior expression of my experience. This experience of the power (of life) seems contradictory to Heidegger's concept "Being-towards-death", in which awareness of the existence of death directs an individual towards authenticity. On the other hand, Heidegger's thinking implicates that death is a good thing, because it directs Dasein towards authenticity.[22] Based on my own experience, power has a similar tendency directing towards authenticity as Being-towards-death, but in a more positive, life-embracing sense.

---

[19]Sheehan's (1978, 229).

[20]Emphasis TK.

[21]Klemola (1998, 82).

[22]Although he does not favour authenticity in comparison to inauthenticity as a way of being, this is anyhow what his thinking implicates. In a later work, *Gelassenheit,* Heidegger (1988, 12–13) suggests that occidental people ought to exercise more meditative thinking, which they are in escape.

8.5 Power

Power can be defined so that it is the ability of every living being to make changes in one's own existence and the world. On the other hand it is an inner experience of the above. The first-mentioned is thus ontic by nature. The inner experience is ontic also as pre-predicative, and ontological as conceptualized in the sense meant by Heidegger.

After crossing the finishing line of the Scenic Route Marathon, my friend Kari said something like "this makes me feel strong" and "during the next few days I will be brave and strong", to which I only said "yes". In my opinion, however, the question is not only about having something strong and positive growing inside us but also about lightening, removal, and loss of importance of the mental burden attached to the ego over the years of our personal history as factors limiting our being. Maybe it was this that Kari was trying to point out.

Power as an experience is an inner, energetic immensity and it can be called "being-towards-life", because as a factual experience the question is about the experience of the power of life, which Being-towards-death is not.[23] In my opinion you cannot have an experience of your own death. Death is only a conceptual fact postulated from the future to the present, which at the moment does not directly concern us.

Epicurus has said that death does not concern us. When we exist, there is no death, and when there is death, we are not there. Ontologically (both in the traditional and Heidegger's sense), Dasein as a concrete being is a dying being and thus experiences Being-towards-death. In certain experiences it is possible to get an experience about and hold of being-towards-life, which is both an ontic (experiential) and ontological property of Dasein's concrete way of being. When Dasein is alive, it is attached to life, it is as a fleshly and sensing being in many ways attached to the "flesh" of the world, to express it in Merleau-Ponty's style.

Being-towards-life refers to the conscious experience that the quality of one's own life can change for the better, towards a more full life, and so to the realization of the possibility of authentication.

When talking about life and death it is essential to see running as an experiential state. Being-towards-death can be claimed to be some kind of an experience of Dasein. Being-towards-death bears no significance to the authentic self, because it does not "worry" about its ego. Thus, Being-towards-death is a moment belonging to the emergence of an ego-self human being. I claim that when Dasein gets experiences of authenticity, the sensation is also oriented to being-towards-life.

My analysis can also be seen as a critique on Heidegger's theoretical and somehow unfleshly spiritless analysis of authenticity. Heidegger does not present any means with which to practice or to seek for Gelassen-zu-den-dingen, and he only talks about superseding calculative thinking as well as in favour of mind-seeking thinking. There is only one piece of advice that he gives: we must just wait.

---

[23] Spiegelberg (1975, 70) agrees with me, since he states that he does not believe Heidegger's "being-toward-death" to be the only valid interpretation of human existence.

Also Levin[24] criticizes Heidegger for this lacking. According to Levin Heidegger was so tied with occidental metaphysics that he could let go of it in his thinking only partially. Levin thinks the main reason for this is that Heidegger denied the role of the body in one's mental growth.

Levin's praise for the partial loosening of the grip of occidental metaphysics means that Heidegger articulates the possibility of new kind of "thinking". But if we seek for concrete support for the promotion of spiritual growth or exercising of meditative thinking, for example, "we find that he has virtually nothing to say", says Levin.[25]

"Power" tells about an individual's ability to be whole, which can mean both inauthentic and authentic being. Power is a way of experiencing one's existence (and at its best also of Being). In it is experienced one of the many means in which a human being is realized. This is more fundamental than an everyday experience, because it roots and grounds an individual to one's own existence – and to existence as a whole.

The experience of power generates various qualitative issues related to both the shape of the body and conscious experiences. For these I will use the term metamorphoses of power, one of which is related to the outer shape of the body and the other to the inner experience. I came across this idea while reading Anne Sankari's article entitled "Body and gym".[26] Sankari borrows Susan Bordo's idea according to which the shape and size of the body has become more and more a sign of the inner order (or disorder) of an individual. This sign is targeted to the individual herself as well as to others. For others I understand it to mean the aesthetic habitus of the body, the way the body looks like and how an individual "carries one's own body". If an individual has had a great desire for strengthening and "enlargening" one's own body, having achieved the target one may feel being "an incarnation of one's own will".[27]

In addition to this, I understand the term "habitus" to cover the degree of vitality of an individual, the amount of mental energy which is visible in different grades and, depending on the amount and quality of exercise, in all of her actions. Long-distance runners with their slim bodies and faces, for example, may give an impression of a "tortured" athlete: hollow cheeks and eyes having the intensive glow of inner energy. As I see it, the latter is significant to a runner. It is an uplifting experience to feel the realization of one's inner energy. Life feels more full and "sustaining". The quality of being improves. A runner has more energy to take action, boredom and triviality are reduced, the amount of meaningful issues increases, life is more pleasant, and getting stuck with negative things gets reduced as one's mind is targeted towards more positive things, which is more meaningful.

---

[24] Levin (1987, 265).

[25] Levin (1987, 265).

[26] Sankari (1994, 170). The example here concerns gym exercises, but I think the idea can well be expanded to other types of physical exercise as well.

[27] Sankari (1994, 170).

The exercising habitus of a body conveys a message about one's bodily way of being in the world, and so shapes up the entire way of being of an individual. For example, just the fact of achieving a better physical condition alone generates growth of inner energy, which enables us to live according to what originates from a new energetic way of being.

8.6 Joy

One of the important and valuable experiences related to running is joy. Having analyzed this experience I have concluded that "benevolent bubbling happiness" is the best way to describe it. It is as if one's mind were euphorically gently floating on a mattress composed of joyous bubbles.

8.7 Devotion, Gratitude

The experience of devotion and gratitude is sublime and reaches cosmic measures. It is somehow egoless and impersonal irrespective of the fact that the experience of oneself as the experiencer is overwhelmingly strong. Being grateful about Being and existence as well as having compassion towards anything living are characteristic aspects of this unique experience. For a runner the gratitude of one's existence and of being in general can be so strong and existence is experienced as something so precious and solemn that it awakens a need to thank something or someone about it (even if we would think that there was no-one to thank, unless we have faith in a personal God.)[28]

8.7.1 Forgiveness

Forgiveness is a modification of devotion and gratitude. They can, depending on the experiential world of a runner preceding the exercise, flow to articulate the emotional relationship the runner has to other person or people. The topography of an experience has some sort of "holes" which are filled up by an emancipating and egoless emotional flow. This filling does not go unnoticed and appears, depending on the situation, in a particularly articulated conceptual form. This flow contains all those experiential qualities that are opened up in the active-passive process, such as joy, unconstrained mind, devotion, gratitude, and so on.

---

[28] See Murphy and White (1995, 27–30).

When running, a state of mind may occur the tone of which is forgiveness, a feeling that makes you forgive.[29] The target of this feeling can principally be any moral being, but in practice we are talking about conflicts in human relationships. Then, all of a sudden when running, without any conscious effort or initiative, one's mind is filled with an unselfish sense of well-being and forgiveness. If before the exercise there had been a quarrel or the relationship with some other person had been repulsively negative and quarrelsome, the negative emotional state will be wiped out. The anger will disappear, melt away.

"Letting loose" from a negative feeling during a run is not caused by a conscious effort, rather it happens on its own, when some entity or process that is carrying through this event is realized in the runner. The runner's mind is filled up with a sense of forgiveness which resembles love for one's neighbour, free from thoughts about guilt. The emotional state is cleared, after which you on your own behalf can start from a clean slate.

The ontological foundation of an emotion lies in a momentary lapse of one's ego in which, to use a scientifically imprecise expression, the ego let's go from itself. To clarify what is meant by this part of the active-passive process, the ego does not consciously let loose rather only notices its occurrence. The expression of letting loose from itself must be understood in a passive sense. There is no-one taking the action although it takes place in the psychophysical entity of a runner.

To conclude this chapter, it is worthwhile to discuss another kind of experience which is unfamiliar to me personally. J.P. Roos writes about his autumn depression which together with a long-lasting flu and heavy drinking in parties almost made him finish running altogether.

> Considering the physical condition in which I had been all the autumn, the best ever and long-lasting like that, the collapse was really dramatic. First I forced myself to run, even long distances, but already during the exercise my thoughts took me only to the gloomy and hostile paths, to the various idiots who had caused me harm during the autumn and to pondering what to do to them. Or, I was thinking about the dismal future of the world, the seemingly emerging conflict between the Islamic and capitalistic world, the terrible domestic recession and the foolish decisions of the government –, so that when I came home, I was either filled with repressed rage and bitterness or so deeply depressed that I could barely lift my arm.[30]

The forgiving angle of running should be understood in such a way that running as a physical exercise is not – like any other kind of physical exercise – a magic trick which instantly or automatically brings a good feeling and peace of mind. It is also to be noted that the time spent for running and the strain caused by it vary, resulting in a different impact. It would be interesting to know whether a 30-km run calmed down one's mind more than a 5-km run. I believe this to be the case. Additionally, if the depression is deep, it takes longer to recoverfrom it. There can

---

[29]I think that this experience is often reached in all other kind of meditative exercises as well.
[30]Roos (1995), Chapter 11.

be many factors causing the depression which one then needs to work on in the right (possibly therapeutic) circumstances. Besides, when the depression is deep, who has the strength to go running?

Roos[31] analyses his depression by making the following conclusions:

> After all it was this depression that made me finish running so that my running diary contained several entirely blank weeks and some weeks with only 5–10 km of running. On the other hand, it was only this break from exercise together with my Christmas holiday which eventually allowed me to get rid of the depression (even writing this book was almost totally on hold for nearly a month). To sum up, it is a good idea to take breaks and there is no reason to worry about them. A human being is not a machine and no action, not even the ones that you like the most, would always appeal to you. You should change your routines and areas of interest time to time.

8.8 True Self, Enlightenment, Absolute

This profound and mystical event (of finding the true self, enlightenment, Absolute) is conceptualized in various ways in different traditions. The event itself is not describable in words, although such attempts are being made. It is beyond description. I interpret it as uncovering of the "fundamental reality" because of the fact that the utterer is always an incarnated subject, a bodily-mental individual.[32] I have written about this as follows:

> Many experiences under the scope of perennial philosophical research are considered mystical. Naturally, this does not mean that they would be somehow supernatural or the products of imagination. The point is that as lived experiences they are not common, but rare. The biggest dispute within the research tradition of perennial philosophy has been whether the mystical experiences are fundamentally similar or varying depending on the culture. Personally I see that the experiences on fundamental reality and the self are the same independent of the cultural differences. Since the experiences are out of the reach of conceptualization, the multitude of interpretations emerges from different interpretational frameworks which vary between cultures.
>
> Luoma[33] writes that those who deny the fundamental unity of the experience are hermeneutically naive, if they from the various descriptions of the experience deduce that similar variation applies to the transcendental reality which the descriptions refer to. Luoma made a summary of Forman's work *The Problem of Pure Consciousness, Mysticism and Philosophy* as follows: A mystical experience represents an immediate and direct touch to an absolute principle (which can be defined in many ways). It is only after this touch that it has been – interpreted in relation to the language and beliefs of one's owntradition. Because

---

[31] Roos (1995), Chapter 11.

[32] It is unclear whether with authentic being and authentic human Heidegger refers to a human who has experienced the experience. My interpretation is that this is the case to some extent, with reference to Heidegger's studies on Master Eckhard and to the fact that Heidegger had familiarized himself with oriental traditions of spiritual growth.

[33] Luoma (1994, 58).

these interpretational categories (thus concepts, beliefs and background assumptions) are not contained in this transcendental experience, mysticism is prevalently similar across cultures.[34]

Kauppi writes that

> it is not mysticism to say in relation to something transcendent that it exists. A mystic makes an attempt to experience the transcendence in such a way that it cannot be seen as intellectual comprehension. She has the conviction that what is transcendental in relation to our capacity to understand is not necessarily transcendental with regard to experience. In this situation, however, we are talking about an experience which is different than the experience which is used as the foundation of our experiential knowledge.[35]

Annemarie Schimmel, who has studied Sufism, a mystic branch of Islam

> defines a mystical[36] experience as some extraordinary and powerful event reached by very few people without methodical exercise. The experience is not reached intellectually –.[37] – Afterwards it is possible to interpret and understand a mystical experience with the help of conceptualization, because humans themselves possess as an experiential foundation an event which is being conceptualized.[38]

Since the question is about the "fundamental reality", and about an incarnated human being as an experiencer, I think that

> humans cannot say anything final about the "fundamental reality", because concepts cannot be utilized comprehensively to describe the being as such. This refers to the way how fundamental reality is in itself and how its existence just is. The fundamental reality is a "suchness", which will always remain beyond human comprehension.[39]

---

[34] Koski (2000, 28–29).

[35] Kauppi (1978, 11).

[36] Mystical does not mean supernatural. In a strong sense of the concept supernatural, it cannot exist for a human being. Every event that a human being can experience, takes place in the world, in the nature. According to this humans cannot get experiences beyond nature or from events outside of it. Consequently, supernatural cannot experientially exist for humans because if something "supernatural" happened, it would take place in the nature, and thus be "natural".

[37] See Schimmel (1986, 3).

[38] This powerful and peculiar experience has in connection with yoga been interpreted to belong to the liberation process (nirvana) of an individual. The question is then about going beyond the everyday being. It is about experiencing and realization of "the undefined" in one's life. In Patanjal's yoga sutras (Johnston 1987, I: 16 – IV: 34) one subject is the emergence of a "spiritual man". In this context we are talking about the "death" and "rebirth" of an individual, by which we mean the "death" of the profane self or ego and spiritual "rebirth" of an individual. The experience is categorical in its strength and will change the human being. (Koski 2000, 106). In occidental philosophy Spinoza refers, as I see it, to the same experience when he talks about "intuitive knowledge". "In philosophical terms the question is about the experience of unity of the being and existence, in which the being is experienced as a totality. Spinoza (1949, V: xxvii) calls the knowledge related to this experience the third kind of knowledge (i.e. intuitive knowledge), which the human being experiences as the broadest possible peace of mind." (Koski 2000, 211).

[39] Koski (2000, 221).

8.8 True Self, Enlightenment, Absolute

These are the **experiential cores** of long-distance running. There can be more of them, and here we deal with only those revealed by this study.[40] For a runner experiential cores are central factors through which other events in the lifeworld of a runner are defined and given their significance. In this situation, the cores experienced as important and significant also affect the way in which unpleasant and negative experiences are seen and understood. If the experiences gained as a runner are significant to one's being as a human, the existential-ontological events that had a positive impact on one's self turning into a whole, are extended to negative experiences as well, resulting in that they feel less important and less negative.

In other words, a runner who has discovered a more positive attitude towards life or something about one's true inner identity will face improved quality of life, and adversities do not shake her as much as earlier. This is the case when we think that a person is an entity, giving every individual phenomenon or experience its significance through the view of life of a human and thus through the interpretational horizon tuned by one's former experiences. Even the moods are noted through the experiential cores that define the totality of the situation. Then, the unpleasant moods can change to good ones.

Next I will take a closer look at running as a meditative exercise.

---

[40]Timo Klemola (1998, 163–170) has written about the phenomenology of rock climbing, discussing experiential cores such as nature, death, trust, fear, other (human being), skill, freedom, looking at oneself, tool, joy, full concentration, and life (1998, 165).

Chapter 9
Going Beyond the Reason and the Wisdom of the Body

In this chapter I will discuss the relationship between a runner and the touch to the world in the context of the runner's more profound essence, including the viewpoint of awakening. The context is related to the questions and processes of authenticity and inauthenticity. The scope of awakening reaches from the area of concepts to those that go beyond it. What is out of reach of the conceptual is beyond reason and rationality.[1] Consequently, the discussion concerns the development and concrete interpretation of Heidegger's thought in meditative thinking and the ideas of Gelassenheit in terms of the actual training of a runner. With the help of the notion of the active-passive process I present how we can go beyond the limits of reason and what role does the wisdom of the body play in it.

9.1 Running as Meditative Thinking

> The goals and motives of a "spiritual physical exercise" are inner.
> The rewards acquired from such sports are quiet and broadminded by nature.[2]

Spiritual physical exercise is an aphoristic spoken language expression. Everything that a human being does is mental or spiritual. In this context mental or spiritual must be seen as a viewpoint to physical exercise and to its goal. It is a different task to try to reach for running a marathon in less than 2 h 30 min than to run with a good feeling and peace of mind (it is, of course, possible to combine the two goals). I will use Heidegger's notion of meditative thinking (mind-seeking thinking), and as mentioned earlier, this notion is related to the concept of Gelassenheit. What is

---

[1] See Klemola (1998, 65–75).
[2] A quote from Mari Verho in an email message 10 Oct 2001 as part of our debate on the meanings of physical exercise.

most essential in this way of thinking about running is getting a hold of the reality or world of another kind of relationship. As the goal of meditative thinking, which is not seen as an external target, is the ontic reality from which all of our thinking originates (a reality which is not emptied in the concepts we have formed about it).[3] No attempts are made to take reality into possession via rational, "calculative thinking", rather by quietening in such a way that the world may have an opportunity to reveal itself as it is, free from our expectations. It is as if we experienced Being with a capital B. In this way we can adopt a new kind of touch to the world and to ourselves. The question is about uncovering the horizon of being-in-the-world in ourselves. I do not write "**opening the horizon**" (which I consider having to do with a conscious action), because we cannot have an influence on it by conscious thinking. All attempts that are made consciously belong to the area of rational, "calculative thinking", which cannot reveal what mind-seeking thinking is capable of doing.

Traditionally, meditative thinking has been considered to be related to the spiritual growth of a human being.[4] When physical exercise contains a meditative dimension, it is important to note that then the bodily and physical existence of human beings can be thematized from the viewpoint of the entire human well-being and meaningfulness of life.

My interpretation is that Heidegger's notion of meditative thinking is related to meditation (or to some of its levels). Therefore I have every reason to make a connection between meditative thinking and meditation and to ask, in order to uncover the essence of meditative thinking (as I see it), what the positive properties of meditation are considered to be based on. Rauhala[5] presents the idea as follows:

> According to meditation psychology, when one's consciousness is emptied, it can restart from a sort of neutral zero-state. In this situation the natural, innate wisdom of the conscious occurrence realizes itself. Originally, that is merely as a result of the neural structure, negativity does not belong to consciousness. Instead, there is only a neutral reflection of the reality as experienced significances. Negativity represents a burden that has accumulated in us over the years of individual evolution. When we manage to blot it out, and repeatedly so via meditation, our consciousness has room for a free, creative space which is no longer governed by any pre-engagements. – When unfavourable experiences of meanings are eventually replaced with a favourable mental relationship with reality, we are naturally talking about mental development. Seeing it in this way, also the concept of mental growth will gain true substance. What speaks in favour of the permanent nature of positive experiential content is the fact that the world view evolving from them is more meaningful, more contributing to living skills and so more pleasing than a negative world view. Motivation to continue striving for the better evolves eventually through the progress as well as from itself. Even a slight change is easily perceived and motivating.

---

[3]The "target" of meditative thinking can thus be seen to be the transcendent, Tao, being, One, Atman, Brahman, God and so on, depending on the explanatory framework in use.

[4]See Koski (2000).

[5]Rauhala (1990, 69–70).

9.1 Running as Meditative Thinking

What is experienced through meditative thinking is experienced as a whole human being, and not merely by rational thinking. Something that has been experienced as a whole human being, through the body and mind, will turn into our "own flesh". It is not, for example, something that we have learned superficially as forms of a good life. Everything that has been personally experienced touches a human being in a different way than superficial knowledge.

> If our understanding does not turn into our "own flesh" and vice versa, it will remain an alienated intellectualism: understanding that has no relation to the activity does not help achieve – (a good life, TK). The growth of both mental and bodily understanding should be visible in everyday actions. According to an Arabic proverb, knowledge without action is like a fruit tree without fruit.[6]

One essential question is, what does a runner strive for by running? In other words, what is the intentional correlate of the consciousness of a runner? How does it structure a runner as a runner and running as running? If the target was, for example, a perennial ideal, it is an individually thematized target adopted through pre-understanding, because the ideal has been interpreted by the individual. According to the idea of the hermeneutical circle the ideal (intentional correlate) is not static, rather something that changes and sharpens up and becomes more versatile in content. Another way of looking at this is to think that a runner can focus on running via the projects of winning, health, expression and the self.[7]

Running is one way of studying and approaching the self and the world. The longer the distance, the more meditative the self-study. What is the significance of going deeply into oneself? The significance lies in the fact that it opens up the experiential horizon of an individual, which also contains the existential aspect. Going deeply into oneself directs an individual to experiencing one's own existence.

Contemplating one's inner self necessitates quietening and calming down. Here we can state that a runner adopts an ontologic-ontic role.[8] It is the structure in which the active-passive process takes place. When running, we place ourselves in an intensive relationship with the world, producing various dimensions related to our own existence and its characteristics. They are individual and have an impact on the continuum with inauthentic and authentic being at its opposite ends. Sheehan writes about his own experiences (from a viewpoint that reduces inauthenticity) as follows:

> When I run and meditate, I abandon my former shelter in the pure simplicity of running as well as the everyday securities included in my life. I abandon — my forefathers, my church, my society, my family, my friends, everyone and everything that I consider valuable. I throw out everything that I have not seen as genuine through my own experience. I abandon everything that I have not learned through immediate dealings and compassion. I challenge all this during the seemingly playful one hour that I spend running on the road by

---

[6]Koski (2000, 48).

[7]Klemola (1998, 5).

[8]With the help of an understanding of Being (in the ontological sense) a runner places oneself as a concrete, bodily being (ontic being) into a running relationship.

the river. — I choose myself, my values, my universe. I choose my own drama, my own life, my own heroes. I search through imagination, reason and intuition for the unique something which I, and nobody else, am here for.[9]

In Heidegger's terms, Dasein provides meaning to Being, i.e. meaningfulness is revealed in the process of Dasein's being-in-the-world, or to be more precise, the fact of Being revealed by Dasein is *meaningfulness*. This meaningfulness is not theoretical nor is it practical, as the opposite of theoretical. Being should not be considered an inner matter of Dasein's mind, rather Dasein's being is meaningfulness. Jean-Luc Nancy has commented on this idea by claiming that meaningfulness has specifically to do with action and behaviour; behaviour is the realization of Being (*vollbringen*).[10] Realization of being is a meaningful action.

Before discussing the call of conscience, next a few words about "anxiety", because I see it as one of the factors that sets up the favourable ground for the call of conscience. In this context we could heuristically ponder whether anxiety was a pre-stage of the call of conscience, as if it were a door through which we could progress to a pre-understanding of call of conscience (e.g. by thematizing it from the viewpoint of the "they" and authenticity).

Anxiety can be seen as an understanding state-of-mind.[11] "(A)nxiousness as a state-of-mind is a way of Being-in-the-world —".[12] "Anxiety brings Dasein face to face with its *Being-free for* — the authenticity of its Being, and for this authenticity as a possibility which it always is".[13] Similarly, in Buddhism humans are considered to possess a Buddha nature which can be actualized. In this sense we say that an individual is-already a Buddha, because the Buddha-nature is already contained in her.

Anxiety thematizes the kind of mental way of experiencing one's own existence which in the call of conscience is placed in its own, understandable position (as part of the growth of understanding the world, similarly to how the call of conscience reveals itself afterwards in an important, constitutive role).

Anxiety as an experience is clearly prominent. It does not hide modestly in quietness, rather shamelessly calls for being noticed. Heidegger writes that "in anxiety one feels 'uncanny'. — ('U)ncanniness' also means 'not-being-at-home' —."[14] Here Heidegger presents an existential pattern that we are used to seeing in connection with Zen-Buddhism.[15] Also there the goal of a human being is "to

---

[9]Sheehan (1978, 233–234).

[10]Nancy (1996).

[11]Heidegger (1978, 227).

[12]Heidegger (1978, 235).

[13]Heidegger (1978, 232).

[14]Heidegger (1978, 233).

[15]Kreeft (1971), in Introduction, makes an interesting remark: "A German friend of Heidegger told me that one day when he visited Heidegger he found him reading one of Suzuki's books. 'If I understand this man correctly,' Heidegger remarked, 'this is what I have been trying to say in all my writings.' This remark may be the slightly exaggerated enthusiasm of a man under the impact

9.1 Running as Meditative Thinking

come home with the help of a way", which is about finding one's true self. Running dissolves or lifts a runner away from anxiety. Running may bring a runner a "feeling of being at home".[16]

"This uncanniness pursues Dasein constantly, and is a threat to its everyday lostness in the 'they', though not explicitly".[17] Uncanniness and anxiety may confront a runner when, for example, she cannot practice for some reason. Could inexclicability and restlessness be uncanniness to some extent? The anxiety triggered by uncanniness makes a runner actualize one's true opportunity to be realized in being-in-the-world. When we take a look at any tradition in which humans are targeted towards authentication, they all seem to have a methodical, continuous exercise in a central position. In the Zen tradition, for example, emphasis is put on lifelong exercise, no matter whether you were a novice or a master. Traditions that have proven their vitality and continuity have probably seen continuous exercise as a necessary prerequisite for keeping their vitality. The reason for that is that everydayness is making constant attempts to draw the exercising person towards the trivial, boring insignificance of grey everydayness. Heidegger calls Dasein's everyday vagueness conventionality.[18] Inauthenticity (with the "they" as the essence) is articulated in a colourfully emphatic way by Heidegger as follows[19]:

> (T)he pallid lack of mood – indifference – which is addicted to nothing and has no urge for anything, and which abandons itself to whatever the day may bring, — demonstrates *most penetratingly* the power of forgetting[20] in the everyday mode of that concern which is closest to us. Just living along — in a way which 'lets' everything 'be' as it is, is based on forgetting and abandoning oneself to one's thrownness. It has the ecstatical meaning of an inauthentic way of having been.

Moran interprets the matter so that everydayness makes Dasein fall, preventing it from confronting the aspects of its existence[21] – or should we say that everydayness as a state of mind keeps Dasein in a fallen state? Anxiety, at least in Heidegger's thinking, is a good thing because anxiety "brings it (Dasein, TK) back from its absorption in the 'world'. Everyday familiarity collapses. — Being-in enters into the

---

of a book in which he recognizes some of his own thoughts, certainly Heidegger's philosophy in its tone and temper and source is Western to its core, and there is much in him that is not in Zen, but also very much more in Zen that is not in Heidegger; and yet the points of correspondence between the two, despite their disparate sources, are startling enough." See Zimmerman (1993).

[16]Heidegger has stated, when reading the books of D.T. Suzuki, that if he understand Suzuki correctly (that is Zen's way to describe man and the world), this is what he has been trying to say in all of his writings (Kreeft 1971, 521).

[17]Heidegger (1978, 234).

[18]Heidegger (1978, 69).

[19]Heidegger (1978, 396).

[20]The emotional state in question makes an attempt to bury the call of conscience to authenticity, TK.

[21]Moran (2000, 242).

existential 'mode' of the 'not-at-home'."[22] In other words, anxiety is an experiential state of mind that appears when Dasein has fallen into the insignificance of an unlived life which feels empty.

In the following two chapters I will discuss the meditative element of running with the help of "call of conscience" and "active-passive process".

9.2 The Call of Conscience

One of the reasons for the fascination of long-distance running is that with the help of it we may get a hold of our deeper essence, and we will find it easier to hear "the call of conscience". I myself understand the concept of call of conscience as an attempt to describe the movements of our "souls" or events which touch us and have something to do with humanity sui generis. These events touch us and "make us move", because they touch us so profoundly and are felt so deep in ourselves. How does Dasein make a connection with itself? Heidegger's answer to this question is that "because Dasein is *lost* in the 'they', it must first *find* itself".[23]

> (I)n order to find *itself* at all, it must be 'shown' to itself in its possible authenticity. In terms of its *possibility*, Dasein *is* already a potentiality-for-Being-its-self, but it needs to have this potentiality attested. — (T)his potentiality is attested by that which, in Dasein's everyday interpretation of itself, is familiar to us as the "*voice of conscience*".[24]

The meaning of conscience is that it "gives us 'something' to understand; it *discloses*".[25] This opening has to do with the openness related to Dasein's way of being which Dasein fundamentally is already at birth to the world. In bodily-mental being-in-the-world Dasein is from the very beginning an open project in which "the world drifts in and out". In Heidegger's analysis, conscience is uncovered as a call. "The call of conscience has the character of an *appeal* to Dasein by calling it to its ownmost potentiality-for-Being-its-Self —".[26]

Pentti Hänninen writes in Juoksija, the Finnish runner's magazine, about conscience, the connection to oneself acquired by running and about life in itself. He writes:

> When I had the time while running, I have sometimes pondered about whether listening to yourself has something to do even with conscience. If you learn to respect and listen to yourself, it is much harder to mistreat your fellow-men. . — I myself have learned to find spiritual content from running – just like many other long-distance runners. I have

---

[22]Heidegger (2000, 233).

[23]Heidegger (1978, 313).

[24]Heidegger (1978, 313).

[25]Heidegger (1978, 314).

[26]Heidegger (1978, 314).

9.2 The Call of Conscience

discovered a direct connection with myself and through that to life itself in me. It is surely a higher power than myself, name it whatever you like.[27]

Hänninen continues in an interesting way by connecting the power of life to himself as a runner in the same way that I experienced during a run when getting prepared for the Scenic Road Marathon. He tells that "at the peak of my physical performance this power is perfectly under my control, but the extra push originating from myself does not take me any further, if life in me does not take care of its own share. It is not my fate to try to control it, rather to adjust my own will and my actions in accordance with it." A self-experienced active-passive process is also clearly exposed here, when Hänninen understands the power of life realizing through the passive state to be beyond his will. He understands that (a) the power is in himself and that (b) it does not emerge or exist under his conscious control.

Sheehan[28] writes that to truly live, to exist as our true selves, we must hear our inner voice and be honest with it. The question is how to hear it. How to hear our own inner voices in order to find our own ways, to be familiar with our souls? The problem is not the difficulty of finding, rather the likelihood that we never find it. This would mean living our lives without really living, without ever hearing the call.[29] "Our tragedy may be an unused soul, an unfulfilled design.[30]"

The connection between Sheehan's idea and Heidegger's notion of the call of conscience is obvious. Because there is no indication in Sheehan's text that he would have been familiar with Heidegger's ideas, one possibility to see the unity in their thinking is that the experience of the inner voice has been produced by running. The experience can be seen originating from the body, because Sheehan has not attempted to generate it with the help of thinking (which would be impossible in any case). Do we then have to draw the conclusion about the presubjective nature of the body that the ontological[31] structure of the body produces this experience? Personally I think this is the case.

Overall, my conclusion is that our ontological structure contains a desire to be something more full, to become a whole. Rauhala[32] also seems to think similarly. According to him "the need for quietening down, recharging and becoming internally a whole belongs to human nature. It is as essential and desired as the exterior need for being active and social." If our being is incomplete, it may appear and be experienced as undefined anxiety and restlessness of being. It is this becoming a whole, being as a whole in our existence, that conscience is calling us for. When conscience is calling, we must possess some property that allows us to accept that

---

[27] Hänninen (2001, 23).

[28] Sheehan (1978, 58).

[29] Sheehan (1978, 58).

[30] Sheehan (1978, 58).

[31] Here I refer to ontology in its traditional sense as the doctrine of being.

[32] Rauhala (1991, 72–73).

call. Heidegger[33] expresses this inner movement of Dasein by claiming that "*it wants to have a conscience*", which suggestively directs and pushes Dasein to the authentic potentiality-for-Being – "Dasein has an authentic potentiality-for-Being in that it *wants to have a conscience*".[34] "'*Understanding the appeal*' means '*wanting to have a conscience*'".[35]

The question is: who is Dasein? What is the ontological structure of Self?[36] Heidegger writes that "what expresses itself in the 'I' is that Self which, proximally and for the most part, I am *not* authentically".[37] My interpretation about the "I" is that it is the conscious human ego, one property of which is being as the "they". The authentic self of Dasein can become expressed and heard first in the I and only through the I.

> Losing itself in the publicness and the idle talk of the "they", *it fails to* hear its own Self —. If Dasein is to be able to get brought back from this lostness of failing to heat itself, and if this is to be done through itself, then it must first be able to find itself – to find itself as something which has failed to hear itself, and which fails to hear in that it *listens away* to the "they".[38]

Hearing one's self means exploring one's own self. The meditative aspect of running refers to this very listening of the self – in running one's own self may be heard. Listening to one's own self must be made through exercise, by concentrating on one's self. In our everyday routines the attraction of the "they" holds Dasein under the influence of the "ego" aloof from the self, thus preventing the possibility of listening to the self.

The call of conscience is

> without any hubbub and unambiguously, leaving no foothold for curiosity. — (This voice of the conscience, TK) gives us to understand – (that, TK) the 'voice' is taken rather as a giving-to-understand. — In the tendency to disclosure which belongs to the call, lies the momentum of a push – of an abrupt arousal. The call is from afar unto afar. It reaches him who wants to be brought back.[39]

I see "returning", "coming home" as experiential discovering of one's own existence, which is authentic being-in-the-world by nature (See Sect. 8.8).

According to Steiner

> its summons are distinct and immediate. The fact that they are not voiced or verbalized does not relegate this phenomenon to 'the indefiniteness of a mysterious voice, but merely

---

[33] Heidegger (1978, 277).

[34] Heidegger (1978, 277).

[35] Heidegger (1978, 334).

[36] Heidegger (1978, 365).

[37] Heidegger (1978, 368).

[38] Heidegger (1978, 315–316).

[39] Heidegger (1978, 316).

9.2 The Call of Conscience

indicates that our understanding of what is "called" is not to be tied up with any expectation of anything like a communication (or message)'. — It is a silent appeal —. [40]

Heidegger writes that the call

> calls Dasein forth (and 'forward') into its ownmost possibilities, as a summons to its ownmost potentiality-for-Being-its-Self. The call dispenses with any kind of utterance. It does not put itself into words at all; yet it remains nothing less than abscure and indefinite. *Conscience discourses solely and constantly in the mode of keeping silent.*[41]

As I have stated already earlier, the speech of conscience is not predicative, rather pre-predicative and experiential. We are dealing with a mystical kind of intuitive insight. Suzuki[42] writes that William James has shown in his book *Varieties of Religious Experience* that mystical experiences contain noetic qualities. Noetic quality means that the experience is conscious and we are capable of having a conscious grip of it, yet we cannot objectify it in a clearly predicative sense.

"Yet what the call discloses is unequivocal, even though it may undergo a different interpretation in the individual Dasein in accordance with its own possibilities of understanding".[43] In other words, every Dasein has realized through its own growth potential as its own kind, and so possesses certain conceptual and comprehensive readiness to interpret the call. Although the call is in this sense ambiguous, it is in some fundamental way the same for all people. How the call is worked upon towards the way that points to the authentic self, depends on each individual ego. Since the call is pointing to something that Dasein is not yet, the only means we have is to try to take possession of the call to the best of our capacity. Because the "ego" is different by nature than the self, the ego cannot but initially take possession of the call and is only capable of understanding its direction and receiving a distant "hint" about the content of the call (the true self). (An analogous example is a child who does not yet walk seeing someone run. The child cannot possess running as real and only receives the call that points to running, for which there is the potential in the child.) Heidegger[44] writes that

> while the content of the call is seemingly indefinite, the *direction it takes* is a sure one and is not to be overlooked. — When 'delusions' arise in the conscience, they do so not because the call has committed some oversight (has miscalled), but only because the call gets *heard* in such a way that instead of becoming authentically understood, it gets drawn by the they-self into a soliloquy in which causes get pleaded, and it becomes perverted in its tendency to disclose. One must keep in mind that when we designate the conscience as a "call", this call is an appeal to the they-self in its Self; as such an appeal, it summons the Self to its potentiality-for-Being-its-Self, and thus calls Dasein forth to its possibilities.

---

[40] Steiner (1987, 104).

[41] Heidegger (1978, 318).

[42] Suzuki (1985, II, s. 34).

[43] Heidegger (1978, 318).

[44] Heidegger (1978, 318–319).

I would not say that the "they-self" perverts the call. My own interpretation about this is that the "I" in some way resists the call to go to the way towards the authentic self, because it poses a threat to the status of the "I". At the time of hearing the call the I is the only conscious apparatus of Dasein with which it can take possession of its own being-in-the-world. Leaving for the way towards the authentic self means deconstruction of the ego, in which the mental structure of Dasein is remodified. The ego undergoes a metamorphosis through deconstruction and rebuilding. Nevertheless, the power of the call is so effective because it originates from the authentic self from the depths of Dasein, making the call "penetrate" through the I and so causing a change. How much and how Dasein responds to the call depends on the amount of calls and their intensity.

"Conscience summons Dasein's Self from its lostness in the 'they'.[45]"The caller does not make itself familiar in any way – "it by no means disguises itself in the call. That which calls the call, simply holds itself aloof from any way of becoming well-known, and this belongs to its phenomenal character."[46] Personally I don't see this as Heidegger does (that which calls the call holds itself aloof). If we say that the caller is "holding itself aloof", we seem to be assuming that the caller knowingly desires to be aloof. The correct expression to me is to say that the caller does not become known because of the simple reason that the caller is not the conscious ego of Dasein, but rather "something" or "it", deep down in the mental structures of Dasein's being-in-the-world.

Dasein contains simultaneously both a conscious and an obscure layer of mind. Heidegger makes an attempt to unwind this dialectic tangle with the help of the "they" (the "I" or ego) and the caller of the call. The starting point here is that phenomenally this entanglement is something that is experienced. This is characteristic of the existential structure of Dasein, through which we can only find out who is calling. In other words, in some obscure way Dasein is both the called and the caller which, nevertheless, is not a sufficient explanation, because the caller does not become clearly possessed in this way.[47]

Heidegger writes about this "something" deep down in the conscious structures of Dasein as follows:

> In conscience Dasein calls itself. — Ontologically, however, it is not enough to answer that Dasein is *at the same time* both the caller and the one to whom the appeal is made. — Indeed the call is precisely something which *we ourselves* have neither planned nor prepared for nor voluntarily performed, nor have we ever done so. 'It' calls, against our expectations and even against our will. On the other hand, the call undoubtedly does not come from someone else who is with me in the world. The call comes *from* me and yet *from beyond me*.[48]

---

[45]Heidegger (1978, 319).
[46]Heidegger (1978, 319).
[47]Heidegger (1978, 319–322).
[48]Heidegger (1978, 335).

9.2 The Call of Conscience

> (I) receive the call as coming both from me and from beyond me, — (of which follows, TK) that this phenomenon is here delineated ontologically as a phenomenon of Dasein. Only the existential constitution of *this* entity can afford us a clue for Interpreting the kind of Being of the 'it' which does the calling. — The fact that the call is not something which is explicitly performed *by me*, but that rather 'it' does the calling, does not justify seeking the caller in some entity with a character other than that of Dasein.[49]

This caller must not be seen as something supermundane or as a god. This phenomenon represents a latent potential for spiritual growth and awakening embedded in every human being. "Ontologically as a phenomenon of Dasein" belongs to man's fundamental structure. This phenomenon has been explored by the methods of listening to the self for thousands of years.

The "it" deserves a brief notion in this context. In the book *Zen in the Art of Archery* the German philosopher Herrigel practices the art of archery.[50] Herrigel tells how he makes attempts to release the bow according to the instructions of the teacher, but despite numerous attempts fails to do so because he cannot free himself from his conscious self and the directing impact that it has. Releasing the arrow does not take place as easily as "snow slipping away from a bamboo leave". In Herrigel's case the problem is how to practice consciously with perseverance yet without specifically attempting to do so.

The only means for an archer is to practise under the guidance of the conscious I, because in order to be able to shoot with the bow one has to consciously settle down in such a relationship with the bow that shooting even becomes possible. How is it possible to simultaneously strive for a goal and do it without specifically attempting to do so? The answer of Herrigel's Master to this is that "It" releases the bow. When Herrigel wants to know what is this mystical "It", his Master replies

> once you have understood that, you will have no further need of me. And if I tried to give you a clue at the cost of your own experience, I should be the worst of teachers and should deserve to be sacked! So let's stop talking about it and go on practising.[51]

On the basis of this answer Herrigel continued his exercises. He writes:

> Weeks went by without my advancing a step. At the same time I discovered that this did not disturb me in the least. Had I grown tired of the whole business? Whether I learned the art or not, whether I experienced what the Master meant by 'It' or not, whether I found the way to Zen or not – all this suddenly seemed to have become so remote, so indifferent, that it no longer troubled me. — I lived from one day to the next, did my professional work as best I might, and in the end ceased to bemoan the fact that all my efforts of the last few years had become meaningless. Then, one day, after a shot, the Master made a deep bow and broke off the lesson, 'Just then "It" shot!' he cried, as I stared at him bewildered. And when I at last understood what he meant I couldn't suppress a sudden whoop of delight. 'What I have said', the Master told me severely, 'was not praise, only a statement that ought

---

[49] Heidegger (1978, 320–321).

[50] See a more detailed analysis in Koski (2000, 143–168). I use Herrigels description because I have not come across anything similar related to long-distance running. See Yamada (2001) for a critical analysis on the same subject.

[51] Herrigel (1987, 73).

not to touch you. Nor was my bow meant for you, for you are entirely innocent of this shot. You remained this time absolutely self-oblivious and with out purpose in the highest tension, so that the shot fell from you like a ripe fruit. Now go on practising as if nothing had happened.'[52]

When a shot is a non-shot, the shooter has to be someone else than the human conscious I. When a human being is self-conscious at the moment of the exercise, someone else, or "It", does not release the shot. "It" is a human being free from ego-consciousness. When a human being does not consciously release the bow, it is performed by someone who possesses a non-conscious attitude towards her action.[53]

Sheehan[54] writes about the change that takes place in the course of running. In the Boston Marathon, for example, half way through the route the marathon turns from a competition to an experience. If the runner has practiced and run long enough, he becomes the running.[55] According to Sheehan this state of being is somehow mystical.[56] At that moment we experience a perfect connection with the ground, air, wind and rain. Sheehan claims that this kind of experience and understanding about being cannot be gained solely by the brain. A runner understands that the universe is the smallest dividend. In this context Sheehan refers to Eugen Herrigel, Zen and the art of archery.[57]

Generally speaking we can state that for someone advanced in meditative exercises the experience of becoming one with one's own breathing is quite familiar. This becoming one is related to the disappearance of the consciousness of the ego and the identification of the meditating person with what one is doing at that moment. The experience is conscious but in a different way than in everyday experience. Everything is breathing. The whole universe is nothing but inhaling and exhaling.[58]

> One of the most significant features we notice in the practice of archery, and in fact of all the arts as they are studied in Japan and probably also in other Far Eastern countries, is that they are not intended for utilitarian purposes only or for purely aesthetic enjoyments, but are meant to train the mind; indeed, to bring it contact with the ultimate reality. Archery is, therefore, not practised solely for hitting the target; the swordsman does not wield the sword

---

[52] Herrigel (1987, 73–74).

[53] Koski (2000, 162).

[54] Sheehan (1978, 215–216).

[55] He writes also that "my running became me" (1978, 219) and "the course — was now running me" (1978, 220).

[56] A Finn Tapio Pekola (1999, 19) also uses in his writings the word "mystical". He formulates his words like this: "Long-distance running is a simple exercise but it contains the whole life. For someone who does not understand it, it is mere sweat, panting and bodily action, but in the depths of its essence it is only spirit, as if it were a wonderful haze, which in a mystical way can hide even the worst tortures of our lives."

[57] Could we possibly interpret this in such a way that Sheehan recognizes similarities in his experiences to the experience that Herrigel refers to?

[58] See Koski (2000), for example 1, 20–128, 149–168.

just for the sake of outdoing his opponent; the dancer does not dance just to perform certain rhythmical movements of the body. The mind has first to be attuned to the Unconscious.[59]

Sheehan[60] mentions Andrew Weil having written about this unification that it "is essential to the wholeness of body and mind and health". Here Sheehan comments that whatever it is, it starts from the body. His idea is that through bodily exercise an individual will get in touch with one's spiritual essence, ones inner self. On page 52 he writes: "The way to relive our life is to go back to the physical self we were before we lost our way." On page 53 he presents a simple but surprisingly wise statement that the body determines our mental and spiritual energy. What I understand him to say by this is that our bodily constitution is very important to the functioning of our spiritual properties.

The call of care as the voice of conscience urges Dasein to the unification of the "they" and the authentic self (or of "It" in Herrigel's terms), which is the harmonization of the conscious and the unconscious. In Heidegger's terminology, this is the most characteristic capability of Dasein's being.[61]

The nature of the call is not predicative rather obscure. Nevertheless, it is clear and unconditional in its own existential requirement. Heidegger speaks about keeping silent and reticence.

> The call does not report events; it calls without uttering anything. The call discourses in the uncanny mode of *keeping silent*. And it does this only because, in calling the one to whom the appeal is made, it does not call him into the public idle talk of the "they", but *calls* him *back* from this *into the reticence of his existent* potentiality-for-Being. When the caller reaches him to whom the appeal is made, it does so with a cold assurance which is uncanny but by no means obvious. — (T)he caller is Dasein, which, in its thrownness (in its Being-already-in), is anxious about its potentiality-for-Being. The one to whom the appeal is made is this very same Dasein, summoned to its ownmost potentiality-for-Being (ahead of itself ...). Dasein is falling into the "they" (in Being-already-alongside the world of its concern), and it is summoned out of this falling by the appeal.[62]

We can claim that the world is uncovered *(alethein)* in the inner experience of the lived body. Is this uncovering different than in "ordinary" life? With the difference to the ordinary I mean that in running we are, due to the strain on the body, in a different relationship with the world than in our daily routines. It is worth noting that with the help of a physical exercise, due to its intensive and profound nature, it is possible to enter into the spirit of approaching this touch between the runner and the world (and its existential-ontological dimension). The entering into the spirit will help open up the bodily-mental experiential horizon. This way the touch of reality will have a larger contacting surface or band to "enter in" a human being.

This pre-predicative relationship to the world can be viewed with the help of the concepts of symbolic and non-symbolic communication. In non-physical culture

---

[59]Daisetz T. Suzuki in his preface of Herrigel's (Herrigel 1987, 5) book *Zen in the Art of Archery*.
[60]Sheehan (1978, 49).
[61]See Heidegger (1978, 317–318.)
[62]Heidegger (1978, 322).

we are typically dealing with symbolic communication. The opposite of this is non-symbolic communication, such as direct connection with the nature or bodily movement, for example. In other words, you do not need to send a symbolic message to your arm in order to make it move. Heilbrun & Stacks claim that in fact our entire lives are deeply entangled with non-symbolic communication.[63]

My interpretation is that Heidegger's "thinking" (i.e. meditative thinking) can be called an inner non-symbolic event. "Thinking" is not a symbolic activity, in which reality is represented or one's own consciousness is reflected or something that is produced through cognitive processes. "Thinking" is quietening generated by the touch of the body and the world, calming and thanking the existence, in which there are no particular conscious requirements posed on the world and the self and in which they are not interpreted nor analysed with the help of conceptual thinking.

In a symbolic environment the touch between the body and the environment is ontically minimal. For example, in a theatre a chair is always in its own place, and the views offered to the viewer's eye do not require much moving of the head, and the body is peacefully settled. When the touch between the body and the world is dynamic (running in a forest, playing floorball in an indoor sports hall, etc.), the dynamism of the ontic touch is quite broad.

A physical exercise is non-symbolic communication with the help of which it is possible to gain the way of being for which I use the term "settle down in Being". Settling down as a term is a bit narrow because it should cover both the nuances of getting settled and settling down. Getting settled is active, conscious and voluntary action, whereas settling down is passive, something that cannot be reached consciously and through one's will. Settling down in Being can be gained by getting settled to the active-passive process. Once we have settled, the possession of the world taking place through the conceptual does no longer play as big a role as it used to (in understanding an individual's position in the world). The speculative reality has settled in another, secondary position as an aid and a tool. In an exercise the experience of one's own existence deepens and may gain an apodictic nature. This kind of an experience fortifies itself and does not call for any ulterior ground.

Before moving on to discussing the active-passive process, I want to thematize it with the help of Heidegger's philosophy. I want to concretize it and open up the issue of what exactly is Heidegger saying about exercising, "thinking", "opening of one's self to questioning". What do these mean from the viewpoint of practising?

The most significant issue is related to the touch between the runner and the world from the viewpoint of an exercise: what is the significance of an exercise in opening to the world. How does an exercise modify a runner? Using Heidegger's terminology, the question is about the relationship between the asker and the asked. All of this tells for its own part about the point of view, the grip to the matter, in the commentaries to Heidegger's texts and above all in the single human being who reads Heidegger's texts and strives forward.

---

[63]Heilbrun and Stacks (1995, 55).

9.2 The Call of Conscience

To quote Steiner, who analyses Heidegger's writing, "the Heideggerian asker lays himself open to that which is being questioned and becomes the vulnerable locus, the permeable space of its disclosure".[64] But what does this mean in a concrete sense, what do we do when "I lay myself open to that which is being questioned"? What kind of action do the words refer to? How does the opening take place, how is opening oneself to what is being questioned operationalized (performed adequately and corresponding to the nature of the phenomenon) and made possible for oneself? Are the texts in Heidegger's commentaries functional only in the sense of a theoretical conceptual apparatus which creates empty, meaningless phrases? What does, for example, the following answer by Steiner tell us?[65] "The 'answer' elicited by authentic questioning is a correspondence, an *Entsprechen*. It accords with, it is a response to the essence of that *after* which it enquires (dem Wesen dessen nach dem gefragt wird)." I see this answer by Steiner as extremely abstract and far from what Heidegger wishes to tell about Dasein. The concrete benefit to the reader remains somewhat thin, mere words on paper.

In what way am I when I open myself to what is being questioned? Can I consciously settle myself in a favourable relationship with what is being questioned in order that I would allow it to come next to me, I would open myself to what is being questioned and would become opened to what is being questioned? Can I consciously have an impact on the opening? If I cannot, does it take place naturally, irrespective of me and other people? If this is the case, why then bother to talk about the issue at all (the issue of questioning the meaning of Being, the prerequisite for which is having been opened to what is being questioned). However, if I can have an impact on the event, we are finally taking a concrete step towards the right direction in clarifying the issue.

How have (a) those who understand Heidegger's philosophy and (b) those who write about it themselves settled in (their) Being and opened to what has been faced and questioned? How have they "released themselves" (Gelassenheit), or have they done that at all? How have they had an impact on it if they have had the opportunity to experience the "unquivering centre of Being"?

How do we open up or attempt to open up to what has been faced, i.e. how do we make questioning about the meaning of Being as present either ready-to-hand or present-at-hand? Heidegger himself emphasizes the presubjective being-in-the-world – thus not only the operations made in consciousness representing the world, but rather concrete existence, which in this context means running.

I understand opening oneself to what is being questioned to mean settling oneself to such a relationship or exercise in which what is being questioned can become questioned. Of course, what is being questioned can express itself without conscious opening one's self to what is being questioned. Persons of this kind have an open and receptive mental structure. They are in some rare way sensitive in an existential-ontological way to the touch between themselves and the world. In a situation like

---

[64]Steiner (1987, 57).
[65]Steiner (1987, 57).

that the asker is an asker without knowing this to be the case. We have to think this way because the "asked" can only be represented to the "asker". And, when this sometimes (very rarely) happens spontaneously, the only sensible way to think of this is that the asker has been an asker without a conscious attempt to be one. In this situation Dasein is sensitive and "open" and is willing to possess conscience in a sensitively "natural way". Because of this natural and sensitive desire Dasein will receive the call of conscience in a profound way (in the sense of pre-ontological understanding of Being). Dasein is a spontaneous, passive caller of itself as well as itself the receiver of the call sent by itself. In this situation Dasein is sensitive to the touch of being.

How does one question the meaning of Being? The following section is my attempt to answer the above-mentioned questions.

9.3 Active-Passive Process

A runner's attitude towards practising is dependent on what she is striving for, whether it is Olympic championship, better physical condition and health, stress-removing and balancing quality of life, or a perennial ideal. In all of these goals, however, the runner is situated in an active-passive process, in which active refers to desired and conscious action and passive to something that "is given to you as a gift".

Spiegelberg[66] sees Husserl making a distinction between two ways in the constitution of humans: The first one is "active" and the second "passive". The passive constitution is receptive by nature. I see this as impacts of one's own body and immediate surroundings to the subject. I see active constitution as conscious, cognitive actions of the subject, which is culturally bound and in this sense relative in its foundation of significance. "Peak experiences" constitute the subject by their uniqueness and on the basis of their apodictic nature. They ensure the subject in an indisputable way. In this sense they are an authority of their own the status of which cannot be invalidated (perhaps at the most relativizable via active constitution).

Involuntary matters such as feelings, ideas and experiences, cannot be realized by desire. The desired things will happen if they happen. The human mind can be an obstacle for the realization of the desired matter, because it has become thematically individually oriented through one's personal history. One's mind needs to be let loose. Sheehan[67] writes that in running one's mind quietens and creativity is freed:

> Creativity must be spontaneous. It cannot be forced. Cannot be produced on demand. Running frees me from that urgency, that ambition, those goals. There I can escape from time and passively await the revelation of the way things are. There, in a lightning flash, I can see truth apprehended whole without thought or reason. There I experience the sudden

---

[66]Spiegelberg (1975, 74–75).
[67]Sheehan (1978, 14–15).

9.3 Active-Passive Process

understanding that comes unmasked, unbidden. I simply rest, rest within myself, rest within the pure rhythm of my running —. But I must wait. Wait and listen. That inner stillness is the only way to reach these inner marvels, these inner miracles all of us possess. — The mystery of all this is that I must let it come to me. If I seek it, it will not be found. If I grasp it, it will escape. Only in not caring and in complete nonattachment, only by existing purely in the present will I find truth. And where truth is will also be the sublime and the beautiful, laughter and tears, joy and happiness.

Sheehan describes in his writing experiential cores which are realised when the ego gets deconstructed. The deconstruction of the ego can occur in the active-passive process. My idea about Heidegger is that the active-passive process is related to Dasein's authenticity and reaching it. Heidegger connects the authenticity met in a person's essence[68] with the experience and means of true being-in-the-world. The description by Sheehan clearly uncovers his experience of a more profound essence. Sheehan often writes about the same topic.

The deconstruction of the ego is composed of exercises targeted at one's consciousness. In many meditative traditions (such as Zen) that have a clearly defined goal of spiritual development, there is an attempt to achieve a receptive and 'empty' state of consciousness. In this state an individual is free from consciousness of the ego and open to the 'touch' of reality. The ego may get deconstructed. When exercising, the disciple is striving for ending the constant monologue which is present in consciousness, because this prevents one's mind from being quiet, calm and placid. This is done by focusing one's thoughts/mind. Achieving the goal through conscious reflection merely by means of thinking is problematic because it only allows us to reach the initiator of the conscious reflection, resulting in a mind filled with a conceptual discourse. Reaching the goal through thinking can be compared to cleaning water with water. When one manages to calm down her mind, something more real may emerge, instead. In order to perform the desired kind of exercise, it has to be consciously unconscious or unconsciously conscious.[69] Here the idea is not to play tricks with oriental esoteric terminology, rather to present the exercise method from the viewpoint of consciousness. That is to say that one has to become consciously attuned to the exercise situation and that consciousness has to direct the disciple. On the other hand, exercising has to be unconscious in the sense that in an exercise there is an attempt towards an empty conscious state not dominated by the ego. The conceptual inner talk of one's mind is come across by focusing it completely on exercising, or in the case of static meditation on a conceptual object. In connection with running I discuss the same thing (consciously unconscious or unconsciously conscious) using the term active-passive process. To repeat myself in this context, what is active in running is making oneself to run. Passive is anything that can take place or emerge when one's mind is calming down and relaxing, resting peacefully upon itself. Sometimes and somewhere it may happen or not happen that the ego, on which the existence of an individual

---

[68]"Dasein's 'Essence' is grounded in its existence", Heidegger (1978).

[69]Koski (1991, 156).

has to some extent been based from the viewpoint of her self-understanding, gets dissolved. This idea on an individual and the conception about her by others is dissolved, Das Man is dissolved. The human doesn't find from herself anything that she could consider, in the true sense of the word, what she really is like. This positive matter is simultaneous with some other experiential cores.

Going beyond the ego is a conceptual regeneration because it calls for and presupposes going beyond the ego. It is difficult for the fact that the ego is the conscious self of a person, through and by the help of which going beyond takes place. The ego-self is the product of a person's whole former life history, which is why it is difficult to direct itself to the road leading to deconstruction. As a conscious structure it aims at preventing dissolving (and then reorganising itself), because it itself is for itself everything that it is. In practical everyday life this means that humans lack the desire to take the path that leads to the deconstruction of the ego. Despite being unhappy with one's way of being, exercising is not considered necessary. Generally speaking a person may admit exercising leading to deconstruction as useful in principle, but not in practice. In the lifeworld one does not see the opportunity of exercising as concretely realisable, because it is the ego that organises the conscious thoughts of the experienced reality of a person. As the ego makes an attempt to preserve itself, the ideas and the experiences about the potential setting out to exercising are articulated as negative thoughts about exercising. To really get initiated, deconstruction calls for a kind of 'letting go from oneself' which, to put it briefly, means turning loose from the behavioural and existential way of being produced by das Man[70]; Zen master Rinzai[71] often asked his disciples (even concretely) to let go. New deconstructions of the ego may repeatedly occur when running and exercising is continuous. In other words, there is an attempt to consciously settle oneself through exercise again and again to the active-passive process, where new deconstructions of the ego are given an opportunity to occur.

Runners run because of a variety of reasons. Very few of them see an exercise as reaching for authenticity or are conscious of this theme. There is no need for that either. If running becomes a way of life, so be it. Due to its nature running can become a reasonable way of exercising and taking care of one's body and mind. Running can justify itself, be its own reason, an activity without any deeper meaning. Or, then the purpose is only the fact that running feels a good way to exist – in this case it can be joy and some kind of simplified beautitude of being.[72]

In a philosophical sense, the active-passive process is that with the help of which we can methodically strive for a goal. The active-passive process is, among other things, a description of the way in which we can strive for authentic being – as we remember, Heidegger does not provide any methodical exercise to guide us

---

[70]Koski (1991, 162).
[71]Rinzai Roku (1976, 45, 47, 49).
[72]See Sheehan (1978, 39).

9.3 Active-Passive Process

(though he thinks that meditative thinking must be practised[73])." Active" means anything that is consciously done, whereas "passive" is anything that "goes beyond" the conscious. The conscious part of the exercise is the event in which we consciously get oriented to the exercise – through the conscious settling of ourselves we extinguish the continuous discourse in one's mind, i.e. we "go beyond" the conscious (this going beyond the conscious is the passive part of the process).[74]

In the active-passive process the touch between man and the world can reach the deep layers of conscience[75] and existence which cannot be reached by the calculative thinking of a rational ego. The event is prepredicative by nature, it is non-symbolic communication with a greater entity than man. I have formerly written about this as follows:

> Disclosure of being (in its existential-ontological dimension, TK) can take place when a person is in a suitable situation and prepared for it. We can place ourselves in such a situation with the help of a physical exercise, and eventually become more and more prepared. — It is active in the sense that with the help of an exercise we make an attempt to reach for disclosure of being (in its existential-ontological sense, TK), which in perennial traditions is one important phase for man in becoming a whole.[76]

In his book *Gelassenheit* Heidegger speaks about how a human being approaches[77] being and can approach it in its being-as-such. "Approaching being" should in my opinion be understood as approaching the **experience** of the disclosure of being. In other words, when we approach being, we come near the existential-ontological disclosure of it. Literally speaking, a human being cannot approach being because she is always in being.

In my doctoral dissertation I wrote:

> The sense in which I talk about the active part of the active-passive nature is nothing else but this 'approaching'. When a human being sets oneself consciously into an active training situation, this is nothing but setting oneself into a *movement which is approaching the* (existential-ontological, TK) *disclosure of being*.[78]
>
> A physical exercise — (can be, TK) human action targeted to reach a perennial goal or ideal, which calls for mental strength and determination. In the active phase of an exercise, that is when you are factually in the middle of an exercise, you are fully committed to it.

---

[73] Heidegger (1969, 47) writes: "It is enough if we dwell on what lies close and meditate on what is closest; upon that which concerns us, each one of us, here and now; here, on this patch of home ground; now, in the present hour of history." He (1969, 50–57) categorically emphasizes, however, in a normative sense that from the viewpoint of a good future for the whole mankind meditative thinking must be practised.

[74] Koski (2000, 205). Heidegger (1988, 12–13) thinks that modern humans should make an attempt to have an experience of the end of continuous inner speech with the help of meditative thinking.

[75] We may speak about preconsciousness, mind and phenomenal consciousness, too. The nature of consciousness is very complicated. See for example http://en.wikipedia.org/wiki/Consciousness: Wikipedia (2014) "An experience or other mental entity is 'phenomenally conscious' just in case there is 'something it is like' for one to have it."

[76] Koski (2000, 58–59).

[77] Nahegehen. Heidegger (1988, 70).

[78] Koski (2000, 59).

The passive[79] part of the exercise is just 'waiting'. This waiting is beyond being active or passive, because it cannot be an intentional correlate.[80] An exercise — sets a human being to[81] a responsive state. When a human is consciously oriented to an exercise, the human — state (of entering into the spirit, TK) is elevated. The exercise is of dual active nature, it is both a method to go near and to be near disclosure. Being close is also part of the exercise, because this is done consciously. One continues the exercise by being close, because — (the occasion, TK) is being waited for without expectation, which means doing so without conscious attachment to expectation, i.e. to the idea of expectation.[82]

Godel[83] writes about yoga and the goal of an exercise as follows: "The state of unconditioned freedom — *cannot be acquired* by training, by effort, by any tension whatsoever, even that of pure desire." I[84] have formerly commented on his ideas, stating that

> he denies the possibility of gaining freedom through exercise. — He does not seem to be aware of the active-passive nature of an exercise in gaining freedom. In the quotation I borrow here he understands an exercise to be only what I myself refer to as the passive part of training. In other words, he does not see training also as going-close and being-close, even though he mentions that different training methods show the direction and that "the truth seeker does employ practical methods, apparently to good advantage —". Godel refers to the goal of yoga (the state of unconditioned freedom), which is harder to reach than (existential-ontological, TK) disclosure of being. Godel is certainly aware of this as he writes "but would the liberative Experience – this sudden upsurge of a non-temporality manifest in us – depend for its realization upon gymnastic exercises imposed by the psyche upon itself?" In other words, as I see it, Godel does not see the physical-mental exercise as a process, which could be realized as freedom.

An exercise has a certain structure that dictates our action. The structure is a good means to perform the phases of the exercise in a certain order, so we do not need to think of how to carry it through again and again. In this sense an exercise can be seen as a method.

---

[79]Passive must be understood in the sense that a human being with her conscious actions cannot have an impact on (existential-ontological, TK) disclosure, rather she can only wait. Waiting can be, depending on the nature of the exercise, very heavy. With this I refer, for example, to the Sufian mystical Islamic tradition where a novice will undergo exercises that last for several years, to different heavy physical Budo arts and arduous Zen meditation in sitting position.

[80]Human consciousness is considered to always be oriented to something. This conscious orientation, intentionality, is in phenomenological tradition seen as a fundamental property so that consciousness is always consciousness about something. See e.g. Koski (2000, 74–77). See the article by Haaparanta (1988, 495) in which she discusses, among other things, goals that cannot be set as goals (intentional correlates) without losing them at the same time as a result of setting them as goals. One's desire to fall asleep is an example of something that cannot be reached intentionally. Conscious desire to fall asleep increases mental activity, making it at the same time harder to fall asleep. When on the contrary you set your mind in such a state in which your body gets relaxed, also your mind does the same. Here in this sense falling asleep originates from the body. You fall asleep when you are so tired that you cannot desire to do so, i.e. when you lose grip of the intentional correlate.

[81]See Heidegger (1978, 172). See also Klemola (1998, 86–87).

[82]Koski (2000, 59–60).

[83]Godel (1971, 9–12).

[84]Koski (2000, 60).

9.3 Active-Passive Process

A method is like a teacher who carries the student to such a relationship with the world in which there are good prerequisites for learning. This is the active part of an exercise. The passive part has to do with the fact that learning does not take place automatically. The teacher cannot teach gaining insight to what has been learned nor the experience of it, because gaining insight and hence learning must emerge from the student herself. It is essential to understand that learning is possible in favourable circumstances.[85]

In an exercise we consciously set ourselves in a waiting state in which we are not consciously waiting but carrying through the exercise. The conscious and active part rests in not stopping the exercise rather continuing with it. Through the exercise we actively set ourselves in a state of waiting, the way of being of which goes beyond active and passive action. What is active is the decision on (1) getting started with the exercise and (2) the duration of the exercise. What is passive in the exercise is the waiting. This means that there is no attempt (not necessarily, TK) in an exercise to consciously gain the waiting state. It is something that emerges spontaneously. Setting what is passive as the intentional correlate is impossible, because passive waiting cannot, due to its essence, be set as a correlate. On the other hand the passive side of an exercise goes further than passiveness (or passive passiveness), because training is very active by nature in the aforementioned sense of activeness in which the training situation is consciously controlled. On the other hand, consciousness also goes further than what is conscious because with a conscious exercise you aim at something that is consciously unreachable.[86]

As I write above that *we consciously set ourselves in a waiting state*, I understand Heidegger[87] to refer to the same idea when he talks about "opting out to what has been faced". According to Heidegger this opting out calls for a "trace of will", which I myself call a "conscious decision" to place oneself to a waiting state. According to Heidegger, however, in opting out this trace is lost, which to me suggests that when the experiential state of passiveness has been reached, one has crossed the active, conscious settlement.[88]

By settling down a runner can attempt to settle herself in such a way that she "gets settled". In this situation her state of mind is by itself attuned towards settling herself. This state of mind is peaceful and tranquil, a harmonious way of being rooted to the world. The occurrence of this settlement is an innate gift from nature. I see it as an anthropological constant.

An exercise is a goal-oriented activity in which a runner enters into the spirit of being responsive and open.

The process is both active and passive, conscious and non-conscious. The active part makes an attempt to reach the goal through the passive and the passive part is enabled only through the active. What is gained through the passive goes beyond the settlement (the active-passive process of an exercise) through which the goal is reached.[89]

---

[85] Koski (2000, 60).
[86] Koski (2000, 60–61).
[87] Heidegger (1988, 58).
[88] Koski (2000, 61).
[89] Koski (2000, 61).

The conscious part of the process is voluntary, and the non-conscious part involuntary, respectively. As mentioned above concerning falling asleep[90] the desired can take place first when the desire loses its grip of the desired. Desire plays a role here in the sense that falling asleep will best take place in certain kind of circumstances. We fall asleep when the active desire to fall asleep turns passive. In the outcome, which is sleep, we go beyond the activeness and passiveness of being awake, because sleep as a state of consciousness is something that we cannot consciously reach awake.

The passive part of the process is thus realized only in running. Flow is passiveness at its best and running is light and relaxed. When this coincides with loosening of the ego and/or calming of one's mind, there is the sensation that I'm not running rather I'm being run or that running takes place in my body (running takes place in the wholeness of my body and mind).

In addition to lightness this event can be described with concepts like ease and joy, as if the whole world is activated. Also colours become more clear and bright. The scenery is sharply and brightly depicted in the eyes. All this sharpens up the way the world is experienced at that moment. The present moment "opens up" and truly appears as the present. In this way emerges a way of being that extends to the "full size of one's existence". The present does no longer feel like a sharp edge from which one's mind constantly keeps slipping to the past or to the future. The inner speech prevalent in everyday consciousness ceases and the mind that is freed from it expands everywhere. If the relationship of the ego to the world can be described with the idea that the ego touches only the surface of the world (just as our eyes only see the surfaces of objects), the tranquil mind penetrates "under the surface of the world" and the runner gets a broader and deeper touch to being.

Flow forms a good basis for the encounter of the caller and the called. When flow takes place, one welcomes the touches of nature with pleasure and interest. The emotions related to this are e.g. ease, lightness, joy, activation of the world and opening of the present. It is "nattering"[91] with nature. In this meditative state the touch of the world is emphasized and becomes consciously present. The world as experientiality is present. Flow is a structure which enables "home-coming" (einkehren).[92] Runner has a euphoric feeling and she is relaxed in every way.

This is a suitable place for the description of my first marathon (in my running diary, 5/1999) that I ran alone: My purpose was to make a long exercise, three times around lake Pyykösjärvi in Oulu, 24 km altogether. I had taken along two bottles of water, one of which I was carrying in my belt bag and another hidden under a tree by the route. It was 8 o'clock in the evening. I remember it well because I happened to

---

[90]Falling asleep is a good example of dealing with the passive and active, because the nature of sleep and factors related to falling asleep are familiar to every one of us.

[91]Easy-going and spontaneous intercommunication without self-reflection.

[92]Flow is not a "home-coming". It is rather a channel through which home-coming *can* happen. In other words flow is the state of mind, which has entered into the spirit, that is one of the "Archimede's points" of asking the meaning of Being, with the help of which one's own being can be levered home.

9.3 Active-Passive Process

start 8 o'clock sharp. Because the intended 24 km went so well and easily, I decided to continue one more round. Having run 32 km I realized that I was only 10 short of a marathon! I carried on running, but my energy was all gone. I remembered that by the route there is a kiosk that I used to visit quite often, and it came to my mind that if it were open, I could try to buy some lemonade and chocolate and pay for them later. I had no inhibition to attempt to do so even though I realized the foolishness of the whole idea. The kiosk was closed. At that point I remembered that when I started the run I came across a little boy on the way home from a birthday party who offered me two candies. As soon as I remembered this I eagerly put the candies to my mouth, but it was extremely difficult to get them digested in my dry mouth, because I had run out of water after the fourth round at 32 km. Despite these drawbacks running felt quite alright, no chafing or anything like that, and my legs were functioning just fine except for slight wobbling. At 40 km I made an extra round of 2.5 km to make sure to cover every metre of a full marathon. When I finished running, I had spent 4 h and 19 min, so it was 19 min past midnight. Back home my wife came to look at me asking where on earth I had been, or whether something had happened. I answered her by telling I had run a marathon and asked her to take a picture of me. The sensation I had was heavy fatigue yet fully light and totally blank.

When one experiences the flow, everything takes place naturally, by itself. This often comes with an aesthetical experience of silence. The silence feels beautiful, it speaks without words. The world is experienced as it is without the boundaries of the ego: the world and existence are beautiful and seemingly perfect in shape, even though there is so much evil in the world (is this because of the idea that the world is like a beautiful vessel which can be filled with many things, even bad ones?). The world becomes more real and close, existence gains depth or the experience of existence gains depth. The runner gains more security for her being.

In flow the colours of nature are strengthened, more clear, bright and intense. Tiny details of nature, such as a leaf fallen down from a tree resting on the tarmac, gain a deeper meaning compared to an everyday experience. They are like pearls which existence is offering us. The world is also in this sense coming close or into the runner. The animals met along the route are like friends whose actions you follow with joy. The runner is experientially blended with nature and sees the occurrences around her as if from inside those occurrences themselves. There is no exterior observer – in this event nature is observing itself in me and through me. In this kind of a situation the world is observing itself. The experiences have an existential-ontological nature.[93] It can be said to be recollection of being (or Being – I can't say for sure). The horizon of existence is expanded.[94]

---

[93] The experiences naturally occur in very many levels and strengths.

[94] The Finnish philosopher emeritus Lauri Rauhala has practised sitting meditation for quite a long time. He states (1986, 57) that also according to occidental psychologists it is "meaningful to think that a new experience sprouts more genuinely from its own terms, after the old, frozen patterns of understanding have been displaced (when, TK) the goal is to gain an 'original state' of the organisation of experiencing that is free from any old 'encumbrance'".

The existential-ontological disclosure of being is contained – as I see it – in uncovering of truth and reality. In the traditions of mental self-education around the world there is the essential element of being freed (cf. my analysis of Godel's ideas). For example in the yoga and budo traditions this has been seen to call for personal training. In occidental traditions the significance of one's personal training is not emphasized, because it is seen that "mercy comes from God" or from some other being that is greater than the person herself. What e.g. in (Zen-)Buddhism is rather seen to be found from inside the person, is in other traditions ontologisized outside the person, where from the essence of true or authentic self is in a way emanated out to the person. This is probably due to the fact that since the rational human ego in its own conceptual possession is not capable of understanding the nature of true self and the ego is not capable of finding it from itself (only hears it as a "call of conscience", which is interpreted to originate from God or other exterior factors), it is considered to come from outside. But, in fact, in occidental traditions as well one shows devotion through ardent prayer, i.e., by practising. The difference in emphasis is in the active-passive process and in the different interpretations and realizations of its nature. Both truth as "wisdom of the heart" (gnosis, which has to do with non-predicative experience, i.e. intuitive knowledge, of the world order) and becoming free must be understood and experienced as part of the human entity.[95] We are talking not only about intellectual understanding because truth as gnosis is not communication of consciousness with concepts or ideas, rather about experiencing the truth.[96] Truth as an experience has thus to do with discovering a personal way of being as an experiential, liberating and apodictic fact.

> This (uncovering of truth and reality, TK) is, in a sense, recollection of being.[97] We must not see it as an epistemological example of structural truth about the world order, for example. Neither are we talking about ontological possession of reality (in the sense of traditional ontology, TK). The world, being — is the basis from which a human being comes from and which forms the grounds for her action. As a (an existential-ontological, TK) human experience aletheia as disclosure of being is an experience that extends to the fundamental structures of human existence, which often has been interpreted as something mystical or divine. Many ways to approach this experience have evolved to promote the mental development of humans for the very reason that it is valuable as an individual experience, which allows us to reach for wisdom and virtue in human life.[98]

---

[95]See Eliade (1989, 164–165).

[96]See Eliade (1989, 208).

[97]Recollection must not be seen (merely) as recollection of ideas like Plato did, rather also as uncovering of being just as being realizes its existence. When we take into account the problematic nature of recollection in human experience, especially in its conceptual description, it is no wonder that recollection can be described in numerous ways and that it has many interpretations resulting from people's different ways of describing what they have experienced. To me recollection represents the utmost concreticity of reality experienced in an existential-ontological opening of being. In this case the question is not about the recollection of an abstract idea, rather about fully experiencing the world.

[98]Koski (2000, 62). See e.g. Sorokin (1971, v–vii).

Chapter 10
Conclusion

The research in physical education has the main stress on the biological and physiological effects of a physical exercise and sport philosophy is mostly analytically orientated. My approach expands the scope of the research to other human aspects as well. I mean e.g. the existential experiences, peak experiences, whose essence I consider ethical. They are fundamental and basis experiences that don't have in colloquial language an accurate conceptual and explicit expression. Their meaning in ethical sense can be seen from the fact that they serve as an inner structuring sings.

Running is a many-sided and in a human sense rich form of physical exercise. It is one way to approach oneself. The longer the distance the more meditative the nature of submerging into oneself is. In my opinion what is interesting is not to study e.g. the various concepts around game theories and the culture of physical education rather how an individual can, with the help of the meanings unveiled by research and through exercising one's body, reach for something that is permanent and humanly valuable in her life.

> *The finger pointing to the moon*
> *is not the moon.*
> *Only a fool would take the finger for the moon.*

This research deals with matters that are hard to conceptualize and to understand – which refers especially to the runners/people who have no personal bodily experience. I have made an attempt to expose what is the significance of these events to an experiencing human being. In this situation the words should be taken as signals or pointers, as something related to experiences. It is important to remember that words and concepts are only a conceptual and rational form of possession of experiences. The foundation of this form lies in the fact that humans have the ability to conceptually interpret the world and their experiences. It is important to understand that the conceptual possession of the world is not the same as the world itself as it is. The French film director Jean-Luc Godard has insightfully stated that a motion picture does not reflect reality, rather is the reality of the reflection of reality.

I find this to be applicable for concepts accordingly: they do not reflect reality, rather are the reality of the reflection of reality. A language as a conceptual system is a good practical tool for understanding the everyday reality. Human activities are practical and meaningful in this sense, when one sees the world on the basis of intersubjectively evolved concepts.

A human is an incarnated being to whom the potential spiritual beings are envious about her body. When running, an individual takes her life into possession in an athletic sense. This relationship is different than that of a bodily and athletically passive person. The athletic relationship to the world is active and it originates from the body itself. To formulate a thesis, physical exercise is essentially doing and acting in the world, while thinking is presenting ideas about the world. It is easy to tell others what to do and to criticise them, while doing and exercising on one's own is not.

I have presented one way to look at an individual and her relationship with running. This perspective has emerged by taking a closer look at Maurice Merleau-Ponty, Martin Heidegger, myself and my own practising. I believe that my athletic past – karate-do, rock climbing, tai chi, gym training, distance running, utility exercising (I do not have a car, not to mention a driving licence, and I move by bicycle) – has had an impact on the fact that at the age of 56 I'm still in good condition, "in a good bodily and mental shape", as the Cartesian saying goes in Finnish. I still get enthusiastic about new things and I'm not afraid of challenges. In 2014 I have together with my wife started to attend Spanish lessons. Gym training and winter swimming are back after a break of several years. As we live in the 5th floor of a block of flats, I prefer walking up the stairs to taking the lift, even when carrying heavy shopping bags. These days I run 3×13 km per week.

Amby Burfoot, the Boston marathon winner in 1968 and the editor of Runner's World says that what he has learned about running is having the courage to get started. He writes about having understood the importance of getting started in his private life especially through participation in running competitions. You must have the courage to take the step of deciding to attend a competition.[1]

Here I would like to return to J.P. Roos's description of competitions and to the "project of winning" included in them, which may become a burden and so reduces the joy and meaningfulness of running. If running turns into a continuous competition against time and other runners, it may cause pressure for a non-competing athlete, reducing the properties that promote quality of life through running. Here the runner is trying to find a balance between the elements that increase and reduce her motivation, and it would be good for a runner to reflect the structures set to oneself and at times to ask oneself about the meaning and purpose of running.

According to Burfoot[2] you must put yourself together, go through various feelings of uncertainty, such as "do I have the strength to reach the finish line", "do I manage to reach my target", "did I do all the preparations correctly", "did I

---

[1] Burfoot (2000, 8).
[2] Burfoot (2000, 18).

10 Conclusion

forget something", and so on. I understand Burfoot's idea in such a way that this kind of a situation prepares us to have courage and take action when confronting something new and unknown. He writes about having learned that if you do not get started, you do not reach anything either. You do not reach even a failure, because also that is something you may learn from. If you do not have the courage to get started, you stay where you are, and your life gets paralyzed when confronting the continuous new challenges and commencements. In this way many a thing is left undone and you live your life partially without actually living it. Something unique and invaluable escapes out of your reach.[3]

> *Nothing started, nothing experienced,*
> *nothing learned, nothing finished.*[4]

Burfoot practised for 10 years targeting to qualify into the Olympics but never reached it. The failure made him to question himself. He was thinking whether he could give up what he had been striving for. Would doing so be a precedent in his life, directing things to go for the worse? The word "failure" did not sound too good in his ears.[5] It is difficult and it takes a lot of willpower to strive for a peak target, but it is equally difficult to let loose from it. The reason for that is that in striving for a peak target, your entire body and mind has been channeled towards it, the target is anchored deeply in your daily practices. You should start to ponder about letting loose when something in you as a runner says "no more" – this is what happened to Burfoot. When you have engaged your entire mental capacity to striving for a goal, giving up the idea turns out to be a really big issue. It takes a lot to be able to give in something that has been one of your focal points and chief supports giving you power and meaning in life. Yet it is also true that you should not cling to it so much that you get hanged. You should be able to give in, admit your failure and still preserve your own security of being. Letting loose may on the other hand prove that the road you chose was a bad or wrong one. You might not have recognized the new or better in case you had continued with perseverance on the path you had adopted. The following quote speaks about the conclusion:

> I kept running, but without expectations and pressures. It became simply a process-path to good health, stress relief, creative thinking, and fun times with friends. More than 20 years later, I can honestly say that running this way is far more enjoyable than striving for the Olympics.[6]

What is essential is that you do not stop but continue running.

The significance of the experiences (both in the sense of "Erlebnis" and "Erfahrung") discussed in this study is that they improve our quality of life and make our lives more full. Life becomes happier and more enjoyable. Our being becomes more peaceful and harmonious and peace of mind increases. Here Heidegger would

---

[3] Burfoot (2000, 8–13).
[4] Burfoot (2000, 13).
[5] Burfoot (2000, 76–77).
[6] Burfoot (2000, 77).

say that Dasein's primordial understanding of Being increases. It becomes more or fully authentic. And, as Sheehan writes, experiences improve your self-knowledge so that you can feel and say consciously based on your own experience that you have lead a whole and full life.[7]

What is important and meaningful for an individual is especially awakening to the idea that as a whole you are more than the understanding of your conscious self about you as a whole, i.e. the idea created by your conscious self about yourself. This is one of the dimensions of increasing authenticity. The question is about finding a deeper side of yourself, which gives you security in making your own decisions. Then it is understood that life has to do with "your own life". In this way the grip of das Man weakens and no longer has the same gravity as before.

The inner talk which so often fills up your mind ceases at the moment when quietness and serenity is present. The impact of this reaches the entire way of being of a runner and everything ready-to-hand, which feels peaceful and provides a sense of presence. I understand the quietness and serenity of the world as calming down and quietening of one's own mind. You do not analyse what is happening at the moment of its occurrence, and this is why you have the experiential feeling that the world quietens although the experience of quiet is your own.

The experiences described above are often also connected to an aesthetic-ethical dimension through the sensation that the world appears to be full-bodied and beautiful. It feels like the world is good just as it is. A runner can, for a heartbeat, have the experience of belonging to being, which has a constructive impact on the runner. This means having a mental rest.

Sheehan writes about his life in which his biggest battle is not against ageing and time rather against boredom, routines and unlived life. These wither life by emptying it from delight, enthusiasm, joy from doing things and happiness. Your life would turn into a grey path, a mentally withering place for performing your necessities and routines. "When I run, I avoid all this. I enter a world where time stops, where now is a fair sample of eternity. Where I am filled with excitement and joy and delight –. I enter a state that will be man's most congenial environment."[8]

For the alienated humans of today, the missing ability of being present is a strongly experienced existential problem. The busy life rhythm disperses your personal life. Some of my friends have said that it is terribly heavy to be focused either in the past or the future, not being able to stop and calm down and to be there at the present moment, trusting that things will get done and that hasting does not make it any easier. Even if you had the time just to be there, the hectic way of life absorbed by both your body and your mind would tear you away from the serenity of being. A busy lifestyle is like a centrifuge the gravity of which is constantly casting you away from the state of serenity which can be found from yourself.

A busy lifestyle and fast pace are not easily removable by rational thinking, because the intensive way of being is adopted as a psychic-bodily way of operation

---

[7]Sheehan (1978, 59).
[8]Sheehan (1978, 123).

10 Conclusion

and structure, which tends to direct us. In other words, the question is not about something that is under our willpower (cf. conscious attempt to be spontaneous).

The experiential cores confronted by long-distance running may help us put an end to this vicious circle. The cores will rearrange the structure of understanding our being – one of those cores is, for example, the existential experience of presence. In presence we "are at that very moment", and the connection between the self and the world is open and giving. An individual is tuned to subtleties and experiencing the whole world as more full.[9]

The experience of presence can also be interpreted as a "non-discursive experience", a bodily experience where there are no concepts. As Klemola puts it, a runner can practise so that the exercise "reveals more delicate nuances from reality and so gives way to a more full and sensitive relationship with the world".[10] And as Sheehan writes[11] after having run the Boston marathon: "The runner relaxing in a shower at Pru Center senses he has united – two existencies (his own and the world's). He has a new and radically altered relationship with other people, the earth, the universe."

An ultra-distance runner Tero Töyrylä[12] writes that the most fundamental "something" is out of reach of speech. Ultra-distance running provides an unusual contacting surface to things that you cannot express by speech. A Canadian friend of his has written about the peculiar attraction of ultra-distance running as follows:

> Just as early poets, apostles and philosophers have said, life cannot be explained merely by logic and sense. Ultra-distance runners know this instinctively. They know about other things, too: they have a connection that those who do not do any physical exercise have lost. They understand perhaps better than anyone else that the doors to the spiritual world open up by physical strain. By running the long and demanding distances ultra-distance runners reply to the call that comes from deep inside the core of our existence, asking who we really are.[13]

Peak experiences have their own central significance to a runner and our relationship to the world. In Sheehan's words "sport is singularly able to give us peak experiences where we feel completely one with the world, where all conflicts are transcended as we finally become our own potential".[14] He also says a few words about the meaning of life. It is uncovered in revelation, which is not a production of sense. Revelation is discovered

---

[9] See Koski (2000, 226–232) and Murphy and White (1995, 35).

[10] Klemola (2004, 37). What is essential here is that this experience can be striven for through (a meditative) exercise. "The question is about exercising your body in such a way that its inner experience builds up with more delicate features. A kind of inner bodily sensitivity is being opened. I have called it exercising and opening bodily consciousness." (Klemola 2004, 37–38.)

[11] Sheehan (1978, 217).

[12] Töyrylä (2003, 55).

[13] Töyrylä (2003, 55).

[14] Sheehan (1978, 195).

where our blood and flesh whisper to our unconscious. The distance runner, the least of all athletes, the least of all men, is continually taking his daily encounter with his universe on that inward journey. Consider your body, he tells us. Not in the memory of past pleasure. Or in anticipation of a glorious future. But for this present moment when you might indeed be in paradise.[15]

When human experience is investigated, we have to remember that there are many kinds of people with a rich variety of experiences. The more you exercise your body and mind, the more profound and uncommon layers of experience you can discover. A person who has not run long distances, not to mention ultra distances, cannot understand the experiences generated by running. She can even deny their existence and consider them products of imagination which have nothing to do with the experiences of ordinary people. At least there is no way to understand them experientially. Klemola writes that in human research the focus typically lies on the ordinary experience and exceptional experiences have been ignored. He continues that

> we lack a closer examination of religious experience or for example an artist's experience at the moment of creation. These experiences would reveal a new angle to questions about the relationship between body and mind or the potential of human experiences as a whole. We easily tend to think that we can understand the nature of a religious experience even if we had no such experience ourselves. – The question is about sensitivity, inner experience, which is gained through exercise. I use the concept of *contemplative body* in a similar sense. It is a body which has undergone various exercises requiring us to internally listen to the body and has so uncovered such experiential opportunities that are not easily revealed to an unexercised body.[16]

Jarmo Pippola remembers

> a summer day in the country, when a warm wind was blowing gently, the rasp of gravel road toned my steps, birds were singing, the sun was bright and the shadows were rich in tone. I felt such happiness in running that I was shivering from the moving experience. Can there be a happier moment than the one in which we experience life as a great gift and privilege? It is wonderful to be able to enjoy the beauty and relaxation of running and to experience to be part of being. It was a strong experience and an emotional burst, and I have gone through that numerous times. Although the beauty of the moment can be a short climax, it will carry you forward over the years, as if inviting you to experience it again. You may discover the same from the smile and uniqueness of your children, from the caretaking and love of your wife, or from the sincerity of your friends.[17]

A runner may experience, for example, a tremendous holiness which goes beyond everything else faced before. Sheehan[18] writes:

---

[15] Sheehan (1978, 128).

[16] Klemola (2004, 89).

[17] Pippola (2002, 12). When I was writing down the last sentence of the quote, I was struck by a strong emotion, and tears came to my eyes – I was able to recognize in his text the familiar sensation of joy and happiness. I said to myself "this is exactly what it is".

[18] Sheehan (1978, 230).

10 Conclusion

> On my afternoon run I had suddenly overreached the confines of time and space. I had become the perfect runner moving easily and surely and effortlessly toward infinity. My ten years of almost daily running had brought me to an area of consciousness, a level of being I never knew existing. – Running that day became for me, I'm sure it has for others, a mystical experience. A proof of existence of God. Something happened, and then – one simply knows, and believes, and can never forget.

This kind of profound existential-ontological experiences, which are related to finding one's position in the world, are about experiencing peace and love, returning home, are always conceptualized via the cultural framework of each individual. Thus for example in Christianity the experience can be associated with the existence of God, and in Zen-Buddhism with discovering one's true self (enlightenment). The impact of the experience is fundamental because it changes us and our relationship to the world.

This is one way of looking at a runner, yet many a question remains unanswered. Where does something "more real" come from and what is it, and what does "real" mean in this context? How should we understand the revelation of reality (truth)? What is the real nature of experiences (especially peak experiences) generated by running? Where from does the experience which I feel coming from inside (if for example I do not believe in a personal God) ultimately come from? In what way can I surely know the true origin of my experience? Although in a sense these phenomena are experientially (quite) clear to us, defining the concepts is a big and difficult task.

When we are not trying to describe these things, we are dealing with metaphysics and are seeking for explanations to these experiences. The fact is that man is part of being, part of the universe. Thereby it makes sense to claim that human experiences are generated by being and are expressed in man. Of course we may ask how being has the "ability" to generate such experiences. Is our only chance to state that the question is about one appearance of being, which becomes conscious in man? Man has simply been built so that this is possible and that this happens. In other words, according to this kind of thinking the fundamental nature of experiences is "an sich", a being as such, which man in an ultimate sense cannot penetrate into or take possession of.

The more and the longer you run
the more securely you can leave behind your ego[19]

This research reveals how we can challenge ourselves through flesh. The challenge takes place when we exercise regularly. There are many obstacles to that, such as feelings of insecurity, laziness, and excessive work load. Our conscious self makes the decision: to quit or to continue. If a runner "wants to possess a conscience", if she is capable of discovering willpower to surpass the ego that resists commencing or demands quitting the practice, she will have the strength to continue. In fact, it is

---

[19] Neil Young sings as follows in his song *Country Home*:
I'm thankful for my country home, it gives me peace of mind.
Somewhere I can walk alone and leave myself behind.

not the self that is challenged through flesh rather the ego. Through challenging the ego we can find something more profound than the ego, something that we can, for example, call the self or true self. I have often encouraged my students to continue and not to give up easily. Give your body a chance to produce something that you do not know yet at this stage of your exercising. By doing so you also give yourself a chance.

Capable of understanding the world and Being and taking possession of it an individual can position oneself in such a relationships with the world that promotes reaching for what is being desired.[20] Long-distance running as a form of exercise and the horizon opening up through it have been examined here. The potentials contained in this horizon can be realized by being active, by taking action, by getting into practising running. The target could be good physical condition on one end and knowing yourself better and realization of your potential at the other end of the target line, thus becoming more whole or a whole (i.e. the theme of authentic self). Long-distance running can be a philosophical way of exploring oneself as loving of wisdom and fronesis (guided by common sense to strive for wisdom and good life). A runner may be able to uncover new experiential cores which she formerly was not aware of – the potentials may be realized and as experiences become something that has both consciously and conceptually been taken possession of.

A potential is not an object which is possessed and which can be "taken into use" when it crosses one's mind. The realization of a potential always calls for a suitable relationship in which it can be realized. The mind is turned to a new, vivid and refreshed position.

The experiential cores in this study were:

1. removal of conflict between subject and object,
2. quietening of mind, silence,
3. getting into the spirit,
4. presence,
5. power,
6. joy,
7. devotion, thankfulness,
8. true self, enlightenment, Absolute.

These experiential cores may have a profound significance to a runner's life and to the level and nature of the realization of her entire being. The experiential cores are centres around which other experiences are organized and direct the life of an individual. New experiences are possessed and interpreted as thematized by

---

[20] As a property of being human, we have the ability to understand Being, to act and to live in the world. The existence of the human species serves as a proof of this, having its foundation in the fact that a human as a bodily-mental being adequately reacts in the world (which is also what Heidegger's concept of "preontological or primordial understanding of Being" refers to). The touch to the world has its conscious correspondence in consciousness, which is the means of orientation for being in the world.

the experiential cores.[21] Often these experiential cores "go hand in hand", i.e. they take place simultaneously or sequentially, fully or partially. In other words, several experiential cores may appear as different layers in a runner at the same time.

For example, the removal of conflict between the subject and object may place a runner face to face with some "great thing" "discovered from oneself". Something discovered from oneself is, on one hand, in this very situation experienced to be discovered from oneself (although a more adequate interpretation would be that the discovery happens through a layer not thematized by the ego). On the other hand the experience is also such that the removal of conflict between the subject and object annihilates the ordinary experience of the ego as a conscious self-monitoring ego – the experience is such that the world is monitoring itself, which takes place in one conscious point, which is an experiencing human being. In other words, then the question is not about one single point rather about an experiential layer of being thematized by the *relationship* between the world and the human being. When we talk about the ego, the relationship to the world takes place through the ego. The ego is oriented to the world from one single "point", while a human being oriented by relationships has numerous starting points of orientation (because the starting point of orientation can be any starting point thematized by a relationship and not an individual as the ego). The crucial matter is opening of humans to the world or opening of being to humans. In this sense a running exercise is a process in which the viewpoint towards reality is changed (or may change) from ego-centric to world-centric.

Two aspects can be distinguished from world-centric being: on one hand it views itself **as** a human (the viewer is an individual person) and on the other it views itself **in** a human being (a being that has become conscious of itself in a human being).[22]

Experiential cores bring us quietness and peace, and through them we experience something "unexplained" that functions as a ground. As Heidegger puts it, it can be called the asked expressed by the call of conscience. There are also other terms, yet it is not the terms and concepts that are essential rather the way it addresses us, which takes place without words. It is a mentally refreshing windless wind, which penetrates through your essence in a soft and quietening way. It is a flash generated by opening the gates of heaven, which penetrates through you.

The results of the research serve the running sport and running culture revealing different kind of running dimensions. A non-runner might motivate to start running when getting better understanding of the different levels of running. The research results make the running culture more familiar by presenting running as well-structured multi-dimensional totality. The results of the study can help an athlete

---

[21]Could it also be so that the interpretative framework thematized by positive experiential cores has an impact on the prepredicative experiences? Then we would talk about a somehow structured prehermeneutical reception of experiences, which has a "positive attitude" towards the touches with the world. It is as if the interpretative preconception had shaped everything that it faces as interesting and acceptable without prejudice.

[22]Koski (2000, 141).

to find some new levels in one's practice and to direct the practice in a new way. Consequently, this makes it possible for an athlete to experience and understand one's practice in a new way. The running exercise itself may in this way help the athlete to discover new existential experiences that help an individual to better understand her own existence.

The results of *The Phenomenology and the Philosophy of Running* serve the culture of physical education by offering a holistic approach to an exercising human being and to revealing the multi-dimensional aspects of man. The ideas of the book can be applied to any type of long-lasting physical exercise such as walking, skiing, swimming, cycling, triathlon, trekking, etc.

One my interests when writing this book was to encourage people to run.

The human body is wise and teaches one if only given a chance.
The body is as an experiential matter open in relation to mind
and provides a channel for reality to step in.

Literature

Abe, Shinobu. 1985. Sport from a viewpoint of sensibility. In *Aktuelle Probleme der Sportphilosophie/Topical problems of sport philosophy*, Schriftenreihe des Bundesinstituts für Sportwissenschaft Band, vol. 46, ed. H. Lenk. Köln: Verlag Karl Hofmann.
Abe, Masao. 1985. *Zen and Western thought*. London: MacMillan Press.
Aristoteles. 1989. *Nikomakhoksen etiikka*. Helsinki: Gaudeamus.
Audi, R. 1995. *The Cambridge dictionary of philosophy*. Cambridge: Press Syndicate of the University of Cambridge.
Austin, M.W. (ed.). 2007. *Running & philosophy. A marathon for the mind*. Oxford: Blackwell.
Aviisi, 2004. Tampereen ylioppilaslehti, 12. Tampere: Tampereen yliopiston ylioppilaskunta.
Burfoot, Amby. 2000. *The Runner's guide to the meaning of life*. New York: Daybreak.
Burfoot, Amby. 2007. Preface. In *Running & philosophy. A marathon for the mind*, ed. M.W. Austin. Oxford: Blackwell.
Chiba, T.K. 1989. Structure of Shu, Ha, Ri, and penetration of Shoshin. http://www.aikidoonline.com/Archives/2001/mar/feat_0301_tkc.html. Reference from 11 May 2004.
Cudahy, Mike. 1989. *Wild trails to far horizons. An ultra-distance runner*. London: Unwin Hyman.
DeWitt, Richard. 2007. Hash runners and hellenistic philosophers. In *Running & philosophy. A marathon for the mind*, ed. M.W. Austin. Oxford: Blackwell.
Dilthey, Wilhelm. 1982. *Gesammelte Schriften XIX* (Grundlagun der Wissenschaften vom Menschen, der Gesellschaft und der Geschichte). Göttingen: Vandernhoeck & Ruprecht.
Douillard, John. 1994. *Body, mind and sport*. New York: Harmony Books, Crown Publishing Inc.
Eliade, Mircea. 1989. *Yoga, immortality and freedom*. London: Penguin Books Ltd.
Fischer-Schreiber, I., S. Schuhmacher, and G. Woerner. 1989. *The encyclopedia of eastern philosophy and religion*. Boston: Shambala.
Fry, Jeffrey. 2007. Running religiously. In *Running & philosophy. A marathon for the mind*, ed. M.W. Austin. Oxford: Blackwell.
Gallagher, S., and A.N. Melzoff. 1996. The earliest sense of self and others: Merleau-Ponty and recent developmental studies. *Philosophical Psychology* 9: 213–236. Available at: http://www2.canisius.edu/~gallaghr/G&M1996.html. Reference from 10 May 2004.
Godel, Roger. 1971. The liberative experience of yoga. In *Forms and techniques of altruistic and spiritual growth*, ed. P.A. Sorokin. New York: Harvard Research Center in Creative Altruism.
Gothóni, René, and Mahapanna (Niinimäki, Mikael). 1990. *Buddhalainen sanasto ja symboliikka*. Helsinki: Gaudeamus.
Haaparanta, Leila. 1988. A note on Nietzsche's moral argument. *The Philosophical Quarterly* 38(153): 490–495.
Hadot, Pierre. 1995. *Philosophy as a way of life*. Oxford: Blackwell.

Hänninen, Pentti. 2001. Sata maratonia – minkä tähden? *Juoksija* 3: 22–23.
Heidegger, Martin. 1969. *The discourse on thinking*. New York: Harper & Row.
Heidegger, Martin. 1978. *Being and time*. Southampton: Basil Blackwell.
Heidegger, Martin. 1982. *The Basic problems of phenomenology*. http://www.marxists.org/reference/subject/philosophy/works/ge/heidegge.htm. Accessed 6 Aug 2014.
Heidegger, Martin. 1988. *Gelassenheit*. Pfullingen: Neske.
Heidegger, Martin. 2000. *Oleminen ja aika*. Tampere: Vastapaino.
Heilbrun, A., and B. Stacks. 1995. Virtuaalitodellisuus vm. 1989 – Interview of Jaron Lanier. In *Virtuaalitodellisuuden arkeologia*, ed. Erkki Huhtamo, 45–63. Rovaniemi: Lapin yliopisto.
Himanen, Pekka. 2001. *Hakkerietiikka ja informaatiojan henki*. Helsinki: WSOY. ISBN 951-0-25417-7. (*The hacker ethic and the spirit of the information age*, 2001, ISBN 978-0-375-50566-9).
Heinämaa, Sara. 2000a. *Ihmetys ja rakkaus*. Helsinki: Kustannusosakeyhtiö Nemo.
Heinämaa, Sara. 2000b. Mitä on fenomenologia, Johdatus *Phénoménologie de la Perception* – teoksen esipuheeseen. *Tiede & Edistys* 3: 165–168.
Heinämaa, Sara. 2002. Loogisista tutkimuksista ruumiinfenomenologiaan. In *Nykyajan filosofia*, ed. Ilkka Niiniluoto and Esa Saarinen. Helsinki: Werner Söderström.
Herrigel, Eugen. 1987. *Zen in the Art of Archery*. London: Arkana.
Ilmarinen, Kari. 1981. Pyhä urheilu. *Juoksija* 6: 16–22.
Johnston, Charles. 1987. *The yoga sutras of Patanjali*. Albuquerque: Brotherhood of Life.
Jokinen, Kimmo. 1994. Uni tiedostamattomasta. In *Uusi aika, Kirjoituksia nykykylttuurista ja aikakauden luonteesta*. Nykykulttuurin tutkimusyksikön julkaisuja, vol. 41. Jyväskylä: Jyväskylän yliopisto.
Kabasenche, William. 2007. Performance-enhancement and the pursuit of excellence. In *Running & philosophy. A marathon for the mind*, ed. Michael W. Austin. Oxford: Blackwell.
Kaelin, Eugene. 1988. *Heidegger's being and time*. Tallahassee: University Presses of Florida.
Kapleau, Philip. 1988. *Three pillars of Zen*. London: Rider & Co Ltd.
Kauppi, Raili. 1978. *Philosophia perennis ja sen merkitys ihmiselle*. Jyväskylän yliopiston filosofian laitoksen julkaisu, vol. 9. Tampere: Tampereen yliopisto.
Kauppi, Raili. 1990. *Varhaisia kirjoituksia & bibliografia 1950–1989*. Juha Varto (toim.), Filosofisia tutkimuksia Tampereen yliopistolta, vol. V. Tampere: Tampereen yliopisto.
Kitti, Tommi. 1997. Muistiinpanoja tanssin itsenäisyydestä. http://www.teak.fi/teak/Teak297/muistiin.html.
Klemola, Timo. 2004. *Taidon filosofia – filosofin taito*. Tampere: Tampere University Press.
Klemola, Timo. 1998. *Ruumis liikkuu – liikkuuko henki? Fenomenologinen tutkimus liikunnan-projekteista*. Filosofisia tutkimuksia Tampereen yliopistosta, vol. 66. Tampere: Tampereen yliopisto.
Koski, Tapio. 1999–2004. Unpublished running diary.
Koski, Tapio. 1991. *Liikunta ja kehollisuus perenniaalisessa filosofiassa*. Filosofisia tutkimuksia Tampereen yliopistosta, vol. 17. Tampere: Tampereen yliopisto.
Koski, Tapio. 2000. *Liikunta elämäntapana ja henkisen kasvun välineenä*. Tampere: Tampere University Press. (*Physical exercise as a way of life and a method for spiritual growth with yoga and zen-budo as examples*. Doctoral thesis, only in Finnish.) Abstract: http://tampub.uta.fi/handle/10024/67035?show=full.
Kreeft, Peter. 1971. Zen In Heidegger's Gelassenheit. *International Philosophical Quarterly* 11(4): 521–545.
Kupiainen, Reijo. 2003. Fenomenologia alkuperän tieteenä. In *Katseen tarkentaminen*, SoPhi, vol. 71, ed. Leena Kakkori, 11–31. Jyväskylä: Jyväskylän yliopisto.
Levin, David M. 1987. Mudra as thinking: developing our wisdom-of-being in gesture and movement. In *Heidegger and Asian thought*, ed. G. Parkes, 245–269. Honolulu: University of Hawaii Press.
Levin, David M. 1989. *The listening self*. London: Routledge.
Levinas, Emmanuel. 1996. *Etiikka ja äärettömyys*. Gaudeamus: Tampere. (Ethique et infini. Paris: LGF, 1982).

Lorenz, K. 1987. *Meyers kleines Lexikon Philosophie*. Mannheim: Bibliographisches Institut.
Luoma, Matti. 1994. *Mystiikka ja filosofia idässä ja lännessä*. Filosofisia tutkimuksia Tampereen yliopistosta, vol. 52. Tampere: Tampereen yliopisto.
Merleau-Ponty, Maurice. 1986. *Phenomenology of Perception*. Suffolk: Routledge & Kegan.
Merleau-Ponty, Maurice. 1987. *Phénoménologie de la perception*. Paris: Gallimard.
Moran, Dermot. 2000. *Introduction to phenomenology*. London/New York: Routledge.
Moreland, J.P. 2007. Running in place or running in its proper place. In *Running & philosophy. A marathon for the mind*, ed. M.W. Austin. Oxford: Blackwell.
Murphy, Micharl, and Rhea White. 1995. *In the zone. Transcendent experience in sport*. New York: Penguin/Arkana.
Nancy, Jean-Luc. 1996. *L'éthique originaire' de Heidegger*. Paris: Galilée.
Nasr, Seyyed. 1976. A foreword in a book, Schuon, Fritjof: *Islam and the perennial philosophy*. Printing place unknown. World of Islam Festival Publishing Company Ltd.
Nishida, Kitaro. 1987. *Intuition and reflection in self-consciousness*. Albany: State University of New York Press.
Oesch, Erna. 2002. Wilhelm Dilthey ja eletty kokemus. *Kokemus*, Acta Philosophica Tamperensia, vol. 1. Tampere: Tampere University Press.
Parkes, Graham. 1987. *Heidegger and Asian thought*. Honolulu: University of Hawaii Press.
Paunonen, Ari. 1999. Monta hyvää syytä juosta. *Juoksija* 6: 32–33.
Pekola, Tapio. 1999. Juoksemisen henkiset vaikutukset. *Juoksija* 7: 18–19.
Pekola, Tapio. 2001. Sisäinen juoksu. *Juoksija* 8: 54–56.
Peussa, Jorma. 2003. Unpublished description of running, Helsinki City Marathon.
Pippola, Jarmo. 2002. Liikunnan sisäinen olemus. *Juoksija* 3: 12.
Pulkkinen, Kati. 2001. Pakkomielteisyydestä. *Juoksija* 7: 8.
Rauhala, Lauri. 1984. *Ihmisolion konstituutiosta ja maailmanjäsennyksestä eksistentiaalisessa fenomenologiassa*. Olio kollokvio. Suomen filosofisen yhdistyksen järjestämä kotimainen tutkijakollokvio, Helsinki 11–12.1.1984. Helsingin yliopiston filosofian laitoksen julkaisuja, vol. 3. Helsinki: Helsingin yliopisto.
Rauhala, Lauri. 1986. *Meditaatio*. Keuruu: Otava. ISBN 951-1-09252-9.
Rauhala, Lauri. 1990. *Humanistinen psykologia*. Helsinki: Yliopistopaino. ISBN 951-570-067-1.
Rauhala, Lauri. 1991. *Humanistinen psykologia*. Yliopistopaino: Helsinki.
Rauhala, Lauri. 1993. *Eksistentiaalinen fenomenologia hermeneuttisen tieteenfilosofian menetelmänä*. Filosofisia tutkimuksia Tampereen yliopistosta, vol. 41. Tampere: Tampereen yliopisto.
Roku, Rinzai. 1976. *The Zen teaching of Rinzai*. Berkeley: Shambala.
Roos, J.P. 1989. *Liikunta ja elämäntapa*. Jyväskylä: Jyväskylän yliopisto.
Roos, J.P. 1995. *Maratonmiehen elämä*. http://www.valt.helsinki.fi/staff/jproos/maresip.htm. Reference from 1 Apr 2004.
Routila, Lauri. 1970. Husserl ja Heidegger. In *Filosofian tila ja tulevaisuus*, ed. J. Hintikka and L. Routila, 77–96. Helsinki: Weilin & Göös.
Saari, Mauno. 1979. *Juoksemisen salaisuudet*. Helsinki: Otava.
Sankari, Anne. 1994. Ruumis ja kuntosali. In *Uusi aika, Kirjoituksia nykykulttuuris*ta *ja aikakauden luonteesta*. Nykykulttuurin tutkimusyksikön julkaisuja, vol. 41. Jyväskylä: Jyväskylän yliopisto.
Schimmel, Annemarie. 1986. *Mystical dimensions of Islam*. Chapel Hill: North Carolina Press.
Schmitt, Richard. 1967. Husserl's transcendental-phenomenological reduction. In *Phenomenology*, ed. Joseph Kockelmans. New York: Doubleday & Company, Inc.
Schrag, Calvin. 1988. The lived body as a phenomenological datum. In *Philosophic inquiry in sport*, ed. J. Morgan and K.V. Meier, 109–118. Champaign: Human Kinetics Publishers.
Sheehan, George. 1978. *Running & being*. Red Bank: Second Wind II.
Sheehan, Thomas. 1998. Elämä luettavana: Heidegger ja kovat ajat. In *Heidegger – ristiriitojen filosofi*, ed. Haapala Arto. Helsinki: Yliopistopaino, Gaudeamus Kirja.
Sinikka. 2004. http://www.pilke.net/hyva_olo/artikkelit/ympari.html. Reference from 5 May 2004.

Sintonen, Matti. 2003. Selittäminen, ymmärtäminen ja ihmistieteet. *Ihmistä tutkimassa*, 9–30. Kuopio: Kuopio University Press.
Sorokin, Pitirim, and Sorokin Preface (eds.). 1971. *Forms and techniques of altruistic and spiritual growth*. New York: Harvard Research Center in Creative Altruism.
Spiegelberg, Herbert. 1975. *Doing phenomenology*. Nijhoff: Hague.
Spinoza, Benedictus. 1949. *Ethics*. New York: Hafner Publishing Company.
Steiner, George. 1987. *Heidegger*. London: Fontana Press.
Stevens, John. 1988. *The Marathon monks of Mount Hiei*. Boston: Shambala.
Suzuki, Daisetz T. 1973. *Zen and Japanese culture*. Princeton: Princeton University Press.
Suzuki, Daisetz T. 1985. *Essays in Zen Buddhism, I-III*. Essex: Rider.
Töyrylä, Tero. 2003. Minun tieni Ateenasta Spartaan. *Juoksija* 9: 51–55.
Värri, Veli-Matti. 1997. *Hyvä kasvatus – kasvatus hyvään*. Vammala: Tampere University Press.
Vapa, Marko. 2001. *Juoksijan hurmos*. An unpublished manuscript.
Varto, Juha. 1990. Liikunnan etiikka. *Liikunnan filosofia, eri tarkastelukulmia*. Filosofisia tutkimuksia Tampereen yliopistosta, vol. XIII, 115–131. Tampere: Tampereen yliopisto.
Varto, Juha. 1992. *Fenomenologinen tieteenkritiikki*. Filosofisia tutkimuksia Tampereen yliopistosta, vol. 30, Tampere: Tampereen yliopisto.
Verho, Mari. 2001. A private e-mail.
Vettenniemi, Erkki. 1994. *Juoksun hurma ja tuska*. Helsinki: Kirjayhtymä.
Wikipedia. 2014. *Consciousness*. http://en.wikipedia.org/wiki/Consciousness. Reference from 25 Aug 2014.
Wisnewski, J.J. 2007. The phenomenology of becoming a runner. In *Running & philosophy. A marathon for the mind*, ed. M.W. Austin. Oxford: Blackwell.
Wittgenstein, Ludwig. 1979. *On certainty*. Oxford: Basil Blackwell.
Yamada, Shoji. 2001. *The Myth of Zen in the Art of Archery*. http://www.texasarchery.org/Documents/myth/MythZenArchery.pdf. Reference from 19 Apr 2004.
Zimmerman, Michael E. 1986. *Eclipse of the self*. London: Ohio University Press.
Zimmerman, Michael E. 1993. *Heidegger, Buddhism, and deep ecology*. Cambridge: Cambridge University Press. http://www.google.fi/books?hl=fi&lr=&id=FPAWupXILkoC&oi=fnd&pg=PA240&dq=Zen+In+Heidegger%27s+Gelassenheit&ots=0U8sUY2VeY&sig=zeGrLFdx4fcQxOMEfTZRoQp_ZiI&redir_esc=y#v=onepage&q&f=false. Reference from 28 Aug 2014.

Printed by Printforce, the Netherlands